THE I.B.TAURIS HISTORY OF THE CHRISTIAN CHURCH

The Church in the Later Middle Ages

THE I.B.TAURIS HISTORY OF THE CHRISTIAN CHURCH
GENERAL EDITOR: G.R. EVANS

The Early Church
Morwenna Ludlow, University of Exeter

The Church in the Early Middle Ages
G.R. Evans, University of Cambridge

The Church in the Later Middle Ages
Norman Tanner, Gregorian University, Rome

Early Modern Christianity
Patrick Provost-Smith, Harvard University

The Church in the Long Eighteenth Century
David Hempton, Harvard University

The Church in the Nineteenth Century
Frances Knight, University of Wales, Lampeter

The Church in the Modern Age
Jeremy Morris, University of Cambridge

The Church in the Later Middle Ages

Norman Tanner

Published in 2008 by I.B.Tauris & Co. Ltd
6 Salem Road, London W2 4BU
175 Fifth Avenue, New York, NY 10010
www.ibtauris.com

Nihil obstat and *Imprimatur*
Francisco J. Egana SJ, Vice-Rector, Gregorian University

Vol 1: *The Early Church*   978 1 84511 366 7
Vol 2: *The Church in the Early Middle Ages*   978 1 84511 150 2
Vol 3: *The Church in the Later Middle Ages*   978 1 84511 438 1
Vol 4: *Early Modern Christianity*   978 1 84511 439 8
Vol 5: *The Church in the Long Eighteenth Century*   978 1 84511 440 4
Vol 6: *The Church in the Nineteenth Century*   978 1 85043 899 1
Vol 7: *The Church in the Modern Age*   978 1 84511 317 9

A full CIP record for this book is available from the British Library

Typeset in Adobe Caslon Pro by A. & D. Worthington, Newmarket, Suffolk
Printed and bound in Great Britain by CPI Antony Rowe

THE I.B.TAURIS HISTORY OF THE CHRISTIAN CHURCH

Since the first disciples were sent out by Jesus, Christianity has been of its essence a missionary religion. That religion has proved to be an ideology and a subversive one. Profoundly though it became 'inculturated' in the societies it converted, it was never syncretistic. It had, by the twentieth century, brought its own view of things to the ends of the earth. The Christian Church, first defined as a religion of love, has interacted with Judaism, Islam and other world religions in ways in which there has been as much warfare as charity. Some of the results are seen in the tensions of the modern world, tensions which are proving very hard to resolve – not least because of a lack of awareness of the history behind the thinking which has brought the Church to where it is now.

In the light of that lack, a new history of the Christian Church is badly needed. There is much to be said for restoring to the general reader a familiarity with the network of ideas about what the Church 'is' and what it should be 'doing' as a vessel of Christian life and thought. This series aims to be both fresh and traditional. It will be organized so that the boundary-dates between volumes fall in some unexpected places. It will attempt to look at its conventional subject matter from the critical perspective of the early twenty-first century, where the Church has a confusing myriad of faces. Behind all these manifestations is a rich history of thinking, effort and struggle. And within it, at the heart of matters, is the Church. *The I.B.Tauris History of the Christian Church* seeks to discover that innermost self through the layers of its multiple manifestations over twenty centuries.

SERIES EDITOR'S PREFACE

Against the background of global conflict involving interfaith resentments and misunderstandings, threatening 'religious wars' on a scale possibly unprecedented in history, Christians and the Christian Church are locked in internal disputes. On 2 November 2003, a practising homosexual was made a bishop in the Episcopal Church in the United States, America's 'province' of the Anglican Communion. This was done in defiance of the strong opinion in other parts of the 'Communion' that if it happened Anglicanism would fall apart into schism. A few years earlier there had been similar rumblings over the ordination of women to ministry in the same Church. A century before that period, the Roman Catholic Church had pronounced all Anglican ordination to the priestly or episcopal ministry to be utterly null and void because of an alleged breach of communion and continuity in the sixteenth century. And the Orthodox Churches watched all this in the secure conviction that Roman Catholic, Anglican and all other Christian communities were not communions at all because they had departed from the truth as it had been defined in the ecumenical Councils of the first few centuries. Orthodoxy alone was orthodox. Even the baptism of other Christians was of dubious validity.

Those heated by the consecration of a 'gay' bishop spoke on the one side of faithfulness to the teaching of the Bible and on the other of the leading of the Holy Spirit into a new world which knew no discrimination. Yet both the notion of faithfulness to Scripture and the idea that Jesus particularly wanted to draw the outcasts and disadvantaged to himself have a long and complex history which makes it impossible to make either statement in simple black-and-white terms.

One of the most significant factors in the frightening failures of communication and goodwill which make daily headlines is a loss of contact with the past on the part of those taking a stand on one side or another of such disagreements. The study of 'history' is fashionable as this series is launched, but the colourful narrative of past lives and episodes does not necessarily make familiar the patterns of thought and assumption in the minds of those involved. A modern history of the Church must embody that awareness in every sinew. Those embattled in disputes within the Church and disputes involving Christian and other-faith communities have tended to take their stand on principles they claim to be of eternal validity, and to represent the will of God. But as they appear in front of television cameras or speak to journalists the accounts they give – on either side – frequently reflect a lack of knowledge of the tradition they seek to protect or to challenge.

The creation of a new history of the Church at the beginning of the third millennium is an ambitious project, but it is needed. The cultural, social and political dominance of Christendom in what we now call 'the West' during the first two millennia made the Christian Church a shaper of the modern world in respects which go far beyond its strictly religious influence. Since the first disciples were sent out to preach the Gospel by Jesus, Christianity has been of its essence a missionary religion. It took the faith across the world in a style which has rightly been criticized as 'imperialist'. Christianity has proved to be an ideology and a subversive one. Profoundly though it became 'inculturated' in the societies converted, it was never syncretistic. It had, by the twentieth century, brought its own view of things to the ends of the earth. The Christian Church, first defined as a religion of love, has interacted with Judaism, Islam and the other world religions in ways in which there has been as much warfare as charity. We see some of the results in tensions in the modern world which are now proving very hard to resolve, not least because of the sheer failure of awareness of the history of the thinking which has brought the Church to where it is now.

Such a history has of course purposes more fundamental, more positive, more universal, but no less timely. There may not be a danger of the loss of the full picture while the libraries of the world and its historic buildings and pictures and music preserve the evidence. But the connecting thread in living minds is easily broken. There is much to be said for restoring as familiar to the general reader, whether Christian or not, a command of the sequence and network of ideas about what the Church *is* and what it should be *doing* as a vessel of Christian thought and life.

This new series aims, then, to be both new and traditional. It is organized so that the boundary-dates between volumes come in some unexpected places. It attempts to look at the conventional subject matter of histories of the Church from the vantage-point of the early twenty-first century, where the Church has confusingly many faces: from Vatican strictures on the use of birth-control and the indissolubility of marriage, and the condemnation of outspoken German academic theologians who challenge the Churches' authority to tell them what to think and write, to the enthusiasm of Black Baptist congregations in the USA joyously affirming a faith with few defining parameters. Behind all these variations is a history of thought and effort and struggle. And within, at the heart of matters, is the Church. It is to be discovered in its innermost self through the layers of its multiple manifestations over twenty centuries. That is the subject of this series.

Contents

To James Campbell and Peter Lewis,

of Oxford University,

brilliant teachers and writers,

who introduced me to the later Middle Ages.

Notes and Abbreviations

References to publications. References to books and articles are given in the body of the text, not in footnotes. For the works referred to frequently, see 'Abbreviations' below. Other references are given in the following form: author, or first word of title, as appropriate, followed by the date of publication and the page(s) referred to, thus: (Hussey 1986: 343). The full title of the book or article can be found in the Bibliography, under the chapter in which the reference occurs.

Dates of birth and death. For most individuals who appear in this book, the year of birth and, in many cases, that of death is not known with certainty. The present policy has been to give dates whenever possible, rather than question-marks (?) or spread-dates (1370/75), but the years given often indicate approximate rather than definite dates.

Abbreviations

c.	*circa*/about
Decrees	*Decrees of the Ecumenical Councils*, ed N. Tanner (Georgetown, 1990), 2 vols. The pagination is continuous through the two volumes, therefore only the page is indicated.
EHD, iv	*English Historical Documents*, vol. 4 (1327–1485), ed A.R. Myers (London, 1969)
Migne, *PL*	J.P. Migne (ed), *Patrologia Latina* (Paris, 1844–64), 221 vols
Norwich	Norman Tanner, *The Church in Late Medieval Norwich 1370–1532* (Toronto, 1984)

MAP I   xiii

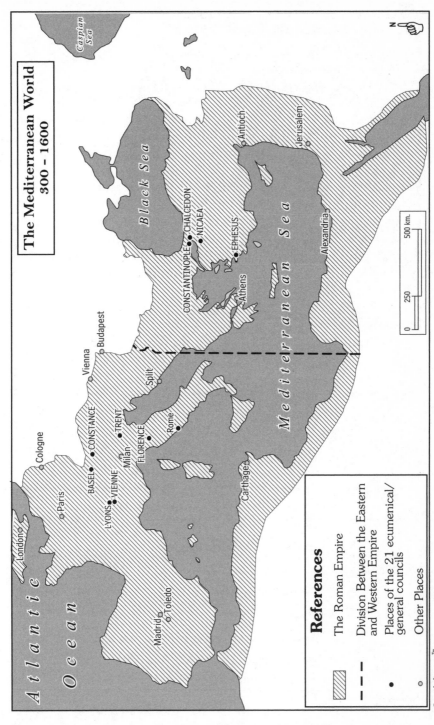

The Mediterranean World
300 – 1600

References

The Roman Empire

Division Between the Eastern
and Western Empire

Places of the 21 ecumenical/
general councils

Other Places

SpatialmapsᵀᵐᵈᵃᵗᵃSpatialmaps™

MAP 2

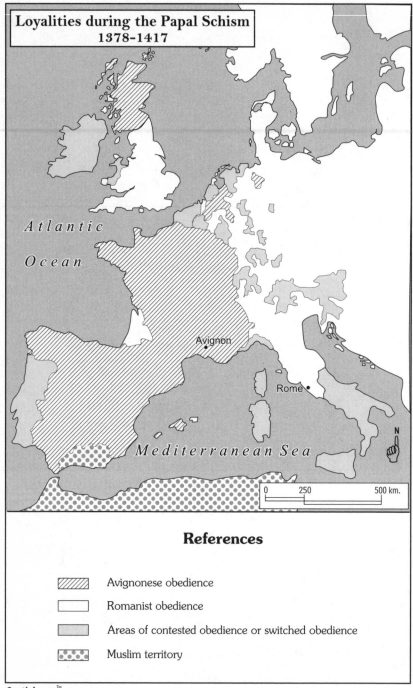

Loyalities during the Papal Schism 1378-1417

Atlantic

Ocean

Avignon

Rome

Mediterranean Sea

N

0   250   500 km.

References

Avignonese obedience

Romanist obedience

Areas of contested obedience or switched obedience

Muslim territory

Spatialmaps™

MAP 3   XV

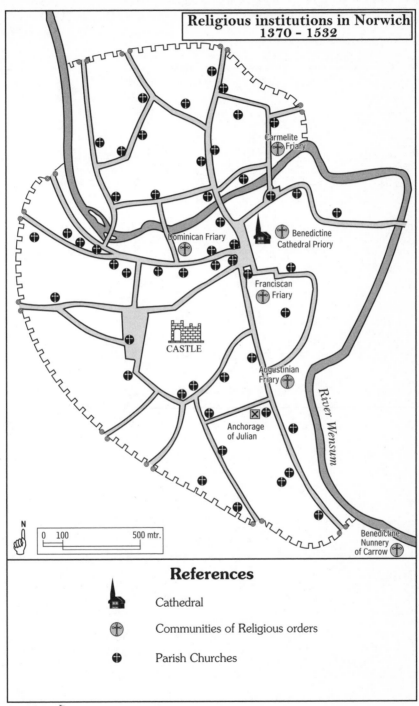

Religious institutions in Norwich
1370 – 1532

Carmelite Friary

Dominican Friary

Benedictine Cathedral Priory

Franciscan Friary

CASTLE

Augustinian Friary

Anchorage of Julian

River Wensum

Benedictine Nunnery of Carrow

N

0   100   500 mtr.

References

Cathedral

Communities of Religious orders

Parish Churches

Spatialmaps^{Tm}

Introduction

Christendom in the later Middle Ages meant the countries from Iceland and Ireland in the west to the Ural mountains in Russia and even beyond in the east, from Scandinavia in the north to North Africa in the south. Precise figures for the total number of Christians are lacking but a figure somewhere in the region of 80 million seems likely. Three-quarters were living in Western Christendom, the countries that remained in communion with Rome; the remaining 20 million dwelt in Eastern Christendom and, for the most part, gave their allegiance to the patriarch of Constantinople. The two centuries between 1300 and 1500 – the period covered in this book – formed a transition between the central Middle Ages and the sixteenth century of Reformation and Counter-Reformation.

Background

To expand on these bald outlines it is important to remember the earlier history of Christianity. Jesus Christ was born and lived all his life, so far as we know, within the Roman Empire. It was largely within this empire that Christianity expanded for centuries. Between the fourth and eleventh centuries there occurred four events of fundamental importance for medieval Christendom – events that are essential for understanding the Church in the later Middle Ages.

First, the Emperor Constantine (306–37) moved the capital of the Roman Empire to the city of Byzantium on the shores of the Bosphorus Sea, and renamed it Constantinople (the 'city of Constantine'). Quickly the empire proved too large and unwieldy to be governed from one capital, so the arrangement of the two capitals became firmly fixed: Rome, capital of the Western half of the empire, and Constantinople, sometimes called 'New Rome', capital of the Eastern half. Regarding the Church, Rome was the centre of the Latin-speaking Western half of Christendom, Constantinople that of the largely Greek-speaking Eastern half (see Map 1).

Secondly, in the fifth century the Western half of the Roman Empire disintegrated in the face of the barbarian invasions, while the Eastern half of the empire (which came to be called the Byzantine Empire, after the original name of its capital city) survived. The intruders, who came from outside the Roman Empire, were called 'barbarians' by the citizens of the empire – not, indeed, because they wore beards (Latin *barba* = beard), as is often thought, but because the Easterners (or Byzantines) could not understand their languages and so suggested, in derision, that all they could say was 'bar, bar', hence 'barbarian'. The result was a seismic shift for Christianity. The new arrivals – Franks settling in Gaul/France, Visigoths in Spain, Lombards in Italy, Angles and Saxons in Britain, Vandals in North Africa, and others – quickly converted to Christianity and gradually brought fresh ideas and approaches, a new dynamism of imagination and creativity. The results were crucial for the development of Christendom in the medieval West, right into the late Middle Ages. The other side of the coin was that Constantinople now saw itself, rather than Rome, as the heir of the ancient world, as the authentic voice of Christianity, as the senior partner in the communion. Tension between the two poles was inevitable.

The third event was the rise of Islam. Mohammed died in 632 and the remarkable expansion of the religion proclaimed by the Prophet began in his lifetime and continued throughout the medieval period and beyond. Christianity was much more affected in the Eastern half of the old Roman Empire than in the Western half. The cities of three of the five major (called 'patriarchal') sees of the early Church were taken by Muslim forces in the seventh century: Alexandria in Egypt, Jerusalem, and Antioch in modern Turkey. Only two remained in Christian hands: Rome and Constantinople. Much of the heartland of the early Church was captured by Muslim armies and in most places the large majority of the people eventually converted to Islam, whether peacefully or under pressure: North Africa, the Near and Middle East, and (with notably fewer conversions to Islam) Greece and much of the Balkans. The freedom of Christians to practise their religion was gradually eroded. By 1300, the start of our period, the Eastern Empire was reduced to a small enclave around the city of Constantinople. Towards the end of the period, in 1453, the empire came to an end when Constantinople was captured by Muslim forces.

In Western Europe, too, Islam made notable advances, but there the tide had turned well before the later Middle Ages. The Western, Latin-speaking half of North Africa was quickly overrun, Muslim armies entered and conquered most of Spain, and even ventured into southern France. The Battle of Tours (sometimes called the Battle of Poitiers – the battle being fought between the two towns) in southern France in 732, in which the Christian army under Charles Martel defeated the invading Muslim army, proved to be a turning point. Effectively it ended the likelihood of Islam gaining a secure foothold in France. Muslim control over most of Spain remained for centuries but eventually waned. By 1300 it had been reduced to the kingdom of Granada in southern Spain, but this too came to an end in 1492 when the city of Granada was captured by the Catholic army of the monarchs of the newly united kingdom of Spain, Queen Isabella and King Ferdinand. Islam, nevertheless, had a profound influence on the medieval West.

The fourth event was the schism between the Eastern and Western Churches, between Rome and Constantinople, beginning in the eleventh century. Earlier tension between the two Churches has already been noted and there had been several periods of schism – times when the two Churches were 'out of communion' with each other – as a result of particular disputes. Matters came to a head again in 1054 when the patriarch of Constantinople, Michael Cerularius, and the legate of Pope Leo IX excommunicated each other. To contemporaries the dispute appeared no more serious than several previous clashes. This time, however, the schism was never healed. The situation was exacerbated in 1204 when crusaders from the West diverted their sea voyage to the Holy Land and went to Constantinople instead. There they captured and sacked the city, deposed the emperor and installed a Westerner (Baldwin, Count of Flanders) in his place, and deposed the patriarch of Constantinople and intruded another Westerner (Thomas Morosini of Venice) in his place. The Byzantines regained control of their capital and the patriarchate within 60 years, but the schism and memories of the crusaders' actions in Constantinople dominated relations between the two Churches in the later Middle Ages. Remarkably, however, efforts at healing the schism continued and they led to the Council of Florence in 1439.

Disasters

The fourteenth and fifteenth centuries witnessed a succession of disasters for Christendom, signalling a period of crisis unparalleled since the collapse of the Roman Empire. Eastern Christendom's loss of lands and faithful as a result of the conquests of Islam, culminating in the capture of Constantinople in 1453, has already been mentioned.

The Black Death plague struck with horrific effect between 1347 and 1350. Coming from Asia as a bubonic and pneumonic plague, it struck Constantinople in 1347 and was carried to Sicily and other places within or bordering the Mediterranean Sea in the same year. During the next three years it spread to virtually all the countries of Europe. There were quite wide regional variations in the resulting mortality but overall perhaps one-third of Europe's population perished, some 20 million people. There were serious recurrences of the plague at approximately ten-year intervals through-out the rest of the fourteenth century and further outbreaks in the fifteenth century. The population of Europe did not recover its pre-1347 level until the sixteenth century. The devastating psychological effects, including preoc-cupation with death and the precarious nature of life, are easy to imagine and can be sensed today in much of the surviving literature and art of the period.

Warfare was endemic in medieval life, even if in proportion to the popu-lation far fewer lives were lost than in the wars of the twentieth century. The 'Hundred Years' War' between France and England was notable in European history in pitting two major countries against each other for over a century. It compounded the gloom of the Black Death and its recurrences. The conflict centred around the claims of the king of England – in many respects well founded – to be the legitimate king of France. War broke out in 1337 and finally ended in 1453 with the expulsion of the English from virtually the whole of France. Indeed, France, on whose soil almost all the fighting took place, was scarred particularly badly. There was the loss of lives on both sides in the major battles and numerous lesser skirmishes as well as in the many sieges of towns. In addition, armies on both sides, includ-ing those of various French nobles who sided with the English, frequently devastated the countryside or sacked towns they had captured. The conflict dominated the politics of Western Europe throughout much of the period under consideration.

The end of the threat of the Muslim conquest of Spain has been noted. The persistent advance of Islam into Eastern and Central Europe – which continued well beyond the end of our period, culminating in the siege of Vienna in 1683 – posed a serious threat to Western Christendom. There was, too, the threat from the Tartars. Coming from the steppes of Russia, they penetrated deep into Central Europe. Their armies of horse-borne warriors for long seemed invincible. In 1242 they captured and sacked the city of Budapest in Hungary. This was the furthest west they came but the waning of their influence was not immediately obvious. A general council of the Western Church, meeting in Lyons in France in 1245, issued this solemn warning:

> The wicked race of the Tartars, seeking to subdue, or rather utterly destroy the Christian people, having gathered for a long time past the strength of all their tribes, have entered Poland, Russia, Hungary and other Christian countries. So savage has been their devastation that their sword spared neither sex nor age, but raged with fearful brutality upon all alike. It caused unparalleled havoc and destruction in these countries in its unbroken advance; for their sword, not knowing how to rest in the sheath, made other kingdoms subject

to it by a ceaseless persecution. As time went on, it could attack stronger Christian armies and exercise its savagery more fully upon them. Thus when, God forbid, the world is bereaved of the faithful, faith may turn aside from the world to lament its followers destroyed by the barbarity of this people. (*Decrees*: 297)

It was only at the end of the period, when Christopher Columbus reached America in 1492, that the wider world was decisively opened up to Europeans. For the rest of the time Europe, and therefore Christendom, seemed gravely threatened both from within and from without. Its very survival as a civilization was called into question.

Crises within the Western Church

In addition to these mainly material disasters, Europe encountered a series of crises within the Church. They are introduced briefly here and will reappear frequently in the rest of the book.

First, the crisis of the Avignon papacy. The institution that came to be called the papacy traced its origins to Peter, the Apostle who had been given a special role of leadership by Jesus Christ and who – according to well-established traditions – had lived and been martyred in Rome. The pope was considered to be the successor of Peter as bishop of Rome and it was in this city that popes had lived, most of the time, until the early fourteenth century. Then, rather suddenly, for a variety of reasons, a succession of popes decided to leave Rome and establish what came increasingly to look like their permanent headquarters in Avignon, a city in the south of France. France was then the most populous country in Europe, it lay at the centre of Western Christendom, geographically and in other respects, and in many ways it was the superpower of the continent. The trauma of the move to Avignon might be compared to a move of the papacy today from Rome to New York.

Pope Gregory XI, the last of the Avignon popes, was persuaded to return to Rome in 1377. He died the following year and there followed the contentious election of his successor. As a result of the dispute, there soon emerged two and later three claimants to the papacy. The countries of Europe were divided in their loyalties. This 'papal schism' paralysed much of the working of the Church, and the development of its institutions, for some 40 years.

The schism was finally resolved by the Council of Constance, which met from 1414 to 1418. In order to deal with the three men who were reluctant, or refused outright, to abandon their claims to be pope, the council felt obliged to assert its right to deal with the situation and, therefore, its authority and indeed ultimate superiority, at least in this emergency, over the papacy. The assertion was broadened after the schism had been healed into wider claims made by subsequent councils regarding the government of the Church. Such claims were viewed by the reunited and revived papacy as a usurpation of its own authority. The result was a long and bitter dispute, principally between Pope Eugenius IV and the Council of Basel, regarding their respective spheres of authority. Eugenius eventually emerged triumphant, but conciliarism persisted. The fifteenth century had discovered a fault-line at the centre of the Church's government.

In addition, the popes of the second half of the fifteenth century seemed to many Christians to be more interested in money and worldly authority, in art and display, than in the spiritual welfare of the Church. The papacy's need to bolster its authority partly explains the motivation, and the promotion of religious art may be considered thoroughly commendable. Nevertheless the 'Renaissance papacy' came in for plenty of criticism. The immorality – including sexual – of several popes added to the concerns.

The problems of the Church extended well beyond the highest levels of authority. Religious orders had been a catalyst for renewal in the Church for many centuries. Yet there were no major new orders in the Middle Ages after the foundation of the four orders of friars – Franciscans, Dominicans, Carmelites and Augustinians – in the thirteenth century. The next two centuries, the later Middle Ages, brought many problems for the existing religious orders and an aura of decline hung over them. The parish clergy, too, were criticized for lack of learning and of attention to their calling, for ill discipline and immorality.

In theological studies the thirteenth century has been considered the high point of the Middle Ages. The towering genius of Thomas Aquinas was not matched subsequently, and his synthesis of faith and reason was attacked from various quarters. The danger of retreating into narrow fideism and fundamentalism threatened. Theological enquiry seemed to lack its earlier confidence. John Wyclif, especially, posed serious theological challenges.

All these problems of the institutional Church and the clerical body, as well as the material disasters mentioned earlier, impacted upon the laity. Precisely how is disputed. At least there appears to have been a waning of confidence in clerical authority and an air of gloom. The later Middle Ages has been called a 'Babylonian Captivity' for the Church. Yet the original exile of the Jewish people in Babylon, painful though it was, proved to be a time of religious deepening and enrichment, a preparation for the coming of Jesus Christ. Should the later Middle Ages be seen likewise in a more positive light? This question leads to a consideration of the historiography of the period.

Historiography

During the two centuries under consideration – which came to be called the later (or late) Middle Ages – the period already appeared to contemporaries as one of unusual crisis and of decline for the Church. In the eyes of Eastern Christendom, the capture of Constantinople by the Muslim army in 1453 seemed almost like the end of the world. Pervading gloom in the Western Church is readily recognized in much of the art and literature of the period, though melancholy was balanced by the renewed optimism of the Renaissance, principally in fifteenth-century Italy.

This portrayal of the later Middle Ages as a period of decline and decadence, including – indeed especially – for the Church, was emphasized further in the sixteenth century. Giorgio Vasari and other historians of Renaissance art, as well as many of the artists themselves, contrasted the primitive nature of medieval art with the brilliant achievements of the new epoch. The description 'Middle Ages' (Latin, *Medio Aevo*, therefore appearing in many languages in the singular, 'Middle Age') quickly became current. The phrase recognized the long period as a unit of time and contrasted it unfavourably with both the glories of the 'ancient civilization' of Greece and Rome and those of the 'new world' of the sixteenth century.

Theologians and apologists of the Reformation in the sixteenth century and later took a dim view of the Middle Ages, especially of the medieval Church. A key proposition for them was that the Church had gone radically astray during this time; hence the need for, and justification of, the Reformation. The deviance was specially marked in the later Middle Ages, they argued.

Attitudes towards the later medieval Church on the part of Catholic writers of the Counter-Reformation were nuanced. These writers had to explain the obvious and remarkable success of the Reformation, but they did not want to justify the Reformation. A distinction was usually drawn. On the one hand, they argued, the Church in the Middle Ages had remained faithful to its doctrinal teaching, so the new doctrines of the Reformation could not be justified. They admitted, on the other hand, that the practice of Christianity had been weakened by abuses and superstitions and moral failures, so that reform in these areas was indeed necessary. Ordinary people, the argument went, had been deceived by the need for moral and practical reforms into also accepting unwarranted doctrinal changes.

There was a further twist to the explanation given by the Counter-Reformation, which centred on religious orders. Many scholars of the Counter-Reformation were members of the new religious orders that had been founded during this time of reinvigoration in Catholic life, notably the Jesuits and Oratorians. These new orders had to justify their existence against considerable opposition, including that of the older religious orders – principally the monastic orders and the orders of friars – some of whose members thought, understandably, that the need to found new orders was an implicit criticism of their own worth. In turn, it was tempting for members of the new orders to underline the laxity and even decadence of the older orders, and of much else in the late medieval Church, as proof of the need to found new orders. The task of the new orders was to remedy the bad moral state of the Church. In this way there was subtle motivation for influential groups within the Counter-Reformation to endorse, partly at least, the Protestant critique of the moral decadence of the late medieval Church, even while they maintained that doctrinal orthodoxy had been preserved.

The eighteenth-century Enlightenment dealt a further blow to the reputation of the Middle Ages. In their exaltation of reason over faith, Voltaire and other personalities of the Enlightenment treated medieval Christianity as a paradigm of superstition and ignorance. In their eyes 'medieval' was almost synonymous with barbarism and stupidity.

The Romantic movement of the nineteenth century brought better understanding and appreciation. In architecture, the neatness and order of eighteenth-century Classicism gave way to a renewed interest in the medieval style. The word 'Gothic', hitherto a term of derision by association with the barbarian Goths, came back into vogue. Nineteenth-century architects tried to recapture the brilliance and imagination of their medieval forebears. The result was the neo-Gothic style, called 'Victorian Gothic' in much of the English-speaking world: St Pancras railway station in London and Richard Upjohn's Trinity Church in New York are fine examples. In art and literature, rationality gave way to emotion and passions – as in the artist Delcaroix or the writer William Wordsworth – and there was fascination with the rugged creativity of the medieval world.

Romanticism began mainly as a secular movement, so that initially interest in the Middle Ages was not primarily religious. Interest in the medieval world, however, could not be separated from some appreciation of its religion, and thus medieval Christianity and the Church were drawn into the debate. Church authorities and theologians, too, began to take more notice of medieval Christendom. For the most part this notice came, at least initially, from Catholics rather than Protestants, since for the latter the period remained something of a taboo, as mentioned earlier. There were, however, some exceptions: among High Church Anglicans, for example, research into the medieval Church flourished as scholars sought to reveal the continuity of the Anglican Church with medieval Christianity; and members of other Churches of the Reformation showed interest and enthusiasm.

Catholics had a variety of motives in this revival of interest in the Middle Ages. Many of them regarded the period as a Golden Age, before the sad divisions of the Reformation, and as a time when Church and state had lived in relative harmony, in contrast to the tensions between the two authorities that had become the norm in many countries of Europe after the French Revolution of 1789. Medieval Christendom was a model to which Catholics could look back with pride – *their* heritage, whereas the Protestants had spurned it – and which they could in some measure try to restore.

It was, however, principally the twelfth and thirteenth centuries, the 'High Middle Ages', that were seen as the Golden Age: the epoch of Thomas Aquinas, the building of cathedrals and numerous parish churches, saints Francis and Dominic and the new orders of friars, the universities of Bologna, Paris and Oxford, the Fourth Lateran Council of 1215, the codification of canon law, and many other achievements. The 'later Middle Ages', the fourteenth and fifteenth centuries, only partly entered into the appreciation. This later period was viewed mainly as one of descent from the high plateau that had been reached in the twelfth and thirteenth centuries, as a time when things began to go wrong. Such an interpretation could conveniently help to explain both the success of the Reformation and the need for the Counter-Reformation. The thesis of cultural and psychological decline was stated most brilliantly by the Dutch historian Johan Huizinga in *Herfsttij der Middeleuwen* of 1919 (English translation, *The Waning of the Middle Ages*, London, 1924).

Around 1950 there began to emerge a new generation of medievalists, many of whom were not committed Christians and as a result did not feel bound by the confessional loyalties, both Catholic and Protestant, that had for long dominated previous scholarship. Among many Catholic and Protestant scholars, moreover, especially after the Second Vatican Council (1962–65) of the Catholic Church, a more ecumenical and tolerant approach prevailed, one that was more respectful of what others had to say. This is not to say that interest in the Middle Ages, including its religion, waned. Far from it. The success of medieval conferences – most notably in the English-speaking world the annual gatherings at Kalamazoo in USA and Leeds in Britain – as well as the numerous institutes, publications and university courses dedicated to the Middle Ages witness to a high level of interest in the period, principally, though not exclusively, in the West. The significant shift has been, rather, to a more eclectic approach.

This more eclectic, enquiring and indeed appreciative approach has impacted notably upon interest in the later Middle Ages. The period has fitted well into the concerns of post-modernism, with its hermeneutics of suspicion and unravelling of traditional discourses. The late Middle Ages was, after all, preeminently a time when the discourses of the twelfth and thirteenth century unravelled, and the disasters and crises of the period made for suspicion on many counts. The fragility of the Church of the time – in terms of both its institutions and the lives of Christians – has been seen in a more positive and sympathetic way. There has been renewed interest in the mystics of the period, both men and women, who have come to be regarded as creative and imaginative rather than as refugees from reality. Lollardy and other movements of dissent have been taken more seriously. Late medieval philosophy and theology have come to be appreciated in their own right, rather than considered simply as symptomatic of a decline from the achievements of thirteenth-century scholasticism. Interest in this 'Age of the Laity', as the Church of the time has sometimes been called, has chimed with the increasing emphasis on the role of the laity in the Catholic Church since the Second Vatican Council. The remarkable women of the period – mystics, dissenters and many others – have fed into feminist studies.

Where these recent developments will lead to in the future can only be surmised. Further opportunities and avenues of exploration into the late medieval Church are likely to open up in the twenty-first century. The topic looks set to retain its recently acquired fascination for some time to come.

Outline of the chapters

So far the Introduction has examined the background, both historical and historiographical, to the study of the later medieval Church. The rest of the book studies this Church and its relations with the wider world in finer detail; yet the background should continue to be borne in mind. The first five chapters focus on the Western Church. Within this framework the first two chapters examine the more obviously institutional dimensions of the Church: Church councils, the secular clergy at various levels from pope to parish priest, and religious orders. Chapter 3 focuses on the laity, who constituted the large majority of the members of the Church, and therefore this chapter is central to the book. Chapter 4 looks at learning and various forms of culture, while Chapter 5 studies dissenting movements and the official Church's response to them. Chapter 6 treats of the Orthodox Church and various other Churches that were partly separate from the Roman Catholic Church. The final chapter examines the attitudes of Christians to outside religions and beliefs and towards the people who adhered to them.

For a fuller description of the contents of the chapters and the conclusions in them, the reader is advised to turn to the introductory section at the beginning of each chapter and to the relevant pages in the Conclusion.

CHAPTER I

Papacy and Councils

The fourteenth and fifteenth centuries were fraught times for the papacy. The fortunes of the popes were enmeshed, for much of the period, with those of a succession of Church councils. It seems right, therefore, to take the two institutions – papacy and councils – together in this chapter.

For most of the fourteenth century the popes resided at Avignon in southern France rather than in Rome. The start of the Avignon papacy is usually dated to 1309, and it ended abruptly in 1377 when Pope Gregory XI returned to Rome. Following his death the next year, there was a dispute over his successor. For almost 40 years two men, and for a while three, claimed to be the rightful pope. Europe was divided in its loyalties. Eventually a Church council, meeting in the city of Constance in southern Germany, managed to end the schism by deposing one claimant, persuading the other two to resign, and arranging the successful election of a new pope, whose legitimacy was soon recognized almost everywhere in Western Christendom.

In claiming authority to deal with the papal schism, the Council of Constance had asserted its supremacy over the papacy. The assertion led to a prolonged and bitter dispute between a succession of popes and councils regarding their respective roles in the Church. Victory seemed at last to be secured by Pope Eugenius IV. He managed to persuade representatives of the Greek Church to come to Florence rather than to Basel in order to discuss reunion between East and West, that is, to come to the council under his control rather than to the rival council in Switzerland that was resisting his authority. The coup was much enhanced at the time by the reunion of the two Churches at the Council of Florence, even though the agreement proved to be fleeting. Eugenius outlawed the council at Basel; it withered and finally dissolved itself some years later.

During the rest of the period under consideration – from 1440 to 1500 – the papacy managed to resist various attempts to revive the authority of councils. The result was an atmosphere of some bitterness and disappointment, especially as the popes of the time seemed to many to be opposing reform itself. A succession of popes came to be closely identified with various aspects of the Renaissance. This movement of cultural and artistic renewal had religious roots and content, yet to many it seemed linked more to paganism and immorality than to truly Christian concerns. Of the popes of the period, some were leading patrons of the Renaissance, and the private lives of some of them left much to be desired. Immorality and financial greed in high places were prominent factors that led, according to the traditional historiography, to the start of the Reformation in 1517.

Such is the skeleton outline of the main events. The fuller picture and the wider implications were, of course, more complex.

Avignon papacy

The move

For a long time before the move, popes had spent considerable time away from Rome. Sometimes this was because they were driven out by their enemies within the city, sometimes they travelled abroad voluntarily. A famous instance was the confrontation between Pope Gregory VII and the Emperor Henry IV in January 1077, which took place not in Rome but at the snow-clad castle of Canossa in northern Italy, where the pope was staying with his friend and ally, Countess Matilda of Tuscany. Another example was Pope Alexander III (1159–81), who was closely involved in the dispute in England between Thomas Becket, Archbishop of Canterbury, and King Henry II. He lived in exile from Rome during the early part of his reign, when the dispute was raging, finding refuge in France and at Benevento in southern Italy. Many other cases could be mentioned.

In the mid and late thirteenth century papal journeys outside Italy were mainly to France, a country with which the papacy came increasingly to be identified. In some cases it would be more appropriate to speak of sojourns rather than brief visits. Pope Innocent IV (1243–54) fled from Rome in 1244 and spent the next seven years in France, based in Lyons. Here he presided over a general council of the Western Church, Lyons I, in 1245. The only other general council of the period was held in the same city, Lyons II, in 1274. In this case, too, the pope, Gregory X, attended the council and presided in person. Several popes of the time were born and lived in France or had French connections. Popes Urban IV (1261–64) and Clement IV (1265–68) were both Frenchmen and had studied at Paris university. Neither of them, during their short pontificates, resided in Rome for long, though they spent the time elsewhere in Italy rather than in France. Martin IV (1281–85) was another Frenchman. He had been archdeacon of Rouen and chancellor of Louis IX before his election. Several other popes of the period had studied at Paris university and spent time in France in various capacities. In addition, many of the cardinals – for example, six of the 14 created by Pope Urban IV in 1261 – and other officials of the papal Curia were French. Altogether the Curia came to have a strongly French character.

Geographically, moreover, France rather than Rome lay at the centre of Western Christendom (see Map 2). Throughout the centuries of the Roman Empire, Rome had been central. It was the capital city of the empire and lay at the centre of the Mediterranean world, which constituted the core of the world within which Christianity spread. Two factors radically altered the situation. First, the rise of Islam meant the gradual loss for Christianity of North Africa and the Near East, and for a long time that of much of Spain. Secondly, the schism between Eastern and Western Christendom, beginning in the eleventh century, meant that most of the countries to the east of Italy that remained Christian owed their loyalty to Constantinople rather than to Rome. Well before 1300, therefore, Rome, lying on the edge of Western Christendom and threatened by the possible further expansion of Islam, was no longer at the centre of a predominantly Christian Mediterranean world.

Avignon, on the other hand, was geographically more central to Western Christendom. It was well surrounded by Catholic lands to the north, south, east and west. It is pleasantly located on the banks of the Rhône, as the visitor today can experience. It was a papal 'fief' – that is, a piece of territory owned by the pope – over which, therefore, the pope had a good measure of authority and control. Rome was still a larger and grander city, even though most of its former glory lay in ruins, but it was prey to fights between the leading families of the city and to the twin scourges of flooding and malaria. The flow of the river Tiber was to be controlled by the construction of embankments only in the late nineteenth century. France, in which Avignon lay culturally and linguistically, even though politically it then formed part of the Holy Roman Empire (centred on Germany), was the largest and most populous country in Europe. Perhaps 15 million people, or a quarter of the total population of Western Christendom, lived within its boundaries. Paris was much the largest city in Western Europe, with a population of around half a million. Its university was the largest and most famous in Europe. In other ways, too, France was the cultural and intellectual leader of Europe.

In all sorts of respects, therefore, the move to Avignon made some sense. Rather than being a sudden change, it set the seal on various developments already under way. Even in terms of the pope's status as bishop of Rome, which was later to prove crucial for the papacy's return to Rome, there was room for discussion. St Peter, it could be argued, had been pope long before he reached Rome towards the end of his life; so likewise his successors were not tied to that city. The exaltation of the papacy from the Gregorian Reform (in the late eleventh century) onwards led to an emphasis on the pope as vicar of Christ and on his authority over the whole Church rather than on his role as bishop of Rome. In these and other subtle ways the papacy became somewhat detached from Rome and another location could be contemplated.

The move to Avignon was gradual and the result of a number of factors. Pope Boniface VIII (1294–1303) and King Philip 'le Bel' (Philip the Fair) of France (1285–1314) had clashed over several issues, principally the king's right to tax the clergy and to appoint bishops within his realm. Boniface died in Rome within a few weeks of the assault upon him at Anagni by Philip's soldiers in September 1303. His successor, Benedict XI, lasted less than a year. The cardinals who met in Perugia in northern Italy to elect the next pope were divided between those who supported the firm policies of Boniface and those who wanted rapprochement with the French king. Eventually, after 11 months of bitter debate, the latter group emerged triumphant. Bertrand de Got, who was archbishop of Bordeaux in southern France and on relatively good terms with Philip the Fair, gained the necessary two-thirds majority among the cardinals and became Clement V. Almost immediately he moved to France and was crowned pope at Lyons in November 1305. After stays in various places in the provinces of Provence and Gascony, he settled with the papal Curia, at King Philip's request, in Avignon in 1309.

As a papal fief, the city of Avignon and surrounding lands were owned directly by the papacy, though its overlord since 1290 had been the king of Naples. For some years it looked as though the sojourn at Avignon might be temporary and a return to Rome was contemplated. Gradually, however, the stay became more definite. A clear sign of stability was the building of an enormous palace for the pope and various departments of his Curia, which remains today in a remarkably good state of preservation. In 1348 Pope Clement VI purchased outright the city and surrounding lands for 80,000 florins from the then overlord, Queen Joanna of Naples. For a while it looked as though the move to Avignon might become permanent.

Popes and Curia at Avignon

All seven of the Avignon popes were Frenchmen. More particularly, all of them came from southern France. The qualification is important because southern France, often called 'Languedoc' (*oc* was the word/*langue* used there for 'yes'), and northern France, 'Languedoil' (where the word for 'yes' was *oïl*), were almost two separate countries. The former looked to the Mediterranean world and southern Europe, and was in large measure outside the control of the king of France; the latter formed part of northern Europe and paid more attention to the king.

Pope Clement V (1305–14) was a native of Gascony in south-western France. A student of canon and civil law at the universities of Orléans in France and Bologna in Italy, he became archbishop of Bordeaux in 1299. Straightaway after his election as pope he sought reconciliation with the king of France, and the papacy acquired an increasingly French atmosphere. At his first appointment of new cardinals in December 1305, nine of the ten promotions were of Frenchmen, including four of his relatives. Further appointments in 1311 and 1312 reinforced the French domination of the college of cardinals.

Clement effectively exonerated Philip the Fair for his part in the assault on Pope Boniface VIII and admitted that Boniface was largely to blame for the crisis. He bowed to the French king's pressure and summoned a general council of the Church to Vienne in southern France. The main business of the council was to condemn and dissolve the military order of the Knights Templar – which had been founded as a religious order in the early twelfth century for the purpose of defending the Christian reconquest of the Holy Land – on the grounds of mismanagement and largely unsubstantiated charges of immorality, principally sodomy, on the part of its members. While Clement insisted that the property of the order be formally entrusted to the sister order of the Knights Hospitaller, King Philip nevertheless seized much of the order's extensive property in France for himself. The council's decision had the horrific effect of enabling Philip to have the head of the order, Grand Master James de Molay, and a considerable number of knights tortured and burnt to death on the grounds of their alleged homosexual practices.

The pope maintained a vigorous foreign policy, intervening in the affairs of many states, including England, Scotland, Hungary, Germany and Venice. He tried to find a middle way in the disputes that riddled the Franciscan order regarding the strictness of poverty to be observed by the friars. His interest in canon law bore fruit in the so-called 'Clementines' (*Liber septimus* was the official title), which was a compilation of the legislation of the Council of Vienne and of various more recent papal and other official decrees. His missionary and academic zeal was evidenced by the encouragement he gave for the study of oriental languages. He tried to promote the decree of the Council of Vienne which ordered the establishment of professorial chairs for the teaching of Hebrew, Arabic and Chaldaic at the papal Curia and at the universities of Paris, Oxford, Bologna and Salamanca (see p 173). The decree remained, however, only partly fulfilled. Sensitive and intelligent, a determined and varied personality yet fragile too, Clement brought a mixture of success and failure, of initiative and compromise, during his papacy.

His successor, John XXII (1316–34), was elected at the age of 72 after a conclave that was for long deadlocked and eventually lasted over two years. Born at Cahors, he studied law at Montpellier university and had been bishop of both Fréjus and Avignon before his election as pope. His long reign made him one of the oldest popes of all time. Despite poor health, he was energetic and administratively capable. He promoted the bureaucratic and financial efficiency for which the papal Curia at Avignon came to be famous. The danger was that Church posts might appear to be up for sale. His appointments of cardinals and officials at the Curia were overwhelmingly of men from southern France. Many of them were his relatives or from his locality. He promoted missionary work in Asia and established bishoprics in Turkey, Armenia, Iran and India. He started the papal library at Avignon and founded a university in his home town of Cahors.

John's interventions in theological disputes were vigorous and sometimes unfortunate. He condemned as heretical, or at least misleading, 28 propositions in the writings of the German mystical writer Meister Eckhart. He sided with moderate Franciscans against those (known as Spiritual Franciscans) who wanted to enforce a strict interpretation of poverty in the order. He had four of the latter burnt to death for their disobedience. Another Franciscan, William of Ockham, he summoned from Oxford to answer charges of heresy and held him in detention in Avignon for five years until he escaped to his friend Duke Ludwig of Bavaria. John condemned Marsiglius of Padua's work, *Defensor pacis*, which advocated lay government of the state, and excommunicated the author. There was also the misfortune of his gloomy views on the 'Beatific Vision', which he taught semi-officially: namely, that after death the souls of the saved will have to wait until the final judgement at the end of the world – rather than immediately or after a time in purgatory, according to the orthodox teaching – before they properly enjoy God. He was obliged on his deathbed to retract this teaching, which was formally condemned by his successor.

Benedict XII (1334–42) was born at Saverdun near Toulouse in southern France and became a Cistercian monk at a young age. He studied theology at Paris university, succeeded his uncle as abbot of Fontfroide monastery and became bishop successively of Pamiers and Mirepoix. As bishop he was indefatigable as an inquisitor, seeking to rid his diocese of the Albigensian heresy. After his election as pope, he revised the teaching of his predecessor on the Beatific Vision. He tried hard to reform the Curia and the clergy: he forbade various types of fees that were customarily paid to curial officials and sought to curtail pluralism (the holding of more than one Church office), non-residence (whereby a bishop or parish priest lived outside his diocese or parish), and various other abuses among the clergy. He also introduced measures of reform for the religious orders of Benedictines, Cistercians and Franciscans. The English regarded him as too closely identified with France, and his efforts to prevent the outbreak of the Hundred Years' War (1337–1453) between the two countries, and to bring hostilities to an end once they had started, were unsuccessful. He started the construction of the papal palace at Avignon, signalling the possible permanence of the papacy in that city and away from Rome.

The early life of Pope Clement VI (1342–52) closely followed that of his predecessor. He joined a Benedictine monastery at the age of ten, studied theology at Paris university, became abbot of another Benedictine monastery and was bishop of three French dioceses in succession before his election as pope. In contrast to his austere predecessor, Clement was pleasure-seeking and worldly in his private life, but generous too. The papal court became known for its banquets and festivities, and Clement was a patron of artists and scholars and a friend of Jews. He purchased the city of Avignon from Queen Joanna of Naples and enlarged the palace begun by his predecessor. His interventions in Italian politics were largely unsuccessful, but in Germany he helped to replace as Holy Roman Emperor the hostile Ludwig of Bavaria with the more accommodating Charles of Bohemia, who reigned as Charles IV. He failed to bring the war between England and France to an end, though he was partly instrumental in arranging the truce of Malestroit between the two countries in 1343.

The expenses of the court at Avignon, as well as lavish gifts to relatives and countrymen, required the raising of fresh taxes and various financial expediencies – a reversal of the reforms of Benedict XII. Opposition in England resulted in two important acts of Parliament: 'Provisors' in 1351, which forbade papal appointments to Church posts in England, and 'Praemunire' in 1353, which forbade appeals from English courts to the pope. Although Clement declined to return to Rome, he fixed 1350 as a 'jubilee year' for the city, encouraging pilgrims from all over Christendom to visit Rome in order to gain the 'indulgences' (leading to reductions in the pains of purgatory) which could be obtained there during the jubilee year.

Innocent VI (1352–62), the fifth of the Avignon popes, came from the Limousin region in southern France. He had been professor of law and a judge before his ordination as priest. He was bishop, successively, of two dioceses and was elected pope at the advanced age of 70. His reign saw a return to the more austere style of Benedict XII. He sought to limit the abuses of pluralism and non-residence and to insist upon adequate qualifications for those appointed to Church offices. He tried, too, to reform various religious orders. He enjoyed good relations with the Emperor Charles IV, and was partly instrumental in arranging the Treaty of Brétigny of 1360, which halted for a while the war between England and France. Innocent stated clearly that he wished to return the papacy to Rome. The desire became a possibility largely through the military campaigns of his legate in Italy, the Spanish cardinal Gil de Albornoz. Through a series of successful military campaigns, Albornoz secured a measure of peace and order in the turbulent papal states. A return to Rome became additionally attractive as Avignon was becoming a prey to marauding mercenary armies – especially, paradoxically, when the Treaty of Brétigny, and various earlier truces, freed troops from fighting in the Anglo-French war.

His successor, Urban V (1362–70), was the only Avignon pope to be officially declared 'blessed' or 'saint' by the Church: he was accorded the lower of the two accolades in 1870, when he was 'beatified' by Pope Pius IX. Indeed Urban was the only pope of the fourteenth and fifteenth centuries to be honoured thus, so that the two centuries represent in this respect a period of exceptional dearth for the papacy. Like Benedict XII, he had been a Benedictine abbot and he continued while pope to live and dress as a monk. He pursued the curial reforms of his predecessor, curbing the greed of officials and checking pluralism. He also promoted learning in the Church and provided many scholarships for poor students. Urban founded a college within Montpellier university and was partly instrumental in the foundation of new universities at Orange in southern France (1364), Cracow in Poland (1364) and Vienna in Austria (1365).

Urban spoke openly of his desire to return to Rome. He took the bold step of returning in 1367 and remained based in Rome for the next three years. While there he was visited by the Emperor Charles IV and by the Byzantine Emperor John V Palaeologus, who submitted to Urban and became a Roman Catholic. Further hopes for reunion between the Churches of Rome and Constantinople proved to be in vain, however. Life in Rome became increasingly difficult and a revolt of the citizens in the spring of 1370 forced Urban to seek refuge elsewhere in the papal states, first at Viterbo and then at Montefiascone. It was no surprise, therefore, that he decided to return to more peaceful Avignon. He entered the city in September 1370 but soon fell ill and died two months later.

The resulting conclave of cardinals took a mere two days to elect Cardinal Pierre Roger de Beaufort, aged 42, as Pope Gregory XI (1370–78). A Frenchman from the Limousin region, he was made a cardinal at the age of 19 by his uncle Pope Clement VI. Subsequently he studied law at Perugia university in Italy and was given important responsibilities by Urban V. As pope he was noted for various initiatives: attempts to call a crusade, the search for reunion with the Greek Church, the reform of religious orders and the repression of heresy, including his condemnation of 19 propositions of the Englishman John Wyclif in 1377. Dominant, however, was his desire to return to Rome, but disturbances in the city and elsewhere in Italy prevented the move for several years. Catherine of Siena came to Avignon and stayed for three months during the summer of 1376, pleading with the pope to return to Rome. Later that year he finally made the move and reached the city in January 1377. The last year of his life was disturbed and an uprising in Rome forced him to retire for a while further south, to Anagni. Gregory died a somewhat broken man, back in Rome, in March 1378.

From papal schism to the Council of Florence

Papal schism

The election of a successor to Gregory XI proved difficult and resulted in the longest papal schism in the history of Christianity. Sixteen cardinals – 11 Frenchmen, four Italians and one Spaniard – gathered 'in conclave' in the papal palace within the Vatican on the evening of 7 April 1378 to conduct the election. Six more cardinals remained at Avignon in France, out of the election. A noisy crowd gathered around the conclave and clamoured for the election of a Roman, or at least an Italian, as pope. The fear was that if a Frenchman was elected, he would return to Avignon, and Rome would once again be deprived of the papacy. As well as the religious significance of the pope residing in the city of Rome, of which he was bishop, his presence there and that of the papal Curia were crucial for the economic and material well being of the city. The vital question was whether the pressure of the crowd was so great as to invalidate the election.

A huge amount of conflicting literature was written about this question during the ensuing schism. Opinions were almost equally divided. There is no doubt that the crowd remained rowdy and threatening throughout the night, and that various officials tried unsuccessfully to restore calm. It seems clear that in the early morning of 8 April at least a part of the conclave decided to vote for Bartholomew Prignano, Archbishop of Bari in southern Italy, though some of the cardinals claimed, at least later, that they did so with reservation, pressurized by the crowd. Prignano was not a cardinal and therefore not present at the conclave but, it was hoped, he would be acceptable as an Italian even though not a Roman. The choice was helped by the split in the French vote, between the southerners – or 'Limousins' as they were called, inasmuch as most of them came from the Limousin region – and those from the middle and north of the country. Unable to agree on a Frenchman, most of the French cardinals came round, at least initially, to supporting Prignano.

Before the archbishop could be fetched, assailants invaded the conclave and demanded a Roman as pope. To assuage them the elderly Roman cardinal Francis Tebaldeschi was presented to them as the one elected. At this point the cardinals took advantage of a lull in the proceedings and escaped from the papal palace, only to reconvene the next day and confirm the election of Bartholomew Prignano, who took the name Urban VI. In the following days the cardinals, or at least the large majority of them, publicly recognized Urban as pope in various ways, including by their presence at his enthronement. Such public recognition, it could be argued, annulled any doubts about the validity of his initial election.

Pope Urban's true character soon became apparent. He was quarrelsome and rude towards a wide range of people, including his potential supporters, both lay and clerical: the cardinals who had elected him, the bishops and officials of the Curia with whom he had to deal, ambassadors and envoys of secular rulers, and sovereigns themselves, including Queen Joanna of Naples and the German Emperor Wenceslas, who were important potential allies. At the very least, arrogance and imbalance of mind were evident. To the issue of the possible invalidity of his election, due to pressure from the Roman crowd, was now added that of his 'incapacity' for the office.

Matters turned bitter during the summer. Most of the cardinals left Rome and gathered together at Anagni, some 40 miles to the south-west. After making various unsuccessful efforts to persuade Urban to resign or at least to seek re-election, the French cardinals formally declared the nullity of his election on 20 July 1378. The Italian cardinals concurred. Two months later, following various further efforts at mediation, the cardinals, now assembled at Fondi to the south of Rome, elected as pope one of their number, Cardinal Robert of Geneva. Born in Geneva in modern Switzerland, he had spent much of his life in Paris and had been bishop of two French dioceses, Thérouanne and later Cambrai. He took the name Clement VII. Initially recognition of him as pope was widespread even within Roman circles, but he was unable to enter the city. On 29 April 1379 his mercenary troops were defeated by Urban's army at the Battle of Marino, which dashed his hopes of taking Rome. After spending two more years in various parts of Italy, Clement retired to Avignon in May 1381.

From that date onwards there were two claimants to the papacy: Urban VI in Rome and Clement VII in Avignon. There were, correspondingly, two colleges of cardinals and two papal Curias. When Urban died in 1389, the cardinals at Rome elected as his successor Boniface IX (1389–1404) and he in turn was followed by Innocent VII (1404–6) and Gregory XII (1406–15). At Avignon, the death of Clement in 1394 led to the election of Benedict

XIII (1394–1423). Europe was divided in its loyalties, largely following the decisions of its political leaders (see Map 2). Central and northern Italy, Germany and Central Europe, Scandinavia and England were solidly or predominantly for Urban. France, apart from the lands under English control, and the kingdoms of Spain, declared for Clement. Scotland, which was often at war with England and traditionally an ally of France, also sided with Clement. Other countries, such as Ireland, Portugal, southern Italy, the islands of Sicily, Sardinia and Corsica, and various territories within the German-speaking world, were less certain in their loyalty or changed allegiance. Religious orders were split down the middle in their loyalty, usually following the national allegiances of their members. The university of Paris for a long time supported Clement and his successor; the universities of Oxford and Cambridge were solid in their defence of the Urbanite line. Saints, too, could be found on both sides. Catherine of Siena was ardent in her support for Urban VI, even though she sharply rebuked him in person and through her letters for his shortcomings, whereas St Vincent Ferrer, the Dominican friar and renowned preacher in France and Spain, was for a long time equally convinced of the legitimacy of the Clementine line of popes.

Three ways of resolving the schism were proposed. The first was the 'way of force', or *via facti* in Latin: for one side to conquer the other. This solution was effectively ruled out by Clement VII's defeat at the Battle of Marino in 1379 and his move to Avignon in 1381, though there were intermittent attempts at armed intervention later, and many attempts, on the part of both lines of popes, to persuade kings and other secular rulers to change sides.

The second way was that of resignation, *via resignationis*, or, as it was sometimes called, *via cessionis*, the way of cession. Urban had been urged to resign by the cardinals soon after his election, but once the two popes had become firmly established in Rome and Avignon, and convinced of their own legitimacy, the call became one for mutual resignation. That is to say, both popes would resign simultaneously and thus make way for the election of a new and undisputed pope. Popes on both sides favoured this solution at various times, at least officially and in public. The difficulty lay in arranging simultaneous resignations. Benedict XIII had been forced to leave Avignon in 1403 on account of the French king's withdrawal of support for him, and he settled elsewhere in France in the lands of his supporter, the count of Provence. Finally in April 1407 both he and Gregory XII, the 'Roman' pope, agreed to meet on 29 September at Savona near Genoa in northern Italy in order to bring about the two resignations. Almost at the last hour Gregory changed his mind and failed to arrive. Further attempts to arrange a meeting followed and at one point the two men came within a few miles of each other. But eventually all was to no avail. Benedict retired to Perpignan in southern France and Gregory found refuge in various places in Austria and northern Italy.

At this juncture, most of the cardinals abandoned their respective popes and came together to summon a council to Pisa in northern Italy. It was set to meet in 1409 for the express purpose of resolving the schism. This third way of resolving the schism, *via concilii*, the way of a council, had been mooted way back in 1378 and continued to be proposed intermittently during the next 30 years. In 1409 it became a reality.

Council of Pisa and afterwards

The Council of Pisa met from 25 March to 7 August 1409. Participation was high: 24 cardinals, that is, almost all the members of the two 'colleges' of cardinals who had previously been loyal to one or other papal claimant; several hundred archbishops, bishops and abbots, or their proxies; representatives of religious orders; deputies of secular rulers, of towns, and of universities – some 500 members altogether, it has been estimated. The Council of Pisa appeared to be a general council of the Western Church, except for the absence of the two claimants to the papacy. Other notable absentees were the German Emperor Rupert, a staunch supporter of Gregory XII, and representatives from Spain, which remained largely loyal to Benedict XIII.

The council's principal purpose was to put an end to the papal schism. Both Gregory XII and Benedict XIII refused to attend or to recognize the council's authority. Each of them, moreover, retained a significant measure of support within Western Christendom. After lengthy proceedings and in view of the 'obstinacy' of the two men, the council declared them to be 'notorious schismatics and obdurate heretics' and the papacy to be vacant. The cardinals met in conclave to fill the vacancy and their apparently unanimous choice fell upon one of their number, Peter Philarghi, Cardinal Archbishop of Milan, who took the name Alexander V. He had been born in Crete, of Greek parents, and entered the Franciscan order as a young man. He was a student at the Franciscan houses of study at Padua in Italy, Norwich and Oxford in England, and Paris. He had lectured at the order's houses in Russia, Bohemia and Poland, at Pavia in Italy, as well as at Paris. He was a personal friend of Gian Galeazzo Visconti, Duke of Milan, through whose patronage he was appointed successively bishop of Piacenza, Vicenza, and Novara, in north Italy, and finally archbishop of Milan. He had been named cardinal by Innocent VII but broke with his successor, Gregory XII, when the latter procrastinated over resigning as pope. With this wide and varied background, the unanimity of his election and his accommodating personality, he might have spelt the end of the schism. Such hopes were dashed by his sudden though apparently natural death less than a year after his election. Philarghi and the other cardinals in the conclave before the election had promised that, if elected pope, they would not dissolve the council until it had tackled the knotty issue of reform of the Church. Once elected, however, he did little to put the promise into practice. His energies went rather into retaining the loyalty of his supporters, both clerical and lay. This policy may be partly explained by the fact that both Gregory XII and Benedict XIII remained threats to his authority, with their restricted but continuing allegiances. When Alexander dissolved the council in early August, he deferred reforms to a future council which was set to meet in three years' time.

His untimely death in May 1410 led to the election of Baldassare Cossa, who took the name John XXIII. Cossa had been a trusted cardinal during the pontificate of Gregory XII but, along with Philarghi, had broken with his master over his delays in resigning as pope. He had been prominent in arranging the Council of Pisa and was himself a strong candidate for the papacy at the election of 1409. He seemed the obvious successor when Alexander V died: the cardinals appear to have been virtually unanimous in choosing him. Soon after his election, however, various unseemly aspects of his past life came to be alleged. It is difficult to distinguish fact from fiction in the accusations, partly because during the process of John's eventual deposition at the Council of Constance in 1415 there were strong motives to discredit his earlier life and to prove his unworthiness as pope. Dubious activities while he was papal treasurer under Gregory XII, as well as during his tenure of various military and naval commands under the same pope, his sexual immorality, simony at the time of his election as pope and a variety of other crimes, were alleged against him. In recent years there have been attempts to rehabilitate his reputation.

Pope John kept to the timetable for a council to follow up Pisa. It duly assembled in Rome in April 1412 and held a number of sessions, sporadically, until its closure in March 1413. It was poorly attended and achieved little apart from a lengthy condemnation of the Englishman John Wyclif. The pope seems to have had little enthusiasm for the council, and reform of the Church, at least through this channel, was put on hold once again. In other ways John appeared to be in favour of reform. He appointed as cardinals the able Frenchmen Pierre D'Ailly and Guillaume Fillastre, and the Italian Francesco Zabarella, and he would have appointed to the same office, it seems, the Englishmen Robert Hallam and Thomas Langley, bishops of Salisbury and Durham respectively, but for the opposition of their monarch, Henry IV. The division of opinion among churchmen was not so much between those in favour and those against reform. Almost all those who spoke out were in favour, at least in principle. The issue was increasingly focusing, rather, on who should initiate and take final responsibility for reform: pope or council?

When closing the Council of Rome in March 1413, John XXIII declared his intention of summoning another council for December of the same year, but without any mention of where it would meet. Other people too were urging a new council, but one with a more specific agenda: that is, to remove the glaring scandal of three men each claiming to be the true pope and then to undertake the desired reform of the Church.

Council of Constance

The initiative in calling the Council of Constance (1414–18) came principally from the German Emperor Sigismund. (He is usually referred to as the Emperor Sigismund, though strictly speaking he held the lesser title of 'king of the Romans' until his coronation as emperor by Pope Eugenius IV in Rome in 1433.) After consulting with John XXIII, Sigismund announced in October 1413 that a new council would begin on 1 November 1414 in the city of Constance in southern Germany. As 'king of the Romans' and effectively 'Holy Roman Emperor-elect', he could, with a measure of respectability, trace his authority back to the first Christian emperor, Constantine I (306–37), and thus claim seniority among European rulers as well as the right to call a general council – it was Constantine who had summoned the first council of the whole Church, Nicaea I, in 325. Thus Sigismund's announcement of the council, which effectively amounted to its summons, could be seen as a return to the practice of the early Church during its first millennium, when all seven plenary (or 'ecumenical') councils – Nicaea I in 325, Constantinople I in 381, Ephesus in 431, Chalcedon in 451, Constantinople II and III in 553 and 680–81, and Nicaea II in 787 (Constantinople IV in 869–70 is usually added in Western sources as the eighth) – were convoked by the reigning emperor or (in a few cases) empress. The announcement by Sigismund was thus a reversal of the medieval trend whereby all general councils of the Western Church after the beginning of the East–West schism in 1054 (that is to say, from Lateran I in 1123 to Vienne in 1311–12) had been summoned by the pope.

Two of the three claimants to the papacy refused to attend the council or to recognize its authority. Gregory XII and Benedict XIII each thought he was the legitimate pope and therefore there was no need of a council to resolve the crisis. John XXIII was wary. In the end he formally convoked the council and decided to attend but on condition that, as he thought, the council would confirm both himself as pope and the deposition of the two other claimants. Once the council had assembled, a consensus soon emerged that, in view of the continuing and significant support for all three candidates in various quarters, the best way forward was to request the resignation of each claimant, including therefore John XXIII, and then to start again with a fresh papal election.

The Council of Constance turned out to be the largest and, in many ways, the most remarkable assembly of the Middle Ages. Its members were at least as numerous as those at the Council of Pisa and it lasted three and a half years, much longer than any previous general council in the Middle Ages. It witnessed a succession of dramatic events and enactments. The human side of the story, including details of the large number of personnel in attendance, remains vividly recorded in the *Chronicle* of Ulrich von Richental (d.1437), a citizen of Constance who wrote from first-hand experience.

A notable feature was the council's organization by 'nations'. The arrangement had begun in embryonic form at the Second Council of Lyons in 1274 and developed at the succeeding general Councils of Vienne (1311–12) and Pisa (1409). It reached its culmination at Constance. Members of the council normally met in their national grouping, or in the one closest to them, while the cardinals sometimes joined their own nation and sometimes met as a separate 'college'. Each of the five nations usually made up its mind on the issue being debated, and then voted as a single unit (so that the voting by nations was 5-0 or 4-1 or 3-2). The five 'nations' were Italy, France, Spain, Germany (which included the countries of Central Europe and Scandinavia) and England (which included Wales, Scotland and Ireland). Spain was not represented as a nation until towards the end of the council, since for a long time it remained largely loyal to Pope Benedict XIII and therefore outside the council. England began the council as part of the German nation but during the course of it managed to acquire the status of an independent 'nation'. The Germans supported the move, content thus to achieve greater control over their own 'nation'. The French, on the other hand, were strongly opposed to England's promotion on the grounds that the country was too small to form an independent nation. English successes in the Hundred Years' War – the Battle of Agincourt was fought in October 1415 – bolstered the country's case for promotion.

France, in fact, had been the chief protagonist of the organization by nations at the start of the council, chiefly in order to reduce the influence of the Italians. For it was from Italy that John XXIII drew much of his support, thereby helping him to block French moves to depose him. That is to say, the large number of dioceses in Italy, and therefore of bishops, would give the Italians a disproportionate influence in the council if the voting was effectively 'one person, one vote', whereas the organization by 'nations' reduced the Italian vote to one of three, or four (after England's promotion), or five (after Spain's entry), and correspondingly increased France's influence (at least until the arrival of England and Spain as nations).

Pope John XXIII opened the council with solemnity in the cathedral of Constance on 5 November 1414 and on 16 November the council held its first session. Three issues were to be given attention: the ending of the papal schism, sometimes referred to simply as bringing 'peace' to the Church; doctrine, which meant principally tackling the teachings of John Wyclif and Jan Hus; and reform of the Church. The Emperor Sigismund arrived on Christmas Day. Many bishops and other representatives arrived early in the new year and then the proper business of the council got under way.

When it became apparent that the council was unwilling to re-confirm John XXIII as pope and to renew Pisa's deposition of the other two candidates, Gregory XII and Benedict XIII, but rather was looking for the resignation of all three men, John appeared for a while to be willing to resign. But then he prevaricated and on the night of 20/21 March fled from Constance secretly and in disguise. He went first to Schaffhausen in Switzerland and then to Breisach on the Rhine, where he had supporters among the German and Burgundian nobility. From this exile John threatened to dissolve the council.

It was in this context of dire emergency that the council formally proclaimed, on 26 March, its legitimacy and the inability of the pope to dissolve it. Then on 6 April it issued the famous decree asserting the superiority of a general council over the pope. The decree is usually known as *Haec Sancta* (English, 'This Holy'), following its first words after the opening invocation of the Trinity (though sometimes it is called *Sacrosancta*, in accordance with an alternative reading to be found in some manuscripts). The key paragraph reads as follows:

> First, it [the council] declares that, legitimately assembled in the holy Spirit, constituting a general council and representing the catholic Church militant, it has power immediately from Christ; and that everyone of whatever state or dignity, even papal, is bound to obey it in those matters which pertain to the faith, the eradication of the said [papal] schism, and the general reform of the said Church of God in head and members. (*Decrees*: 409)

Much has been written about the significance of the decree. On the one hand, obviously, it emerged from a particular crisis: that of three claimants to the papacy and, most immediately, of the threats coming from the candidate most favoured by the council at the time, John XXIII, to dissolve it. On the other hand, the language of the decree does not limit itself to the particular crisis. The council claims authority over the pope not just regarding 'the eradication of the [papal] schism,' but also 'in those matters which pertain to the faith ... and the general reform of the Church of God in head and members'. In basing these claims upon its status as a general council, moreover, Constance seems to be claiming the same or similar authority for other general councils of the Church.

J.N. Figgis, the noted constitutional historian, described *Haec Sancta* in the following words:

> Probably the most revolutionary official document in the history of the world is the decree of the council of Constance asserting its superiority to the pope, and striving to turn into a tepid constitutionalism the divine authority of a thousand years. The [conciliar] movement is the culmination of medieval constitutionalism. It forms the watershed between the medieval and the modern world. (Figgis 1907: 41)

This is strong language and in many ways the Council of Constance saw itself as conservative rather than revolutionary, as returning to the balanced and conciliar forms of government of the early Church that had been jeopardized by developments towards papal monarchy and absolutism since the Gregorian Reform movement of the late eleventh century. Through the surviving documentation, we are quite well informed about the meetings and discussion within the council that led up to the promulgation of *Haec Sancta*. There was a fair range of opinions among the members of the council, between moderate and more extreme conciliarists. But the large majority, it seems clear, wanted to put some firm checks on the papacy and to institutionalize Church councils for this purpose.

John XXIII soon withdrew his threats to dissolve the council. He was taken prisoner and brought before the council, where he was tried for his misconduct and formally deposed as pope on 29 May. A broken man, John acquiesced in the decision and accepted his deposition. He was held in strict confinement for several years and set free only in 1419, when he made his submission to the new pope, Martin V. He died a few months later and was buried in the baptistery next to the cathedral in Florence. On his magnificent tomb – the work of Bartholomew di Michelozzo and Donatello – is carved the papal insignia: an indication that he was widely regarded as having been, for a while, the true pope.

Gregory XII, who had refused to recognize the council at the start, quite quickly came to terms with it. In July 1415, under pressure from the council, he announced his resignation as pope, convinced that he had been the true pope until that moment. At the same time he convoked the council afresh, but without recognizing its earlier enactments, including *Haec Sancta*. He was given an honourable retirement as a cardinal legate and died soon afterwards in 1417, shortly before the election of Martin V. Benedict XIII adamantly refused to resign. He moved in 1415 from Perpignan in southern France to the castle of Peniscola on the Mediterranean coast of Spain and remained there until his death, convinced to the end that he was the sole legitimate pope but supported by a diminishing band of adherents. He was visited at Perpignan by the Emperor Sigismund but firmly rejected his overtures to resign. The council dispatched other envoys to him during the next two years, in further painstaking but unsuccessful efforts to obtain his resignation. Finally, in July 1417, the council 'divested' him of any claims to the papacy, in language that implied that he had never been the true pope. At his death in 1423, a successor was elected who took the name of Clement VIII, but he was persuaded to resign in 1429, thereby bringing an end to this line of papal claimants.

Which was the true line of popes? The Catholic Church has never given a definitive answer to the question, though in recent years the papacy has clearly favoured the 'Roman' line of Urban VI to Gregory XII – as indicated, for example, by the list of past popes in *Annuario Pontificio*, the Vatican yearbook. No crucial religious importance hangs on the answer, inasmuch as none of the possible popes made major doctrinal statements, so that from this point of view it is not essential to know who was the genuine pope at any given time. Interesting and of some significance, however, was the permission given by the 'Roman' pope Innocent VII to the Benedictine abbot of St Osyth in Essex, England, to ordain monks to the priesthood, inasmuch as it confirmed an important precedent that someone other than a bishop might ordain a priest.

In terms of historical rather than religious or theological interest, the following points may be noted. The Clementine (or Avignon) popes have been the least favoured of the three lines. In addition to the widespread rejection of Benedict XIII after he was 'divested' of his claims to the papacy by the Council of Constance in 1417, as mentioned, there is the fact that when later popes chose for themselves names that had been taken by 'Clementine' popes, they added the same number as had been assumed by the earlier Clementine pope of that name, thereby implying his illegitimacy. Thus Clement VII (1523–34) took the same number as the earlier Clement VII (1378–94), Benedict XIII (1724–30) the same number as Benedict XIII (1394–1423).

Regarding the other two lines, the evidence is more complex and somewhat conflicting. When John XXIII was deposed by the Council of Constance in May 1415, and Gregory XII resigned in July 1415, the council did not pronounce, one way or the other, on the legitimacy of their claims to have been pope. Nor did any later general council. When later popes chose a name that had been held by a 'Roman' (or Urbanite) pope, they always added one to the number, thereby implying the latter's legitimacy. Thus Urban VI (1378–89) was followed by Urban VII (1590), Innocent VII (1404–6) by Innocent VIII (1484–92), and Gregory XII (1406–15) by Gregory XIII (1572–83). Regarding the 'Pisan' popes, the papal insignia on the tomb of John XXIII has already been noted. Further support for the legitimacy of this line was shown by Pope Alexander VI (1492–1503), inasmuch as in taking the number VI, rather than V, he seemed to imply the legitimacy of the first Pisan pope, Alexander V (1409–10). After the second Pisan pope, John XXIII, no pope took the previously popular name of John for centuries, thereby skirting the question of his legitimacy. When Giovanni Roncalli finally broke the deadlock in 1958, he took the name John XXIII. The number implied the illegitimacy of the previous John XXIII, but of course this is difficult to square with the opposite logic in the sequence of Alexanders!

Already in 1415, when attempts to resolve the scandal of three claimants to the papacy dominated proceedings, the council was giving some attention to other matters. The council's eighth session, on 4 May 1415, issued condemnations of many teachings to be found in the writings of the Englishman John Wyclif (d.1384) and condemned him personally as a heretic. In July of the same year the council turned its attention to the Czech priest Jan Hus, who held similar views to those of Wyclif, though for the most part in a more moderate form. Hus had been given safe conduct to come to the council, but this protection was gradually disregarded after he arrived in November 1414. He was imprisoned, condemned in person and in his writings, and then burnt at the stake on 6 July 1415 – a fate he bore with great fortitude. Jerome of Prague, his friend and associate, suffered a similar death at the hands of the council in May of the following year. The three men condemned by the council will be treated more fully in Chapter 5. Here it may simply be noted that their condemnations dispel any notions that the Council of Constance, or indeed the 'conciliar movement' more generally, can easily be equated with liberal democracy or considered a direct precursor of movements in that direction from the eighteenth century onwards. It is noticeable, too, that Jan Hus remained safe and was relatively well treated as long as John XXIII remained at the council and retained some authority over it: the threats to his life began after the pope's departure.

In October 1417 the council enacted the important decree *Frequens*, which sought to institutionalize general councils on a regular basis:

> The frequent holding of general councils is a pre-eminent means of cultivating the Lord's patrimony. ... We therefore enact, decree and ordain, by a perpetual decree, that general councils shall be held henceforth in the following way.

The first shall follow in five years immediately after the end of this council, the second in seven years immediately after the end of the next council, and thereafter they are to be held every ten years for ever. They are to be held in places which the pope is bound to nominate and assign with a month before the end of each preceding council, with the approval and consent of the council, or which, in his default, the council itself is bound to nominate. Thus by a certain continuity, there will always be a council in existence or one expected within a given time. (*Decrees*: 438–9)

In the final months, the council turned its attention to moral and disciplinary reform of the Church. The results were limited. The main decrees of this nature were enacted in March 1418, just a few weeks before the end of the council. They restricted some exemptions of religious orders from episcopal authority, limited various abuses pertaining to benefices, once again forbade 'simoniacal' purchase of Church offices (simony, the sin of buying a Church office, named after the case of a certain Simon, who tried to buy spiritual gifts from the Apostles, as described in Acts 8.18–22), imposed various limits on tithes and other Church taxes, and issued a decree entitled, 'The life and good conduct of clerics', which dealt principally with the dress and tonsure of priests. There is nothing far reaching, nothing indeed comparable with the reform decrees of the major council of the thirteenth century, the Fourth Lateran Council of 1215.

Sometimes the failure of the late medieval Church to reform itself – and therefore the need of the Protestant Reformation of the sixteenth century – is seen as a consequence of the failure of the conciliar movement and of the papacy's opposition to that movement. But the very limited reformed decrees promulgated by the Council of Constance, and by other general councils of the fifteenth century, do not suggest that they would have brought about more radical reform – and thereby preempted the need for the Protestant Reformation – if they had been given more encouragement. The councils, it is true, met mostly in an atmosphere of pressure and crisis, so that they never really enjoyed the necessary calm that might have enabled them to debate or promulgate all the decrees they desired. Even so, what they managed to enact gives little hint of their anticipating the radical developments that were to take place in the following century. In many ways, indeed, in terms of doctrine and the protection of vested interests, the councils in question appear more conservative than the papacy.

The failure of the Council of Constance to move on to further reforms was partly the result of a split among the five 'nations'. Members of the French nation, particularly, urged that the council remain in session until the reform programme had been properly debated. The other nations, led by the English and supported by the Germans, urged rather that the council had been going on for long enough already, that the participants were tired and that reform should be postponed until the next council, which would be in only five years' time according to the decree *Frequens*. It was the latter view that won the day and the next council was duly assigned to the city of Pavia in 1423.

When Pope Martin V finally dissolved the Council of Constance on 22 April 1418, he confirmed everything that had been enacted by it 'in a conciliar way' (Latin, *conciliariter*). At the time this seemed sufficient confirmation and some of the 'concordats' that Martin made with the rulers of various countries immediately after the end of the council contained more explicit approval of the conciliar decrees, including *Haec Sancta* and *Frequens*. Nevertheless the question of papal approval of the decrees of Constance, especially *Haec Sancta* and *Frequens*, would return to haunt the Council of Basel and indeed the Catholic Church more generally for centuries to come.

The next council duly met in Pavia in northern Italy in April 1423. It soon transferred further south to Siena. Its achievements were minimal – little more than a few decrees of administrative reform, somewhat similar to the relatively minor reform decrees of Constance. Attendance at the council was thin, and Pope Martin, who did not attend in person, showed little enthusiasm for it. Much of his energy was taken up with consolidating his political position in Italy. Insofar as he favoured reform, he seems to have regarded the matter as the responsibility of the papacy rather than of a council. Early in 1424 his legates dissolved the council, apparently against the wishes of the majority of participants. At least the stipulations of *Frequens* were observed, so that shortly before the dissolution it was agreed between pope and council that the next meeting would be held in Basel in Switzerland in 1431.

Council of Basel–Florence

Before the Council of Basel convened in July 1431, Martin V died in February 1431 and Eugenius IV was elected as his successor. In the early stages attendance at the council was thin, but the number of participants built up gradually, so that the assembly came to resemble, in terms of participation and duration, the Council of Constance rather than the brief and thinly attended Councils of Rome (1412–13) and Pavia-Siena (1423–24). Pope Eugenius soon showed hostility to the council and dissolved it in December 1431. The council refused to recognize the dissolution, on the grounds that the pope could not dissolve a general council without its consent.

Two tense years followed, during which support for the council grew. An important success for the council was the arrival of a large delegation of Hussites from Bohemia in early 1433 and the beginnings of an agreement with them. Negotiations were continued after the departure of the delegation and resulted in the *Compactata* of Prague (see p 152).

Eventually Eugenius climbed down. In December 1433 he formally recognized the council, including its acts of the preceding two years, and at the same time confirmed Constance's decrees *Haec Sancta* and *Frequens*. Tension between the two parties persisted. Eugenius was still smarting under the humiliation of his climb-down, while the council issued a number of additional measures that could be perceived as hostile to the papacy and the Roman Curia, particularly in the area of Church reform.

Reform of the Church was a major preoccupation of the council during the next few years. The measures enacted went beyond the reform decrees of Constance; even so they were modest. There was very little anticipation in them of the momentous changes that would come with the Reformation and the Counter-Reformation in the following century. There were several decrees limiting papal authority in the appointment to benefices and in taxation of the Church, and various decrees limiting the pope's authority over the present council. Every bishop was instructed to hold an annual synod in his diocese, which was to attend to necessary reforms, and archbishops were to hold a synod every three years for the whole province – instructions that might have borne good fruits if they had been observed. Priests were forbidden to keep concubines, and various other measures relating to the good order and behaviour of the clergy were enacted. A fierce decree obliged Jews to attend Christian sermons, forbade various forms of social intercourse between (unconverted) Jews and Christians and forbade Jews who had converted to Christianity to return to their former ways.

Lying in the background of the council were the proposed discussions that would lead, it was hoped, to reunion between the Eastern and Western Churches. The presence of an army of Ottoman Turks virtually at the gates of Constantinople gave urgency to the situation. Already in September 1434 the council appeared to have reached agreement with the Byzantine emperor and the patriarch of Constantinople that a delegation from the Eastern Church should come to Basel to discuss reunion. Further measures were taken by the council but without bringing about the arrival of the Eastern delegation.

A vital twist in the story occurred in 1437. Pope Eugenius, who never came to Basel, instructed his representatives at the council to institute a vote on whether the assembly should be moved to another city. An important reason was to choose a city that would be closer to Constantinople and would therefore avoid the arduous trans-Alpine journey for the Eastern delegation. Another obvious motive was to choose a city that would be closer to Eugenius and more under his control: he had been expelled from Rome by the hostile forces of the mercenary leader Francesco Sforza in 1434 and was subsequently based mainly in Florence. The vote was taken in May 1437. Approximately two-thirds of the council members voted to remain at Basel, one-third to move.

Pope Eugenius followed the vote of the minority and ordered the council to move to northern Italy, first to Ferrara, where various sessions were held in 1438, and then to Florence, where the council met from 1439 onwards. The majority refused to accept the move and continued to meet in Basel. From 1438 onwards, therefore, there were two councils meeting simultaneously. Relations between the two assemblies grew increasingly bitter: each one refused to recognize the legitimacy of the other and excommunicated its members.

In 1439 the council at Basel deposed Eugenius as pope and elected in his place the Duke of Savoy, who took the name Felix V. The duke was a widower, the father of five children. A devout man, many people nevertheless considered his married and lay status made him unsuitable to be pope. Few, moreover, wanted a repetition of the papal schism, when two and later three individuals had claimed the papacy. This sad episode, which had divided and traumatized Europe between 1378 and 1417, was well within living memory. Felix V never had much support outside the Council of Basel and he finally resigned his claim to be pope in 1449. What was widely seen as Basel's mistake in electing Felix as a rival pope strengthened the position of the Council of Florence and of Eugenius IV.

Equally important in Eugenius's victory over the Council of Basel was that the delegation from the Church of Constantinople chose to come to Ferrara, and then to Florence, rather than to Basel to discuss reunion with the Western Church and that a formula of reunion was indeed agreed upon at Florence. The choice was made, it seems, for several reasons: Italy was easier than northern Switzerland to reach from Constantinople, the Eastern delegation had doubts about the legitimacy of the council at Basel, and the pope and the cities of Ferrara and Florence were attentive and generous, for the most part, regarding the details of payment for travel and accommodation.

The delegation from Constantinople was substantial. It was led by the heads of state and Church, the Emperor John VIII Palaeologus and the patriarch of Constantinople, Joseph II, and it included a number of bishops and theologians of the Orthodox Church. There followed at Ferrara and Florence over a year of discussions between the Orthodox delegation and bishops and theologians of the Catholic Church. Eventually agreement was reached in a decree of reunion, which was published on 6 July 1439.

This important decree, which is usually known by the opening words in the Latin text, *Laetentur Caeli* ('Let the heavens rejoice', expressing the joy of reunion; the decree was officially published in both Greek and Latin), reached agreement on the four main doctrinal issues that had been in dispute between the two Churches for a long time.

The first issue, which formed a major theological controversy, concerned *Filioque*, Latin for 'and from the Son'. The word had been inserted into the Creed by the Catholic Church in the early Middle Ages, to the anger of the Orthodox Church. It denoted that within the Trinity – the three 'persons' in one God, according to Christian theology – the Holy Spirit comes 'from the Son' as well as from the Father. The Orthodox Church regarded the insertion as misleading or even heretical and, perhaps more pertinently, as contrary to proper order, inasmuch as it had been introduced without their consent. *Laetentur Caeli* ruled, as a compromise, that the word could be justified on theological grounds but that members of the Orthodox Church were not obliged to include it when they recited the Creed.

The second issue concerned the bread used in the Eucharist. Should it be leavened or unleavened? Leavened bread was customary in the Eastern Church and seemed better to symbolize the risen Christ. Unleavened bread had for long been customary in the West and was more practical for keeping in the tabernacle – when awaiting distribution to the sick or while people prayed before the tabernacle, as were the practices in the West – since it lasted much longer than leavened bread before decomposing. The simple compromise reached was that each Church should follow its present custom: unleavened bread for Catholics and leavened bread for Orthodox.

The third issue concerned purgatory, the passage through which people destined for heaven might have to pass in order to 'purge' their sins in this life. Purgatory was prominent in the doctrine and devotional life of Catholics in the Middle Ages, featuring in much art of the period and in the multiplication of Masses and prayers for the dead. Orthodox theologians regarded the doctrine almost as an invention of the Catholic Church and largely ignored it. *Laetentur Caeli* recognized purgatory but in a careful and moderate way, thereby implicitly discouraging exaggerated attention to it.

Fourth was the extent of papal authority. Agreement was reached on this thorny issue by asserting the authority of the pope over all Christians, while stating – in a sentence that was open to somewhat varying interpretations (following different nuances in the Greek and Latin texts of the decree) – that this authority must be seen within the context of Church councils (which the Orthodox regarded as central to Church government), and by asserting the authority of the patriarch of Constantinople, subject to the overall authority of the pope, within the Orthodox Church.

Reunion with the Eastern or Orthodox Church was the most dramatic success of the Council of Florence. The council went on to achieve reunions with groups in several other Churches which had become separated from the Catholic Church: the Armenian, Ethiopian and Syrian Churches (see pp 169–72). Although the groups were relatively small communities within their respective Churches, the reunions added further prestige to the council and to Eugenius. The council was moved by the pope from Florence to Rome in 1443 and was finally dissolved in 1445. Meanwhile the council in Basel was losing support, owing in good measure both to its rash election of Felix V and to the achievement of *Laetentur Caeli* in Florence. Many of its leading supporters, including Aeneas Silvius Piccolomini, the future Pope Pius II, transferred their loyalties to Eugenius. The council moved from Basel to Lausanne, still in Switzerland, in 1447. It finally dissolved itself two years later, following Felix's resignation of his claims to the papacy; in return Eugenius lifted the excommunications and other penalties that had been imposed upon its members.

Reunion with the Eastern Church proved fleeting. Patriarch Joseph of Constantinople, who had backed the decree of reunion, *Laetentur Caeli*, died in Florence shortly before its promulgation. When the rest of the Eastern delegation returned to Constantinople, support for the reunion quickly declined and eventually evaporated. There was hostility to the decree at the popular level, several bishops on the delegation who had signed the decree changed their mind, and Emperor John VIII Palaeologus did not press for its confirmation. The possibility of further discussion of reunion effectively came to an end with the capture of Constantinople by the Turks in 1453 and the resulting loss of freedom for the Orthodox Church. For the papacy, however, and its struggle with the Council of Basel, *Laetentur Caeli* proved to be a triumph. When Eugenius died in 1447, secure in Rome since 1443, after many years of enforced exile, he could justifiably regard his reign as crucial to the restoration of papal authority.

Renaissance papacy

The last half-century of our period, ending in 1500, saw a transformation in the style of the papacy. The popes lived fairly securely in Rome. There was no serious talk of permanently moving again to Avignon or to anywhere else outside Rome. The threat posed to papal authority by the conciliar movement of the first half of the fifteenth century became less menacing in the second half of the century. The popes became somewhat identified with the Renaissance, though some caution is needed here: the identification was emphasized by later historians and to some extent was their construction. The popes in question had many other concerns and interests besides the promotion of art, architecture and scholarship. In many respects they were more medieval than modern or Renaissance figures. Even so, most of them devoted considerable time and attention, for a variety of motives, to rebuilding the city of Rome, to the patronage of art and to the promotion of scholarship.

Conciliarism

Conciliarism was by no means dead in the later fifteenth century, even though it was less overtly threatening to the papacy. The decree *Frequens* of the Council of Constance, which had ordered the holding of general councils every ten years (see pp 19–20), fell into abeyance. The popes remained opposed to this prescription of *Frequens*, fearing the reappearance of the ghost of conciliarism, while the mechanism for calling a council, in the absence of papal summons, could not be realized. Pope Pius II issued the fierce bull *Execrabilis* in 1460. The bull forbade appeals from the papacy to a general council, in direct opposition to the Council of Constance's decree *Haec Sancta*. No further general councils were held until the early sixteenth century, when the Fifth Lateran Council (1512–17) took place. Pope Julius II's main purpose in summoning this council, which was held within the Lateran basilica in Rome, was to outmanoeuvre a rival council that had been summoned to Pisa by various cardinals – who were supported by Louis XII of France – in fulfilment, it was argued, of the requirements of *Frequens*. The Fifth Lateran Council achieved little, despite its long duration, and does not reveal a renewed papal enthusiasm for general councils. It was only with the Council of Trent (1545–63) that another truly effective general council of the Western Church took place.

Despite the absence of general councils, support for them remained widespread and quite strong. The need to promulgate the bull *Execrabilis* partly acknowledged this. Many Christians of impeccable orthodoxy advocated the summoning of a general council for the reform of the Church and recognized the final superiority of such a council over the papacy. Thomas More, the Englishman executed by Henry VIII for his opposition to the king's divorce and for his loyalty to the papacy, was an example. Similar views in support of councils were widely held in university circles in the late fifteenth and early sixteenth centuries. When Martin Luther broke with Rome, he initially appealed to a general council to resolve the crisis. Conciliarism, at least at the level of general councils, was terminated within the Catholic Church for many centuries mainly by the new situation created by Reformation and Counter-Reformation as well as by the comprehensiveness and success of the Council of Trent, which for a long time made the calling of another general council appear unnecessary and almost superfluous.

Seven popes

The second half of the fifteenth century brought seven popes: Nicholas V (1447–54), Callistus III (1455–58), Pius II (1458–64), Paul II (1464–71), Sixtus IV (1471–84), Innocent VIII (1484–92) and Alexander VI (1492–1503). Five were Italians and two Spaniards, Callistus III and Alexander VI. It is important to look at their reigns in the round, not to focus exclusively on those aspects that have interested later Renaissance historians.

Nicholas V's important reign witnessed the consolidation of papal authority within Rome and the papal states, the successful termination of the Council of Basel and the end of the renewed papal schism. Nicholas enjoyed good relations with the leading families of Rome. Within the papal states he balanced firmness with respect for the aspirations of various regions and cities for a measure of self-government. His tact and good sense allowed the Council of Basel (which moved to Lausanne in 1447) to dissolve itself peacefully in 1449. In the same year he persuaded Felix V to renounce his claims to the papacy, in return making him a cardinal and providing him with a substantial pension. Nicholas obtained the support of the Emperor Frederick III and other rulers in Germany by reaching concordats with them on matters of taxation and appointments to Church benefices. The obvious perils of these policies were too much friendship with the powers of this world and the development of state Churches that were almost independent of Rome.

Nicholas is rightly regarded as the first Renaissance pope. He was a scholar himself as well as a patron of scholars and artists. He is often considered the effective founder of the Vatican Library, mainly thanks to his enormous collection of some 1,200 Greek and Latin manuscripts which came to the library. As pope he was responsible for the rebuilding of numerous churches, palaces, bridges and fortifications both in Rome and elsewhere in the papal states, and he employed many artists to adorn these and other buildings, most notably Fra Angelico. A central aim of these enterprises was to promote the Christian message by making the Church a leader of culture. He was the co-founder, together with Bishop Turnbull of Glasgow, of the university of Glasgow in Scotland.

Another achievement was his successful proclamation of 1450 as a jubilee year, when many pilgrims flocked to Rome to gain the indulgences offered there. The end of his life was shrouded with misfortune. There was a plot against his life in January 1453, and the capture and sack of Constantinople by the Turks followed in May. Nicholas tried to rally Christendom by calling a crusade, but to no avail.

Callistus III's short reign of three years was dominated by his efforts to re-launch the crusade called by his predecessor. Christian forces defeated the Turks before the city of Belgrade in Serbia and their fleet off the island of Lesbos, but the further goal of recapturing Constantinople proved quite out of reach. The pope spent money on the crusade rather than on cultural and artistic projects, so that the Renaissance found little support from him. A native Spaniard, he favoured his relatives and compatriots with posts and salaries. He made his nephew Rodrigo Borgia, the future Alexander VI, a cardinal at the age of 25 and vice-chancellor of the Roman Curia. He pleased France by declaring the innocence of Joan of Arc, quashing the earlier condemnation of her for witchcraft and heresy.

Pius II became pope with a mixed background. A well-known humanist scholar and writer, he was a leading supporter of the Council of Basel – acting for a while as secretary to Felix V, the man recognized as pope by the council – until 1445, when he transferred his allegiance to Eugenius IV. In that year, too, disturbed by a serious illness, he abandoned his rather dissolute way of life – having been the father of several illegitimate children as well as the author of the popular romance *De duobus amantibus* (usually rendered in English as *Euryalus and Lucretia*) – and underwent a religious conversion. He was ordained a priest the next year. Subsequently he enjoyed the confidence of Popes Nicholas V and Callistus III, was appointed bishop of Trieste in 1447 and of Siena in 1449 and cardinal in 1456.

As pope he continued his literary career by composing his memoirs and various other works. He devoted much time, though with little effect, to organizing a crusade to check the Turkish advance into Europe. Alongside this warlike approach, he wrote his remarkable 'Letter to Sultan Mohammed II', in which he provided a detailed refutation of the Koran and an appeal to the sultan to abandon Islam, be baptized and accept the crown of the former Byzantine Empire! He showed his continuing hostility to conciliarism by promulgating the bull *Execrabilis* (see p 26). Pius played an active role in European politics and pursued the vision of a united Christian Europe, though with mixed results. Like his predecessor, he favoured his relatives and compatriots (from Siena) with appointments and gifts, thus encouraging the nepotism that increasingly became a feature of the papacy. As a Renaissance figure, he is noted more for his own literary and oratorical achievements than for his patronage of other artists and scholars.

Paul II was the nephew of Eugenius IV. He enjoyed his uncle's patronage as well as that of Nicholas V and Callistus III. His seven-year reign provided a mixture of splendour and fragility. He delighted the citizens of Rome with sports, carnivals and other entertainments. He completed the magnificent Palazzo San Marco (now the Palazzo di Venezia) in the centre of Rome, which he had begun building while still a cardinal, and made it his chief residence in the city. His attitude to Renaissance art and culture constituted a strange blend of encouragement and hostility. Likewise he could be both generous and mean in his dealings with people. He tried to rally Christian rulers to defend Central Europe from further incursions of the Turks and he called a crusade against them in 1470, even entering into an alliance with the Persian prince Uzun-Hassan. Following his predecessors, he remained hostile to the summoning of a general council as well as to the special privileges and liberties claimed by the French Church. He hoped to reconcile the Russian Church with Rome through a marriage between Ivan III of Russia and a Catholic princess, but he died suddenly of a stroke before the arrangements could be completed.

Sixtus IV was the most brazen Renaissance pope of the fifteenth century. He had become a Franciscan friar at a young age and rose to become head of the order. With this Franciscan background he might have been expected to promote simplicity and poverty but the outcome was different. His personal life, however, remained austere.

Turkish advances continued even into Italy, notably through the capture of Otranto in the south in 1480. Pius devoted much attention to equipping a fleet to resist this expansion and he proclaimed a crusade against the Turks in 1481. Otranto was recovered in the following year, though this was due more to the sudden death of Mohammed II than to the papal galleys. He continued papal opposition to the French monarchy's claims to virtual independence from Rome with regard to appointments to Church offices within France, as they had been expressed in the so-called 'Pragmatic Sanction of Bourges' of 1438. Sixtus IV followed his predecessors' firm opposition to calling a general council and to any revival of conciliarism. He kept alive Paul II's negotiations with Ivan III of Russia for the reunion of the Russian Church with Rome, but to no avail. At the request of Ferdinand and Isabella of Spain, he established the Spanish Inquisition to tackle the problem of heresy in their realms and he approved the appointment of Tomás de Torquemada as its first head (grand inquisitor).

Sixtus was unashamed in the promotion of his family. Soon after his election as pope he appointed as cardinals two of his youthful nephews, Pietro Riario and Giuliano della Rovere (later Pope Julius II). He enriched them with gifts and Church offices and fell under their influence and that of Pietro's intriguing brother, Girolamo. Many other relatives were advanced and rewarded. Indeed, six of the 34 cardinals he appointed were his relatives. He became closely involved in the internal affairs of various city states in Italy, notably Florence, where he was linked to the 'Pazzi conspiracy' in 1478, and Venice. Sixtus was central to the transformation of Rome from a medieval to a Renaissance city. He opened up new streets, widened and paved old ones and built the elegant bridge over the Tiber that was named after him, the Ponte Sisto. He built several new churches in Rome in the new Renaissance style, including Santa Maria del Popolo and Santa Maria della Pace. Best known, in this respect, was the construction of the chapel that lies at the heart of the pope's quarters within the Vatican and which still bears his name, the Sistine Chapel. He engaged artists to decorate its walls and so initiated the brilliant adornment of the chapel that would be completed with the frescoes of Michelangelo. Sixtus drew to Rome many painters and sculptors and remains famous for the 'Sistine choir', which he founded principally for the accompaniment of church services conducted by the pope. Scholarship, too, remains in his debt, thanks to his promotion of the Vatican archives and his munificence towards the Vatican Library. But his generosity and ambitious initiatives saddled the papacy with huge debts at his death.

The eight years of Innocent VIII's papacy followed in the weaknesses, and in few of the strengths, of his predecessor. Before his election as pope he had lived and studied in various Italian cities and earlier had led a some-what lax life, being the father of several illegitimate children. His court, like Sixtus IV's, was colourful and loose and papal debts continued to grow. He engaged closely in Italian politics, with largely disadvantageous results, and was active, like many of his predecessors, in promoting his family. His attempts to halt the Turkish advance proved largely fruitless. He entered into a curious arrangement with the Ottoman sultan Bayezid II. In return for receiving from the sultan 40,000 ducats annually and the gift of the Holy Lance (which was supposed to have pierced Christ's side at his crucifixion), Innocent obliged him by keeping in close confinement in Rome Bayezid's brother and potential rival Jem, who had fallen into the pope's hands in a roundabout way: Jem had escaped from his brother Bayezid to the island of Rhodes, but had been detained there by the grand master of the Knights of St John and subsequently handed over to the pope. Granada, the last Muslim stronghold in Spain, fell to the army of Ferdinand and Isabella in 1492, a few months before the pope's death. On receiving the news, Inno-cent responded by awarding the Spanish monarchy the hereditary title of 'Their Most Catholic Majesty'. But Innocent left the papal states in semi-anarchy: further violence and disorder broke out after his death.

Alexander VI was the most notorious of all Renaissance popes. Born in Játiva near Valencia in Spain, he was promoted by his maternal uncle, Pope Callistus III, who made him a cardinal at the age of 25. Family affairs and the accumulation of wealth dominated much of his life and reign. He kept a string of mistresses and fathered through them at least ten illegiti-mate children. He was the only pope of the period known to have kept a mistress after his election to the papacy: Giovanni and Rodrigo, who were openly acknowledged as his children while pope, were borne to him by Giulia Farnese in 1498 and 1503 respectively. The best known of his children were the beautiful Lucretia Borgia, for whom he arranged a succession of magnificent marriages, and the notorious Cesare Borgia, whom he made a cardinal at the age of 18 and later laicized when it became clear that Cesare preferred a military career. For a time the papal states became subordinated to the interests of the Borgia family, led by the pope.

By the Treaty of Tordesillas in 1494 Alexander assigned the 'New World' of the Americas to the authority of Spain and Portugal, reaching an agreement with the monarchs of the two countries regarding the line of demarcation between their zones. He was co-founder, together with the local bishop William Elphinstone, of the university of Aberdeen in Scotland in 1494/95. For all the difficulties in his personal life, he was devout after a fashion and defended orthodoxy. He celebrated the jubilee year of 1500 in style and by granting many indulgences. His quarrels with Girolamo Savanarola, the famous Dominican preacher in Florence, ended tragically with the latter's excommunication and his torture and execution by burning at the stake in Florence. Alexander was an important patron of Renaissance artists. He richly restored the papal fortress, Castel Sant'Angelo, next to the Vatican, he employed Pinturicchio and other artists to embellish the 'Borgia apartments' within the Vatican palace and he engaged Michelangelo to draw up plans for the rebuilding of St Peter's Church. He died suddenly in August 1503 when, it seems, a poisoned cup of wine, intended for a guest, was given to him by mistake.

Conclusion

The papacy and the councils of the Church during the fourteenth and fifteenth centuries should be studied in their own right, without looking back at them too much from the vantage point of the sixteenth century. The danger with the latter approach is that later preoccupations and concerns are introduced into the earlier period, resulting in distortions. More particularly, it is important not to see the period too exclusively through the lenses of Reformation and Counter-Reformation.

During the two centuries there were the serious challenges that have been outlined: the sojourn of the papacy in Avignon, the long papal schism and the conciliar movement, the worldliness and bad example given by some of the late fifteenth-century popes. Challenges just as serious had confronted the papacy in earlier centuries and the institution had survived them, indeed developed through them. There was no reason to expect otherwise in 1500, as, indeed, despite the challenges of the Reformation, was to prove the case. Another point to remember is that medieval people were well able to distinguish between people and the offices they held. They lived long before the advent of the mass media, so that most people were quite unable to grasp or image the personalities of individual popes. They themselves lived in a tough world and would have recognized the difficult decisions that popes had to take just to survive. While they appreciated idealism, they were realistic about what most people were able to accomplish. They were also fairly tolerant and understanding of people's private lives.

The councils of the period must be seen in a positive light, not just as challenges to the papacy. They represented, and were seen by many people of the time, as a healthy development in the life of the Church, as well as the revival of an institution that had served the Church well during its first millennium. Tension between papacy and councils was in many respects creative rather than destructive. Neither side was advocating the abolition of the other: debate and sometimes conflict concerned the precise relationship between them.

Finally, the papacy's interest in the sometimes ambivalent values that came to be associated with the Renaissance should be appreciated. Those who subsequently embraced the Reformation used this interest as one more stick, conveniently at hand, with which to beat the papacy. Catholics of the Counter-Reformation defended the basic doctrinal orthodoxy of the popes in question but their appreciation did not extend much further. The moral failures of the popes and their worldly lifestyles seemed to provide for later Catholic apologists a convenient explanation for the success of the Reformation without the need to justify its teachings. Yet appreciation of the beauty and dignity of creation, and the recognition of human achievement, which were central features of the Renaissance, are right in line with the Incarnation, the central belief of Christianity that God came in human form in the person of Jesus Christ, thus setting God's seal of approval on the basic goodness of creation and humanity. In many ways, therefore, and despite all their faults, the popes of the Renaissance were promoting a healthy and more positive vision of Christianity, a move away from the rather negative spirituality of excessive emphasis upon suffering and the Cross, and of retreat from the world, which was widely prevalent – as exemplified, for example, in Thomas à Kempis's *The Imitation of Christ*.

In short, when the Reformation and Counter-Reformation are removed from the immediate frame of reference, the papacy especially, but also the general councils of the period, take their place within a more balanced scenario, much less as part of an impending doom.

CHAPTER 2

Clergy and Religious Orders

At the start of our period, in 1300, clergy and religious orders represented what might be called the 'old order' of the Church – twin pillars that had supported the Church for many centuries. They still represented the old order at the end of the period, in 1500, but by then various important changes had taken place or were imminent. First, several newer religious movements, which challenged the old order in various ways, had developed during the intervening two centuries. These new movements will be discussed in Chapter 3. Secondly, the clergy and religious orders had come in for plenty of criticism and by 1500 they stood on the eve of the Reformation. In all the countries that accepted the Reformation, religious orders were swept away and clerical ministry was radically remodelled – changes that represented a radical critique of the situation in the late medieval Church. In countries that remained Catholic, the Counter-Reformation promoted new religious orders and sought to reform the diocesan clergy in a variety of ways. The measures taken in both sets of countries suggested that not all had been well with clergy and religious orders in the later Middle Ages.

This chapter will follow, as far as possible, the distinction between diocesan (or secular) clergy and religious orders, while recognizing the overlaps between the two. The first group, all men, consisted mainly of priests who belonged to a diocese and whose principal responsibility was towards the parishes of the diocese. They were variously described as diocesan clergy, in that they belonged to a diocese and were subject to its bishop, or parochial clergy, because most of them worked in parishes, or, more ambivalently, as secular clergy, inasmuch as they did not renounce the 'world' (Latin, *saeculum*) in the way that members of religious orders professed to do, but rather remained within it. The latter group were members of religious orders – Benedictines, Franciscans, Dominicans and many others – whose loyalty and responsibilities were more towards their order than to a diocese. They comprised both men and women who took 'vows', principally the three vows of poverty, chastity and obedience. The men, many of whom were priests, were often called collectively 'regular clergy' because they lived under the

Rule (Latin, *regula*) of their order. Thus 'regular' and 'secular' clergy could be distinguished. The women who belonged to religious orders are best called (collectively, in English) nuns, though there were many variations among them.

Diocesan (or secular) clergy

Pope and cardinals

The popes of the period have been treated at some length in the previous chapter. They held the highest office in the Church on earth and therefore headed the diocesan clergy as well as the regular clergy and the Church as a whole. They traced their origins back to the Apostle Peter and the special authority given to him through Christ's promise, 'You are Peter and upon this rock I will build my Church' (Matthew 16.18), and through other words and gestures of the Lord. The reigning pope could claim to be the heir of this authority through a continuous succession of bishops of Rome stretching from Peter to himself. While the pope was placed at the top of the hierarchy in the Church, his ministry was, in principle, one of service to the Christian community. 'Servant of the servants of God' was a title that Pope Gregory I (590–604) had taken to himself and which medieval popes continued to use.

The paradoxes of high authority, the fact that holders of the office were frail human beings, often leading notably sinful lives, and the service involved in all authority, were themes familiar to medieval people and a source of some delight. The 'feast of fools' or of the 'boy abbot/bishop', whereby on certain days the young and inexperienced ruled their elders and betters, and the artistic motif of *la danse macabre*, whereby popes and other authorities were portrayed as skeletons a few years after their death, stripped of the insignia of office and of all else, were widespread conventions in the Middle Ages. *La danse macabre* was especially popular in the later Middle Ages, following the horrors of the Black Death in the mid-fourteenth century and its recurrences. While, therefore, the awesome authority of the pope was accepted, indeed generally welcomed as an essential and necessary part of God's plan, the personal lives of the popes were not taken too seriously. A certain distance was recognized between the papal office and the person of the office holder. As is abundantly clear from the last chapter, the fortunes of both the papal office and its holders were quite disturbed during the two centuries under consideration.

Cardinals, too, have already featured prominently, principally in their roles of electing the pope and settling disputed papal elections. The title 'cardinal' comes from the Latin *cardo*, meaning a 'hinge', and the office drew its origins from the early organization of the Christian community in

Rome, which was divided into some 24 districts or parishes, each headed by a priest, who was sometimes referred to as a 'cardinal' inasmuch as he was a key figure, or 'hinge', in the local church. The decisive development in the office came in the late eleventh century, when popes began to appoint as 'cardinals' the principal office holders in the Roman Curia, and the election of a new pope was entrusted to them. In the twelfth century the office was extended beyond Rome to some archbishops of major dioceses in Europe. Conrad von Wittelsbach, Archbishop of Mainz, who was appointed cardinal by Pope Alexander III in 1163 with special permission not to reside in Rome, appears to have been the first case.

In the later Middle Ages, following these developments, 'cardinal' remained a mixture of title and office and there were two main categories: the principal office holders in the Roman Curia as well as some other ecclesiastics living in Rome, and, secondly, various important bishops and archbishops of sees elsewhere in Europe. Those in the second category were nominated by the pope on an individual basis: it was only much later that holders of various major sees, such as Paris or Vienna or Madrid or, as of the nineteenth century, Westminster, were appointed cardinals almost automatically. During most of the later Middle Ages the number of cardinals remained close to the original number of 24, rarely rising above 30. The total grew temporarily during the papal schism between 1378 and 1417 when each of the two and later three claimants to the papacy maintained a separate college of cardinals. The Council of Basel attempted in 1436 to fix the limit at between 24 and 26. It was only in the following century that numbers grew dramatically: Pope Sixtus V in 1586 established 70 as the ideal number, based on the analogy of the 70 'elders' of Israel (Numbers 11.16), and much later Pope John XXIII (1958–63) inaugurated further increases.

The later Middle Ages witnessed the high-water mark of the college of cardinals. Never before or since did cardinals enjoy such collective authority and importance within the Church. The position was attained largely through difficulties in the Church, principally those of the papacy during the papal schism and the Council of Constance. During this time cardinals acquired a semi-official position in the constitution of the Church through their oversight of the papacy and the council. With the subsequent recovery of papal authority, the papacy sought to prevent any re-emergence of the cardinals' collective power that might pose a threat to its own authority, in a manner that paralleled its opposition to the conciliar movement. Individual cardinals remained important and interesting figures, and the election of a new pope remained their collective prerogative. Outside the elections, however, cardinals who were members of the Roman Curia were mainly reduced to the level of papal officials, subordinate to the papacy, and thereby lost much of their independence. Even for other cardinals, the title indicated more an honour than a substantial post. These trends, towards honour rather than substantial position, and of subordination to the papacy, continued through the Counter-Reformation and afterwards. Never again would the college of cardinals provide a serious alternative to papal government.

In terms of lifestyle and clothing, the thirteenth to fifteenth centuries brought in many of the features that came to be traditionally associated with cardinals, as can be seen from the surviving portraits and architecture of the period. The right to wear the large red hat with appendant tassels, six on each side, symbolizing the 12 tribes of Israel, was granted to cardinals by Pope Innocent IV during the First Council of Lyons in 1245 and was only abolished by Paul VI in 1965. The red habit, which later developed into a soutane, was granted by Boniface VIII in 1294; the red biretta, zucchetto and mantello were granted by Paul II in 1464. Red was chosen in semi-conscious imitation of the purple clothes of senators and officials of the ancient Roman Empire. Peter Damian, in the late eleventh century, made the comparison with senators even before the widespread introduction of red. He spoke of cardinals as 'spiritual senators of the universal Church', whose function, like the senators of ancient Rome, was to ensure obedience to the universal laws of Christ and, like consuls, to rescue captives 'from the power of the devil' (Migne, *PL*, vol. clxv, col. 540). They were styled 'Lord cardinal' (Latin, *Dominus cardinalis*) until the title 'Eminence' was introduced by Urban VIII in 1630. The palaces of late medieval cardinals that still survive, principally in Rome, bear witness to the large households they were expected to maintain. Many of them were noted patrons of Renaissance art and scholarship.

The cardinals provided a rich mixture of qualities and personalities. There were scandalous cases, yet it would be wrong to focus on them exclusively. The large majority of cardinals in the fourteenth century, when the papacy was based at Avignon, were Frenchmen, especially southern Frenchmen. In the fifteenth century the balance shifted decisively towards Italians, a trend that was to last for centuries. Appointments 'in family', such as the four relatives appointed as cardinals by Clement V, and the six appointed by Sixtus IV, as well as youthful cardinals, such as Pietro Riario and Giuliano della Rovere, also appointed by Sixtus, and the 18-year-old Cesare Borgia, appointed by his father Alexander VI, have been mentioned (see pp 5, 29, 31). Many cardinals came from wealthy and prestigious families. Some families provided a succession or quasi-dynasty of cardinals, such as the Orsini and Colonna families in Italy. Yet many cardinals came from families of modest or poor means, showing that the late medieval Church could act as a social mixer. The backgrounds of cardinals who subsequently became popes have been outlined in Chapter 1, and Chapter 4 portrays some cardinals of intellectual distinction: Pierre D'Ailly, Jean Gerson and Nicholas of Cusa.

Three other cardinals, chosen almost at random, may help to fill out the picture: Henry Beaufort, Cardinal Bishop of Winchester in England, and the Italian cardinals and brothers, Domenico and Angelo Capranica.

Henry Beaufort (c.1375–1447) was one of the several illegitimate children of John of Gaunt and his mistress Catherine Swynford, and therefore a half-brother to Henry IV of England. He was bishop of Lincoln from 1398 to 1404, and from then until his death bishop of the even richer see of Winchester. For the best part of half a century he played a prominent part in religious and secular affairs in England and in Western Christendom. He attended the Council of Constance as part of the English delegation and was a candidate at the papal election in 1417. The man elected, Martin V, immediately created him a cardinal and employed him in 1420 and again in 1427 and 1428 to organize crusades against the Hussites in Bohemia. He was appointed papal legate to Germany, Hungary and Bohemia. He was a leading member of the English government during much of the reigns of Henry V and Henry VI, which were dominated by the war in France. His enormous wealth enabled him to become the king's chief creditor and his leading financier in this war, yet during it Beaufort generally favoured peace rather than an aggressive foreign policy. A complex and in many ways sympathetic character, he played some role in the patronage of art and architecture – including the completion of Winchester cathedral – and in promoting works of charity, though perhaps not on the scale that might have been expected in view of his wealth. His religion appears conventional for the time and he showed little interest in reform. His passions seem to have been for money and politics. A liaison while he was a young bishop of Lincoln brought him a daughter, his only known offspring.

The Capranica brothers came from the small town of that name near Rome. At least two other brothers of theirs in this very religious family were prominent churchmen: one was prior of the Knights of Jerusalem, the other an archbishop. Domenico and his younger brother Angelo showed their loyalty to a succession of popes in the mid-fifteenth century, who rewarded them with cardinalates and gave them many appointments and offices. They were prominent churchmen of their time and might be described as conservative reformers, known especially for their integrity of life and for their promotion of learning and of concern for the formation of the clergy – 'Renaissance cardinals' in the good sense. Domenico was a serious candidate for election as pope at the conclaves in 1447 and 1455, Angelo in 1464. Domenico left a large library of some 2,000 volumes which eventually passed into the Vatican Library. He is best known for Collegio Capranica in Rome, which he founded in 1458 for the education, in theology and canon law, of poor students for the priesthood. This successful college still flourishes today in remarkable continuity with its foundation, and Domenico's elegant tomb may be seen nearby in the church of Santa Maria sopra Mineva.

Archbishops and bishops

Western Christendom was divided into some 800 dioceses in the late Middle Ages, each with a bishop or archbishop in charge. A few dioceses also had one or more auxiliary bishops. Many dioceses dated back to the time of the Roman Empire and most of the others had been founded well before 1300. Indeed dioceses represented the oldest and most basic organization of the Church, with bishops tracing their origins back to the Apostles. The later Middle Ages saw a few developments. Within Christian territory, 16 new dioceses were carved out of existing dioceses in southern France by Pope John XXII in the early fourteenth century, various new dioceses were created in the recently Christianized countries of Central and Eastern Europe and Scandinavia, and some reorganization of boundaries and new dioceses resulted from the final stages of the *Reconquista* in Spain and Portugal. Nevertheless much of the diocesan map in the West remained stable during the last two centuries of the medieval period.

Dioceses varied greatly in geographical size and in population. Central and southern Italy had numerous small dioceses, accounting for nearly half the dioceses in Western Christendom. The bishop there often resembled a dean or parish priest – in modern terms – rather than the remote figure prevailing in large dioceses. The situation in these parts of Italy was close to what had been normal in much of the Mediterranean world in late Antiquity. Whereas most of this Christian world had been swept away by the Islamic conquests – principally in North Africa and western Asia – it had remained largely intact in much of Italy. In contrast were the large dioceses of England, Germany, Scandinavia and the Slavic countries. The number of dioceses in England remained fixed at 17 from the late twelfth to the early sixteenth century, for a population that may have reached 5 million in the early fourteenth century. Though even in this country there were wide divergences between the small or thinly populated dioceses of Rochester and Carlisle and the large and well-populated dioceses of York, Lincoln and Norwich. Seventeen was fewer than the peak number in the seventh and eighth centuries, when the population of the country was but a fraction of its late medieval figure. In the middle, overall, in terms of size and Christian population, were the dioceses in northern France, Scotland and Spain, though in these countries too there were wide variations. In practice, therefore, a diocese could mean many different things, even though in canon law it remained a relatively clear and well-defined entity. The work and status of the bishop varied accordingly.

Dioceses were grouped – in numbers that varied between two and a dozen or so – into provinces. In each province, the senior or most important diocese was governed by an archbishop, who, as well as being the 'bishop' of his own diocese, had a certain authority over the other bishops of the province. Precisely what this authority comprised was far from clear, even in canon law. It was generally considered to include the right to visit and inspect other dioceses in the province, at least periodically, and to correct a bishop if necessary. Thomas Becket, Archbishop of Canterbury in the late twelfth century, had famously shown how difficult it was to exercise these and other archiepiscopal rights over bishops of his province who disagreed with him. Similar difficulties were common throughout the later Middle Ages and they were accentuated by the loosening of central authority during the papal schism and the conciliar movement. As a result, prudence often turned out to be the better part of valour.

The qualities and lifestyles of bishops and archbishops in the later Middle Ages mirrored to a considerable extent, and for the most part in a lower key, those of popes and cardinals. There were scandalous cases; there was the scourge of pluralism (whereby an individual was bishop of several dioceses) and the evil, frequently accompanying pluralism, of non-residence (whereby the bishop lived outside his diocese). The scarcity of popes of the period who have been declared 'blessed' or 'saints' (see p 8) was paralleled by the relatively small number of bishops and archbishops who have been recognized in the same way, even though the period saw a fair number of other people who have been declared saints or blessed. There are various possible reasons for the dearth. Heroic ages, such as the first centuries of persecution of Christians, or during the evangelization in Europe of the newly arrived barbarian tribes, or during the remarkable Christian achievements of the twelfth and thirteenth centuries – which was also a time of sharp conflicts between Church and state, and therefore an age of bishops who stood out for their courage – were more likely, it might be thought, to produce Church leaders who caught the popular imagination than the internally troubled later Middle Ages. Writers in the later Middle Ages consistently pointed to the great importance of the office of bishop and many holders of the office during this time came decently close to the ideal. The English episcopate, for instance, produced a generally good record of capable and conscientious men, even though outstanding individuals are missing.

Antoninus of Florence (1389–1459) provides a good example of a saintly bishop whose renown nevertheless remained largely local. Born the son of a notary of Florence, he entered the Dominican novitiate in that city at the age of 15. He held various positions of responsibility within his order and returned to his native city in 1436 to found the priory of San Marco. He engaged the architect Michelozzi to adapt an existing building to the needs of the new priory and the artist Fra Angelico, who had been a fellow novice with him, to decorate it. The result, still resplendent today, is a magnificent and deeply religious yet simple building. Antoninus featured prominently at the Council of Florence (1439–45) as host and theologian. As a moral theologian he permitted the lending of money at interest for the purpose of commerce and industry – teaching that was agreeable to the Medicis, the leading banking family in Florence, who were prominent patrons of the San Marco priory. He was appointed archbishop of Florence by Pope Eugenius IV in 1445 and spent his last 14 years in that office, renowned especially for austerity of life, indefatigable preaching throughout his diocese and generosity towards the poor. A reformer, yet also a man of peace and unity, he managed to a remarkable degree to hold the confidence of most sections of Florentine society as well as that of the papacy. He was canonized by the Medici pope Clement VII in 1523.

Parochial and other diocesan clergy

The majority of the diocesan (or secular) clergy were involved in parishes, one way or another. Indeed the *cura pastoralis* (pastoral care) of the parishioners was their principal *raison d'être*, alongside their own salvation and holiness; thus they were often called 'parish (or parochial) clergy'. Regarding the number of parishes, there are quite precise figures for England: some 9,000 in the year 1300. The figure could probably be multiplied by about ten, to about 100,000, to arrive at the total in Western Christendom (England's population was somewhat less than a tenth of Western Christendom's; see pp xvii, 38). This network of parishes, each normally containing one parish church, was a central feature of the genius of the medieval Church. It meant that Christianity was present at close range and (for the most part) sympathetically to almost everyone. A large measure of the responsibility for administering this presence fell to the parochial clergy. In each parish, normally living besides or near the parish church, was at least one priest (the parish priest) and often several others (his assistants).

The standards of education and behaviour of the parish clergy of the time have been much debated, from the Middle Ages to the present day. There were the abuses of pluralism and non-residence, as among bishops, though such cases among the parish clergy were usually mitigated by the parish priest in question employing a substitute, who was expected to do the work in return for receiving a portion of the absentee's wage. Some of the criticism came from members of religious orders and may partly be seen as self-justification – exalting the regular above the secular clergy. Other criticism came later as ways of explaining and partly justifying the Reformation and Counter-Reformation (see pp xxiii–xxiv). Some criticism came from the laity and must be seen within the general framework of anti-clericalism. It is noticeable, however, that few writers attacked the parish clergy who were trying to do their duty; towards religious orders and other branches of the Church criticism could be more direct and unforgiving. Relatively few of the parish clergy, moreover, leapt to their own defence, at least in writing.

Plenty of legislation outlined the recommended standards for parish clergy. The most comprehensive came in the canons of the Fourth Lateran Council in 1215, which were incorporated into canon law and remained authoritative throughout the later Middle Ages. Subsequent legislation reinforced rather than altered its requirements and it was not until the Council of Trent in the sixteenth century that a comparable body of new laws was enacted for the diocesan clergy.

The importance of preparation for the priesthood was clearly stated in Canon 27 of the Fourth Lateran Council, 'On the instruction of ordinands'. 'To guide souls is a supreme art,' it began, and then continued:

> We therefore strictly order bishops carefully to prepare those who are to be promoted to the priesthood and to instruct them, either by themselves or through other suitable persons, in the divine services and the sacraments of the Church, so that they may be able to celebrate them correctly. ... For it is preferable, in the ordination of priests, to have a few good ministers than many bad ones. (*Decrees*: 248)

Canon 11 of the same council, 'On schoolmasters', provided more details about the desired academic preparation, both before and after ordination to the priesthood:

> Zeal for learning and the opportunity to make progress is denied to some through lack of means. The third Lateran council [in 1189] decreed that in every cathedral church there should be provided a suitable benefice for a master who shall instruct without charge the clerics of the cathedral church and other poor scholars. ... We confirm this decree and add that not only in every cathedral church but also in other churches with sufficient resources a suitable master ... shall be appointed ... to teach grammar and other branches of study ... to the clerics. The metropolitan church [of the archbishop] shall have a theologian to teach scripture to priests and others and especially to instruct them in matters pertaining to the cure of souls. (*Decrees*: 240)

Seminaries, as colleges at which all future parish priests studied for several years, entered the Catholic Church only later, as a result of the legislation of the Council of Trent in the sixteenth century, though there were a few precursors in the fifteenth century such as Collegio Capranica (see p 38). Universities will be treated later (see pp 109–11), but at most only 10 per cent of the parish clergy had studied at a university. For the others, the large majority, the canons of Lateran IV are important in showing that academic preparation for ordination to the parish ministry was taken seriously.

The Fourth Lateran Council issued a number of other canons dealing with the lifestyle and duties of the secular clergy, including therefore the parish clergy. These canons, too, remained foundational for the later Middle Ages. Canon 14 insisted on their celibacy: 'Let all the clergy live in a continent and chaste way ... so that they may be worthy to minister in the sight of almighty God with a pure heart and an unsullied body.' Canons 15 to 18 attended to moderation in food and drink, to dress, and to inappropriate occupations and pastimes:

> Clerics should carefully abstain from gluttony and drunkenness. They should temper the wine to themselves and themselves to the wine ... since drunkenness obscures the intellect and stirs up lust. We forbid clerics to hunt or to fowl, so let them not presume to have dogs or birds for fowling. (*Decrees*: 242–3, Canon 15)

> Clerics should not practise callings or business of a secular nature, especially those that are dishonourable. They should not watch mimes, entertainers and actors. Let them avoid taverns altogether, unless by chance they are obliged by necessity on a journey. They should not play at games of chance or of dice, nor be present at such games. They should have a suitable crown and tonsure, and let them diligently apply themselves to the divine services and other good pursuits. Their outer garments should be closed and neither too short nor too long. Let them not indulge in red or green clothes, long sleeves or shoes with embroidery or pointed toes, or in bridles, saddles, breast-plates and spurs that are gilded or have other superfluous ornamentation. ... They are not to wear buckles or belts ornamented with gold or silver, or even rings except for those whose dignity it befits to have them. (*Decrees*: 243, Canon 16)

The Council of Constance seems to have had this legislation in mind in its decree of March 1418 'On the life and probity of clerics': 'We renew and order the careful observance of all the laws currently in force regarding the clothing, tonsure and habits of clerics, as to both shape and colour, and their hair-styles, and the style and uprightness of their lives' (*Decrees*: 499). Lateran IV also dwelt at some length on the obligations of the parish clergy towards the spiritual welfare of their parishioners: the need to keep parish churches clean and in good order (Canon 19), their responsibilities regarding the sacraments of confession and the Eucharist (Canons 1, 20 and 21), regarding parishioners wanting to marry (Canons 50–2), and towards the sick and dying (Canon 22).

But what was the reality – how far was the legislation observed? As we are dealing with a large number of men trying to live up to high ideals, it is not surprising that there were failures. The Council of Constance, in the decree cited, admitted that it was renewing legislation precisely because 'the laws have been heeded far too little by both the secular and the regular clergy'. On the other hand, it would be wrong to focus exclusively on the negative side. The frequent call to high standards may have helped many to reach decently near the mark. Partial answers to the questions are scattered throughout this book. It is noticeable that Geoffrey Chaucer (1343–1400), in *The Canterbury Tales*, while scathing in his portraits of the monk and the friar, is very appreciative of the parish priest:

> A good man was there of religion,
> And was a poor parson of a town,
> But rich was he of holy thought and work.
> He was also a learned man, a clerk,
> That Christ's gospel truly would preach;
> His parishioners devoutly would he teach.
> …
> Wide was his parish, and houses far asunder,
> But he left not, for rain nor thunder,
> In sickness nor in mischief to visit.
> …
> He was a shepherd and not a mercenary,
> And though he holy were and virtuous,
> He was to sinful men not despising,
> Nor of his speech dangerous or unworthy,
> But in his teaching discreet and benign.
> To draw folk to heaven by fairness,
> By good example, this was his business.
> …
> A better priest I trust that nowhere none is,
> He waited after no pomp and reverence,
> Nor maked him a spiced conscience,
> But Christ's law and his apostles twelve
> He taught, but first he followed it himself. (Prologue, lines 477–528)

The parish clergy formed the core of the diocesan clergy. Within the parish clergy there existed a variety of grades and callings. At the centre was the parish priest, who was entrusted with official responsibility for the spiritual well being of the people living within the parish – the 'cure of souls' of his parishioners. He was likely to be aided in this task by one or more assistant priests, on either a tenured or a more casual basis. They were variously described as curates, assistant parish priests and stipendiary priests, or by other titles.

Chantry priests, whose principal function was the 'chanting' or saying of Masses and prayers for the dead, were numerous, especially in the towns. They were normally members of the diocesan clergy and many of them were attached to parish churches. Thus many of them said or sang their chantry masses in the local parish church and assisted the parish priest in his parochial duties in various ways.

A number of diocesan priests were not attached to parish churches, though most of them were in various ways at the service of the parochial system: members of the bishop's administrative staff; the clergy of the cathedral church; chantry priests who celebrated their chantry Masses, and perhaps gave help, in non-parochial churches, mainly those of religious orders or in those attached to colleges of secular priests; teachers in schools – many of the schools were attached to parish churches and often the schoolmaster was the parish priest or his assistant priest – and in universities.

Most of these arrangements are described in more detail in the third part of this chapter, 'A case study: Norwich'.

Religious orders

Distinct from the diocesan clergy, though with various points of contact and overlap, were the religious orders. For religious orders of men, total membership looks to have been somewhat, but not much, lower than that of the diocesan clergy: somewhere, therefore, between a quarter and a third of a million men at any given time, with the low point, in absolute terms, coming – as with the diocesan clergy and the population as a whole – after the Black Death of 1347–50. This was a sizeable and fairly constant proportion, therefore, of the adult male population throughout the later Middle Ages. In addition there was a much smaller number of women who belonged to female religious orders.

For men, religious orders may be divided into two main categories: first, the old monastic orders, principally the Benedictines, Cistercians and Carthusians; secondly, the more 'active' orders founded in the twelfth and thirteenth centuries, most notably the four orders of friars – Franciscans, Dominicans, Carmelites and Augustinians. The number of men appears (in the absence of precise figures) to have been roughly equal in each of the two groups – if anything rather larger in the second group (active orders). The origins and development of these religious orders before 1300 have been treated in previous volumes of this series. With regard to the later Middle

Ages, two general points should be remembered.

First, there was no foundation of a major new religious order, for men or women, during the period 1300 to 1500. This was an unusually long absence in the history of the Western Church. Before, there had been a succession of foundations and major reforms from the time of St Benedict in the sixth century to the friars of the thirteenth century. Afterwards, the founding of the Society of Jesus (Jesuits) in the sixteenth century initiated a long period, almost uninterrupted until recent times, of important new foundations. Maybe, therefore, the absence of new foundations in the fourteenth and fifteenth centuries reflected the general sterility and decline of religious orders, and indeed of the Church more generally, in this period. On the other hand, new orders cannot simply be predicted or manufactured, as if they are the inevitable results of good health in the Church: there is something more mysterious in their arrival. The thirteenth century, moreover, had been exceptionally productive of new orders, principally the four orders of friars, so that a pause thereafter may have seemed necessary just to digest the creativity of that period. The pause was especially necessary, it might be reckoned, inasmuch as the decline in the population of society at large, beginning with the Black Death, meant that there was much less room or need for new orders: those already in existence could adequately cater for vocations to these ways of life. There was also the disruptive effect of the papal schism from 1378 to 1417, whereby all the main orders were internally divided in their loyalties between the two (and briefly three) papal claimants. This schism both disrupted the religious orders of the time and damaged the likelihood of new orders being founded. Finally, the period saw major developments in the religious life of the laity, much of which was linked to and brought about through the initiative of members of religious orders; in some cases, too, membership of the new movements was partly clerical, as with the Brethren of the Common Life. These developments will be discussed in the next chapter. They were positive developments even while they cut some ground from under the religious orders: they can be considered fruits of religious orders as much as evidence of their decline.

Secondly, a mixture of historiographical issues have tended to present religious orders in the later Middle Ages in a poor light (see pp xxiii–xxiv). Anti-clericalism in the period often included hostility towards religious orders. Subsequently the Reformation rejected religious orders more or less outright, and those of the later Middle Ages with particular vehemence. Writers of the Counter-Reformation often acknowledged the decadence of religious orders in the late Middle Ages, partly as a way of explaining (without justifying) the success of the Reformation and partly to justify the need to found the new orders of the sixteenth century and afterwards.

Finally, the decline of religious orders became part and parcel of the wider issue of the alleged decline of the Church, and of European civilization more generally, in the later Middle Ages.

Where does the truth lie? At the very least, religious orders played a major role in the later medieval Church and therefore merit serious consideration.

Monastic orders

The society and landscape of later medieval Europe were powerfully influenced by the monastic orders. Almost all the monasteries had been founded at an earlier date, many much earlier, so that they were already venerable institutions by 1300. Although few new monasteries were founded during the fourteenth and fifteenth centuries, most of the existing houses survived the period, in many cases with somewhat reduced communities yet with even larger buildings.

The large buildings and imposing churches of monasteries frequently dominated the local scene, as can still be imagined today from their ruins or from surviving buildings. The archetypal monastic building, or rather complex of buildings, was that of Cluny in the province of Burgundy in eastern France. Its colossal church, measuring some 550 feet in length, had been built in the late eleventh and twelfth centuries and it remained the largest church in Western Christendom until the building of St Peter's in Rome in the sixteenth century. The monastery came to an end in 1790, caught up in the French Revolution, and almost all the buildings were pulled down soon afterwards. Surviving drawings of the buildings, as well as the transept and central tower of the church that remain today, still convey some idea of their former magnificence. The community comprised some 140 monks around the year 1500, a decline from the peak numbers in the early twelfth century but still a sizeable community. Cluny had been founded in the early tenth century as a reformed Benedictine monastery. It soon established many semi-dependent houses, which developed into a huge family of over a thousand 'Cluniac' monasteries by the twelfth century, stretching far and wide through Western Christendom. Subsequently there were troubles and some decline, yet much of the network survived into the later Middle Ages and afterwards.

The fortunes of the Cistercian order provided a somewhat parallel example. This order, too, started as a reform of Benedictine monasticism, at the monastery of Cîteaux (hence 'Cistercian'), which lay, like Cluny, in Burgundy. The decisive impetus came with the entry into the monastery in 1112 of the young Bernard, better known as St Bernard of Clairvaux. The reform movement rapidly grew into an independent religious order with the foundation of new monasteries in almost every country of Western Christendom. For a while the order captured the leadership of Western monasticism. Its emphasis on simple services in church, austerity of life and the importance of manual work, especially farming, contrasted with the more ceremonial and elaborate worship and lifestyle of Cluniac monasticism. By the late Middle Ages, however, similarities between the two orders – Benedictines and Cistercians – were more obvious than differences. The Cistercians built large churches and extensive living quarters, even while the style was relatively simple – buildings that the visitor today can glimpse or imagine at Rievaulx or Fountains in England, at Valla Crucis on the Welsh border and in many other places. The concentration on sheep farming led to the acquisition of large estates. In the later Middle Ages the order met with various difficulties, notably the frequent appointment of abbots who effectively were absentees, called abbots *in commendam*, that is, men, often appointed by the local lord and sometimes by the papacy, who were not monks and sometimes were lay men. Nevertheless the number of monasteries – though usually not the number of monks in each house – continued to grow from some 500 in 1200 to almost 750 on the eve of the Reformation.

Forming a looser communion was the large number of Benedictine monasteries. Each monastery was basically autonomous, though there were some groupings according to national and other factors. Unity and identity among them were provided primarily by the Rule of St Benedict, which each monastery claimed to follow. Many Benedictine monasteries were already venerable institutions by 1300, some of them dating back to the early origins of the order. Many of them had large churches and monastic buildings – witness the surviving ruins of the monasteries of St Albans and Bury St Edmunds in England – as well as extensive property; though it should be remembered that many monasteries were quite small and poor institutions, struggling to make ends meet. Benedictine monasteries were affected in various ways by the travails of the later Middle Ages, including the Hundred Years' War, the Black Death plagues, the papal schism and other troubles of the Church. Nevertheless the large majority of them survived through the period and remained a fundamental pillar of the late medieval Church.

What about the internal life within these outwardly impressive institutions? Many factors are involved in any answer to this complex question. At the heart of a monk's life should be prayer and closeness to God – the word 'monk' comes from the Greek *monos* meaning 'alone', so that the monk should be 'alone' with God – which are scarcely open to human disclosure or historical verification. The later Middle Ages was neither a heroic nor a pioneering epoch in Western monasticism. Even so, large numbers of men sought to follow these difficult ways of life, and their readiness should be respected. There were, moreover, some reform movements, such as the one centred on the Benedictine abbey of San Giustina in Padua in the fifteenth century and extending to a family of monasteries in northern Italy. Perhaps the large buildings and extensive property should not be judged too harshly. In 1300 such assets represented an inherited situation, the result of past donations and acquisitions; the next two centuries saw shrinkage as well as further acquisitions of this kind. Public opulence could be combined with considerable personal austerity on the part of individual monks. Corporate wealth was generally accepted at the time, even welcomed, if those responsible performed their duties to the local community, and many monasteries fulfilled this role partly as major local employers and partly through their assistance to the poor through alms and by other means. To some extent, monasteries held the place of today's social services and providers of employment.

Even so, too rosy a picture should not be drawn. Alongside the support, there was hostility to the wealth and lifestyles of many monasteries. There was relatively little opposition to the suppression of monasteries in those countries that accepted the Reformation – another indication that all was not well. Some ferocious attacks on individual monasteries occurred in the later Middle Ages. To take one example, in the course of the Peasants' Revolt in England in 1381, the wealthy Benedictine monastery of Bury St Edmunds was ransacked and the abbot murdered. Yet this monastery provides an intriguing case of the complexity of reality. Recent studies show that while, on the one hand, there was frequent tension between the citizens – at least the urban elite – of Bury St Edmunds and the monastery, which boiled over in 1381 and on other occasions, there were plenty of more positive and fruitful exchanges between the two groups. Books kept in the monastery's large library, and those known to have been borrowed from it and presumably read by individual monks, as well as a variety of other evidence, liturgical and otherwise, suggest a monastic community that was remarkably alive both intellectually and spiritually. Its most famous monk, John Lydgate (1370–1450), epitomized the strengths and some of the weaknesses of the monastery. A distinguished poet and scholar, Lydgate wrote plentifully on secular as well as religious topics. The majority of his poems bear the mark of a pious and learned man and he was highly regarded as a poet in fifteenth-century England. He appears to have been appreciated and well respected by his fellow monks, yet he also cultivated a wide circle of friends and spent much time outside his monastery, including a spell in royal service in France. Norwich cathedral priory (see pp 57–62, 67–9) provides striking parallels with Bury St Edmunds abbey.

Of all monastic orders, the Carthusians showed most vitality in the later Middle Ages. The order had been founded in the late eleventh century by St Bruno for men who wished to live as hermits with a measure of community support. Each monk had his own small house in which he lived, worked and prayed. The houses were usually arranged around a large courtyard and a few activities were done in common: some meals, some services in church and occasional recreation. The monks – normally between 12 and 20 in each monastery – were helped by a similar number of lay brothers who lived in separate quarters and looked after the material well being of the community. The monastery was called *Cartusia* in Latin or Charter-house in English (hence the adjective 'Carthusian'), after the 'Chartreuse' mountains in the French Alps where the first monastery, called 'La Grande Chartreuse', was established by Bruno. The order, which was centralized and tightly governed, grew steadily throughout the twelfth and thirteenth centuries to reach some 70 houses by 1300. The next two centuries saw further growth, to nearly 200 monasteries on the eve of the Reformation, situated in most countries of Western Christendom. The eremitical lifestyle was unusual and was recognized at the time as being so. Nevertheless it chimed well with the greater individualism that was a mark of both religious and secular life in the later Middle Ages. It may be seen, too, as a return to the more eremitical lifestyles that were features of religious life in the early Church, as characterized preeminently by the 'desert' hermit-saints Anthony of Egypt and Pachomius.

Carthusians exercised an attraction, indeed fascination, that extended well beyond the walls of their monasteries. Many of the Charterhouses founded in the later Middle Ages were situated in towns and they played a significant spiritual role in urban life. Thomas More spent some years in the London Charterhouse before he married in 1505, and even as chancellor of England he would return there for prayer and inspiration. Ludolph of Saxony (1300–78), the German Carthusian, was a well-known spiritual writer, popular with the laity especially for his *Vita Christi*, which contained a series of meditations on the life of Christ with doctrinal, spiritual and moral instructions, and extensive quotations from early Christian authors. Denys van Leeuwen (1407–71), also known as Denys Ryckel or Denis (Dionysius) the Carthusian, occupied a similar position in the fifteenth century. A monk at the Charterhouse at Roermond in the Netherlands, he wrote extensively on a wide range of topics: Scripture, early and medieval Christian authors, moral theology, mysticism – hence his title *Doctor Ecstaticus* (Ecstatic Doctor) – and Islam. His writings achieved popularity in his lifetime and even more so after his death. He was willing to leave his monastery when deemed necessary and in 1451–52 he accompanied Cardinal

Nicholas of Cusa to Germany in the cause of Church reform and to preach a crusade against the Turks. Rather like John Lydgate, he was a monk both inside and outside the cloister. In various ways, especially through their spirituality, Carthusians exercised a distinctive influence upon the late medieval Church, more pronounced than their numbers would suggest.

Friars and other male orders

The twelfth and thirteenth centuries had been a prolific period in the foundation of new religious orders. The growth of towns in the twelfth century, and the Church authorities' more or less concurrent drive for priestly celibacy, had seen the emergence of various orders and groups of priests who lived in community and staffed a church in a town. Many of them followed, in whole or in part, the Rule that St Augustine had written for his cathedral clergy at Hippo in North Africa in the early fifth century. The thirteenth century saw the new orders of friars, principally Franciscans, Dominicans, Carmelites and Augustinians. The word 'friar' comes from the Latin *frater*, meaning brother. The emphasis, accordingly, and contrasting somewhat with the more solitary lifestyle of monks, was on 'fraternal' living and working within the friary and on helping the wider community. The first order of friars to be founded, and the principal inspiration in this new movement in the Church's history, was the Order of Friars Minor (OFM), better known as Franciscans after their charismatic founder St Francis of Assisi. Following soon afterwards was the Order of Preachers (OP), better known as Dominicans after their founder St Dominic. The thirteenth century saw the emergence of many other orders of friars, some of which survived for only a short time. Of those that endured, the most important were Augustinians and Carmelites. The former took the Rule of Augustine and adapted it to the lifestyle of friars. Carmelites traced their origins back to hermits living on Mount Carmel in the Holy Land, and ultimately to the Old Testament prophet Elijah. They sought to combine a friar's life with that of a hermit.

Franciscans. Already in the thirteenth century the Franciscan order had encountered difficulties. There were divisions between those who sought to preserve the extreme ideals of poverty that had been proclaimed and lived by their saintly founder, and those who sought a poor yet more liveable and institutional lifestyle, who regarded buildings and churches as necessary for orderly life and ministry; between those who saw the order as a mainly lay movement, somewhat after the example of Francis who became a deacon but never a priest, and those who accepted the priesthood as necessary for the order's ministries; between those who accepted studies as part of the preparation for priesthood, and learning as good in itself, and those who kept to the reserve shown by Francis, who reckoned that learning was liable to 'puff up' its seekers. Those favouring austerity and simplicity were often called 'Spiritual Franciscans', while those who promoted the more institutional lifestyle and apostolate were called 'Conventuals'. Needless to say, there were many overlaps and nuances between the two groups, and most friars probably stood somewhere in the middle. To take but two examples of overlap, many of the more intellectual Franciscans were 'Spirituals', and most of the intellectuals among the Spirituals were priests.

While the differences could be divisive, even destructive, they were also creative. It was the genius of Francis, somewhat unintended, to open up major issues and yet to leave them unresolved and open to further development. Thus the order acted as a catalyst more than a clear blueprint for thought and action. From the nine or so companions who received verbal approval from Pope Innocent III in 1209 or 1210, the order grew rapidly throughout the thirteenth century to reach an estimated 50,000 friars by 1300. This was the peak figure for the order and was around double that of the next largest order of friars at the time, the Dominicans. A microcosm of the energy and creativity of the thirteenth century, the Franciscan order exercised a wide influence over the Church's activity: spiritual, missionary, intellectual and organizational.

The fourteenth and fifteenth centuries saw continuing creativity as well as troubles. The number of friars declined but no more, proportionally, it seems, than the population of Western Christendom as a whole. The order in the early fourteenth century saw two exceptionally brilliant and original theologian-philosophers, Duns Scotus (1265–1308) and William of Ockham (1285–1347), both from the British Isles, teachers at Oxford and Paris universities, who exercised a lasting influence throughout the later Middle Ages. Subsequently the order produced no figures of comparable intellectual stature, yet Franciscans continued to play a leading role in European education as teachers and writers.

A Franciscan friary, normally including a large church open to the public, was to be found in almost every major city of Western and Central Europe and in many medium-size towns. Thereby the friars reached deep into urban society and beyond: through the services and sermons held in their churches, the hearing of confessions, and more personal contacts, and through 'missions' in the countryside. The effects are difficult to verify, and less talked about than in the thirteenth century when the Franciscans were new on the scene, but they were surely extensive and profound. The outreach included responsibility for their 'second' order, Franciscan nuns, and for the 'third' order, lay men and women who sought various forms of association as 'tertiaries'. Paradoxically the frequent and copious legislation of the general chapters of the order that attempted to limit the friars' involvement with their second and third orders indicates the extent to which many people appreciated and wished to be associated with the lives and work of Franciscan friars in the later Middle Ages. Plenty of other evidence points to similar conclusions.

Franciscan friars maintained a tenuous foothold in Jerusalem and the Holy Land as well as in Persia. John of Montecorvino established a successful mission in China in the early fourteenth century, though this was largely terminated with the conversion of the Mongols to Islam, and there were Franciscans working in the Crimea and its neighbourhood as well as among the Bashkir people. The advances of Islam on various fronts, and a hardening of Muslim attitudes towards Christianity, made Franciscan missionary work outside Christendom difficult. There were no personalities in the order to match Francis of Assisi and Bonaventure of the thirteenth century. At the institutional level, the election of a Franciscan pope in the thirteenth century, Nicholas IV (1288–92), was not repeated in the next two centuries. Cardinal Bertrand de la Tour (d.1332) was an influential Franciscan at the papal court in Avignon, but Franciscan bishops appear to have been fewer in the later Middle Ages than in the thirteenth century; though the distancing from bishoprics, one may surmise, would have met with Francis's approval.

Relations between the order and the papacy were especially tense in the first half of the fourteenth century. Pope John XXII (1316–34) resolutely opposed the Spiritual Franciscans' advocacy of extreme poverty and he had four friars burnt at the stake in 1318; he also imprisoned and excommunicated William of Ockham. (These events formed the background to Umberto Eco's bestselling novel, which appeared in English under the title *The Name of the Rose* as both a book and a film.) Tensions remained within the order between 'Spirituals' and 'Conventuals' and they eventually resulted in the formal separation into two and later three orders in the early sixteenth century: Friars Minor, Conventuals and Capuchins. The papal schism, from 1378 to 1417, split the order into two and briefly three allegiances. But for all the troubles, many of which were indeed creative, the order – perhaps better described as a movement – remained at the heart of the later medieval Church, so that some knowledge and appreciation of its fortunes and vicissitudes is essential to an understanding of the Church of the time.

Dominicans. Developments in the Dominican order were both similar and different to those of the Franciscans. In terms of numbers, probably the peak was reached around 1300 with some 25,000 friars, about half the number of Franciscans. Thereafter there was some decline, but not markedly so as a proportion of the total population of Western Christendom. Like the Franciscans, the Dominicans made for the towns, so that often there were friaries of both orders in the same town and with lifestyles and works that were, at least outwardly, rather similar. The Dominicans, too, had a second order of nuns and a third order of lay 'tertiaries'.

Dominican friars remained prominent in the universities and in teaching throughout Europe, though none of them approached the intellectual stature of their thirteenth-century confrère Thomas Aquinas. Aquinas was canonized (declared a saint) by Pope John XXII in 1323. This stamp of official approval increased his authority as a theologian chiefly within the Dominican order and, to a lesser extent, in the Western Church as a whole. Yet, there was an anti-intellectual streak in the order's best-known writers of the later Middle Ages: Meister Eckhart (1260–1328), Henry Suso (1295–1366) and Johann Tauler (1300–61), who sought to go beyond academic and conceptual theology to mysticism. The development is somewhat paradoxical in view of the order's thorough commitment to theology in its Rule and during its early years, and is doubly interesting in that it contrasts with the paradox of the Franciscan friars – while Francis of Assisi and his order early on were almost hostile towards learning, the order went on to produce two intellectual giants of the later Middle Ages, Duns Scotus and William of Ockham. Once again we find complexity within the later medieval Church and are warned against sweeping generalizations.

Dominicans as a whole remained loyal to Church authorities and were creative. Of those who became popes, just as there was one in the thirteenth century, Innocent V (January to June 1276), so there was one in the fourteenth century, with an almost equally short reign, Benedict XI (1303–4), then a gap until Pius V in the late sixteenth century. A good number of friars became bishops and cardinals, and Dominicans remained prominent in the Inquisition (see pp 153–5). Of missionaries beyond Europe, the best known was Ricoldus de Monte Croce (1243–1320), who laboured in Palestine and modern Iraq and who wrote *Impugnatio Alcorani*, a critical study of Islam. Fra Angelico was an artist of genius.

The Dominican order remained relatively united through the late Middle Ages, though it suffered with the rest of the Church from the divided loyalties resulting from the papal schism. Attempts to reform various provinces of the order, mainly in the late fifteenth century, led to some dissensions between houses that accepted reforms and those that did not. Divisions within the friaries in Tuscany, where Fra Girolamo Savanarola was a leading reformer, provided a case in point. Nevertheless the order was not rent by internal dissensions to anything like the extent of the Franciscans. The Rule drawn up by Dominic and the early companions was clear, the ideals and way of life expressed in it were practical, and Dominic himself was an understanding personality – all somewhat in contrast to the soaring ideals of Francis and his Rule – and these factors helped to preserve unity in the later Middle Ages.

Preaching lay at the heart of the Dominican way of life, as indicated by the order's official name, 'Order of Preachers'. The order produced perhaps the most powerful and popular preacher of the later Middle Ages, Vincent Ferrer (1350–1419). For many years he preached to huge crowds in France, Spain and Italy, often in public places rather than in churches, moving people to repentance and conversion by his eloquence and devotion. Savanarola was a more controversial figure. His fiery sermons divided Florentine society and alienated Florence from Rome. His criticisms of Pope Alexander VI led to his excommunication; the city of Florence was placed under an 'interdict' (church services were forbidden, other spiritual and material penalties were imposed) and eventually Savanarola was burnt at the stake. Some Dominicans wrote preaching manuals – books to help their confrères and other priests to prepare and deliver their sermons. One of the best known was *Summa predicancium* by the Englishman John Bromyard (d.1352).

Carmelite and Augustinian friars. The two orders of Carmelite and Augustinian friars gained official papal approval in the middle decades of the thirteenth century, though the Carmelites claimed a much earlier foundation, going back even to the Old Testament prophet Elijah. Both orders remained smaller than the Franciscans and Dominicans, with an estimated 8,000 Augustinians in 350 friaries, and several thousand Carmelites in 150 houses, in 1300. But whereas the number of friars in the two older orders declined in the fourteenth and fifteenth centuries, those of the Carmelites and Augustinians continued to grow during the same period – roughly doubling in terms of both friars and friaries for the Carmelites, and increasing by around half for the Augustinians. The two orders followed the Franciscans and Dominicans in many ways regarding work and lifestyle. They, too, established their friaries mainly in towns and made notable contributions to the universities. Yet they also retained their own characteristic features, especially regarding the eremitical lifestyle: Carmelites remembered their forebears who had lived as hermits on Mount Carmel in Palestine, and the official title of the Augustinian order was 'Order of Hermits of Saint Augustine'.

Notable Augustinian friars, at both ends of the later Middle Ages, were

James of Viterbo (1255–1308), who wrote in favour of the papacy's authority over secular rulers and was appointed archbishop of Benevento and later of Naples; Giles of Rome (1243–1316), the philosopher and political theorist, who was elected general (head) of his order and later became archbishop of Bourges in France; and Giles of Viterbo (1469–1532), who was versatile as scholar and preacher, as an advocate of Church reform, and who served as general of the order. The English Augustinian friar John Capgrave (1393–1464) was a scholar and writer of wide interests, well known for his historical works. His *Chronicle of England to 1417* was the first history of the country written in English. Martin Luther became an Augustinian friar just after the end of the period, in 1505.

Other orders of men. In addition to the orders outlined above, the later medieval Church embraced smaller orders of friars as well as a variety of other orders. Of the smaller orders of friars, there had been many foundations in the thirteenth century, but few survived the prohibitions against new religious orders that were promulgated by the general councils of Lateran IV in 1215 and Lyons II in 1274. Of those that did survive into the later Middle Ages, notable was the order of Servite friars, which was founded by seven merchants of Florence in 1232 and was officially approved by Pope Benedict XI in 1304. Its work focused on the care of the poor and the sick and on the education of youth. The 'Order of the Most Holy Trinity' (Ordo Sanctissimae Trinitatus), or Trinitarians, had as its principal purpose the ransoming of Christians captured by Muslims. Founded in 1198, it grew to some 800 houses in the fifteenth century. Most of the smaller orders, including the Servites and Trinitarians, had second orders of nuns and third orders of associated lay men and women – outreaches into the wider Christian community. The orders of the Knights Templar and Knights Hospitaller are treated elsewhere (see p 5). These smaller orders formed an integral part of the late medieval Church.

Nuns

Throughout the medieval period the number of women in religious orders, or nuns, was much smaller than the number of men in religious orders. It was only much later, beginning in the nineteenth century, that women came to outnumber men in this respect. There were several reasons for the imbalance in the later Middle Ages. Various social factors meant that women had much less freedom of choice than men to enter a religious order, especially women coming from outside the upper ranks of society. Many religious orders of women, moreover, arose as branches of orders of men, rather than as orders that had been founded by women in the first place and had them primarily in mind. In families of religious orders, accordingly, the order for women was often called the second order, the first being that for men. The Benedictine and Dominican orders are examples. They were founded by St Benedict and St Dominic primarily as orders for men, but each had a second order of women – founded jointly (at least according to tradition) by Scholastica, the sister of Benedict, in the case of Benedictine nuns, and directly by Dominic in the case of Dominican nuns. Franciscan nuns took their inspiration from both Francis of Assisi and the remarkable and quite independent-minded Clare of Assisi. It was only later, in the sixteenth and more notably in the nineteenth and twentieth centuries, that religious orders more clearly and exclusively focused on women began to emerge on a large scale. As a result of these limitations, many women seeking a committed religious life searched for it as beguines, or as tertiaries of religious orders, or within a family – forms of religious life that will be discussed in Chapter 3.

It is noticeable that while a fair number of women in the twelfth and thirteenth centuries became famous as members of religious orders, the same cannot be said of the next two centuries. Hildegard of Bingen, the Benedictine abbess in the twelfth century, and the three remarkable nuns at the Cistercian abbey of Helfta in the thirteenth century, Mechtild of Magdeburg, Mechtild of Hackeborn and Gertrude, were not followed by comparable figures subsequently. In the later Middle Ages, women well known for their holiness of life and writings – who were numerous – were mostly beguines or anchorites or tertiaries or married women. The difference can be seen either as a sign of the decline of female religious orders or, rather, as indicative of developments in feminine piety.

Focusing on the lack of well-known personalities should not obscure the many women who chose this demanding and appreciated way of life. Geoffrey Chaucer in *The Canterbury Tales* perhaps summarizes well the overall situation. He portrays the two nuns – the prioress and her companion nun – with a mixture of sympathy and criticism. They are treated in the *Tales* much more kindly than the monk and the friar, yet not as favourably as the parish priest. The prioress is polite and sprightly, yet she relates an unpleasant anti-Semitic tale. The other nun's character is not developed but her tale of the 'chaste marriage' between St Cecilia and a pagan knight is typical of Chaucer's refined ambiguity, perhaps intended to illustrate both high ideals and some naivety on the part of the nuns of his time.

A case study: Norwich

Norwich, the capital city of East Anglia, the eastern region of England, had a population in 1300 that has been variously estimated by recent historians as lying somewhere between 12,000 and 25,000. (The large variations are partly explained by differences of opinion regarding where the boundaries of the city should be drawn: should they be the legal boundaries of the city as a corporation, or rather the wider limits within which people linked to the city actually lived?) The population of the city, following national trends, had been growing steadily during the twelfth and thirteenth centuries, reached a peak in the early fourteenth century and went into sharp decline as a result of the Black Death in 1348/49 and subsequent outbreaks of the plague. Recovery began slowly in the middle of the fifteenth century, but the city's population in 1500, the end of our period, was still well below what it had been in 1300.

Throughout the late Middle Ages, Norwich was one of England's half-dozen most important regional capitals, second in population only to the national capital, London. It was never in the first rank of European cities, alongside Paris or Venice or London, or a few other cities, but clearly in the second rank. Close links with the Low Countries and further afield, through trade and in other ways, meant that it was a city of European standing as well as an English provincial capital. Comparison might be made with Siena in northern Italy, a city that was similar to it in population as well as in religious energy and creativity. Norwich, therefore, provides a revealing case-study, from an urban setting, on the clergy and religious orders.

Numbers in the city

Norwich abounded in clergy and religious orders (see Map 3 for the parish churches and religious houses). For numbers, the most accurate figures are for 1492, through the records of the bishop of Norwich's visitation of the city in that year. Eighty-nine priests were listed as belonging, in various functions, to the 46 parish churches in the city – either priests in charge of the churches, or their assistants or chantry priests attached to the churches. Some 25 priests were attached to the three colleges of secular priests (communities of diocesan clergy without parochial responsibilities). The bishop of Norwich had his principal residence in the city, and half a dozen priests were living in the city and were mainly occupied in assisting him in various ways with diocesan administration. Altogether, therefore, there was one bishop and some 120 priests of the diocesan (or secular) clergy.

Five religious orders of men had communities in the city in the later Middle Ages: Benedictine monks, and the four orders of friars, Franciscans, Dominicans, Carmelites and Augustinians. The Benedictine monks lived in the large cathedral priory (called thus because the priory was attached to the cathedral and the monks were responsible for conducting religious services in the cathedral and for maintaining the building). The visitation records of 1492 listed 46 monks at the cathedral priory, though this figure probably included a small number of monks living in dependent houses of the priory outside the city. The number of friars in 1492 can only be guessed at because the four friaries do not appear in the visitation records. They were large friaries, and various evidence suggests some 40 to 55 friars in each house in the early fourteenth century. For the late fifteenth century, a minimum total of 120 friars, or some 30 in each house, seems likely.

For no other year in the Middle Ages are there figures of comparable precision to those available for 1492. Fragmentary evidence suggests, however, that the proportion of diocesan clergy and members of male religious orders to the total population of the city remained fairly constant throughout the late medieval period. In absolute terms, certainly, the numbers were larger in 1300 than in 1492; they dropped dramatically in the aftermath of the Black Death and its recurrences, and there was some recovery in the second half of the fifteenth century. Allowing for the uncertainty about the total population of the city, it may be estimated that in 1492, as indeed at other times in the late Middle Ages, between 4 and 6 per cent of the male population, and a correspondingly greater proportion of the adult men, were secular priests or members of religious orders. High as these figures may appear, they were not unusual for late medieval England. Similar percentages are indicated for London, York and Lincoln, for example, and higher figures for the university towns of Oxford and Cambridge. In other countries of late medieval Christendom, similar figures are indicated for many towns and cities, even higher in some cases. It should be noted, however, that the proportion of secular and regular clergy to the total population was generally higher in towns and cities than in the countryside, in England as elsewhere, except of course in the immediate vicinity of large monasteries.

For women who wished to join a religious order in Norwich, the only possibility was the Benedictine nunnery of Carrow in the suburbs of the city. The community appears to have fluctuated between some nine and 17 nuns during the later Middle Ages, with a dozen as the average. Even allowing for the fact that far fewer women than men joined religious orders in late medieval Christendom as a whole, the imbalance in Norwich was striking. It was compensated for by the remarkable number of women living other forms of committed religious life in the city, notably as anchorites – most famous among them was Julian of Norwich – and in communities resembling beguinages, and some joined nunneries away from the city.

Geographical and social origins

Chaucer and Langland described late fourteenth-century London as a magnet attracting priests from outside the city (*The Canterbury Tales*, Prologue, lines 507–11; *Piers Plowman*, B Text, Prologue, lines 83–6). How far Norwich acted in the same way cannot be known with any accuracy because the origins of priests residing in the city are not known at all fully. However, a variety of evidence, notably the lists of men ordained to the diocesan priesthood, which are preserved for Norwich diocese with remarkable completeness for the years 1413 to 1445 and which usually mention the home town of the ordinand, suggest that as many diocesan priests originated in the city of Norwich as were living in it: that the citizens, therefore, were indeed productive of vocations to the diocesan clergy. It also appears that, overall and perhaps unsurprisingly, while a fair number of priests who had grown up in Norwich went away and worked elsewhere, probably the majority remained in the city.

For the regular clergy, the evidence is more fragmentary and suggests greater mobility both into and out of the city. For the Benedictine cathedral priory, the home towns of a fair number of the monks are known with some certainty. While a small number of them originated in the city, the majority, it seems, came from outside. According to the records of the visitation of the priory in 1492, only three monks had Norwich as their second name (e.g. John Norwich), and most of the others were named after towns and villages elsewhere in East Anglia, many of them lying near estates of the priory. It appears, therefore, that the priory recruited many of its monks from families living on or near to its extensive estates. The names of the obedientiaries (monks who held offices – called 'obediences' – within the priory and cathedral), which are known quite fully throughout the later Middle Ages, support a similar profile of the monks' origins.

Each of the four friaries contained a *studium* (that is, the friary acted as a house of studies for student friars preparing for ordination to the priesthood). Most of the student friars came to Norwich from elsewhere in England, some even from abroad, in order to pursue their studies for ordination at the friary. Of the few friars who can be clearly identified as sons of citizens of Norwich, some are to be found living in their home town, others living elsewhere. Mobility, and willingness to go wherever sent, was part of the friars' way of life.

The citizens' wills, which survive in quantity from 1370 onwards, show that a remarkably high proportion of their sons were becoming secular priests or entering religious orders. Altogether some 1,500 such wills survive from 1370 to 1532 (the eve of the English Reformation). Between 10 and 11 per cent of the sons mentioned in the wills were described as secular priests or members of religious orders. The figures, indeed, understate the true situation since they do not include children who became priests or entered religious orders after their parents made their wills. The testators came predominantly from the upper ranks of Norwich society. That such a high proportion of the sons of the upper bourgeoisie chose these ways of life is very significant and shows that the older and more institutional ways of religious life still had considerable appeal for a class of young men that might be expected to have produced its fair share of radicals. The proportion of sons so choosing showed no sign of decline on the eve of the Reformation; indeed it was slightly higher between 1490 and 1532 than between 1370 and 1489. The sons in question were almost exactly divided between diocesan (or secular) priests and members of religious orders. The surviving evidence suggests that the majority of the latter chose religious houses away from Norwich, while a much higher proportion of the former were living in the city – findings that support other indications, mentioned earlier, about provenance. Regarding age of entry into the priesthood, usually no information is given in the wills, but there is evidence that some men became priests later in life. Eight diocesan priests living in Norwich mentioned their wives and/or children in their wills. None of the wives was said to be still alive, so the assumption must be that the men were ordained to the priesthood some time later in life, after their wife's death.

Of the daughters mentioned as nuns in their parents' wills, almost half were at Carrow priory in the suburbs of Norwich. This finding supports other evidence of the close links between the priory and the city. The priory was the only nunnery in or near Norwich and it gave board and lodging and other forms of accommodation to a number of lay people from Norwich and elsewhere. Some girls from the city went to the convent for education and no doubt some of them later became nuns there. The other daughters mentioned in the wills were nuns at convents elsewhere in East Anglia.

Education and learning

Late medieval Norwich provides relatively plentiful evidence of quite high levels of education and learning among the clergy of a provincial capital. The evidence provided by the registers of the bishops of Norwich regarding appointments to benefices in the city shows that the number of rectors and vicars of parish churches in the city known to have been university graduates rose steadily from 12 out of 158 between 1370 and 1449, to 23 out of 71 between 1450 and 1499, and to 25 out of 60 between 1500 and 1532. The proportion among the unbeneficed parish clergy (those who were not rectors or vicars) was much lower, as would be expected. Thus at the 1492 visitation of parishes in the city, four of the 45 stipendiary and chantry priests, and just one of the 25 parish chaplains, were styled 'Magister'.

Regarding religious orders, the fullest picture comes from the Benedictine cathedral priory. In 1360 the priory had two monks studying at Gloucester College, the Benedictine house of studies within Oxford university. They
were the priory's most illustrious members in the later Middle Ages: Adam
Easton, later a cardinal and author of *Defensorium ecclesiastice potestatis*, and
Thomas Brinton, later bishop of Rochester and a renowned preacher. More
than a century later, in 1492, the bishop of Norwich complained during
his visitation of the priory that young monks were not being sent 'to the
university of Oxford to study, and this to the great scandal and injury of
the monastery'. He ordered that the priory should always have at least two
monks at Gloucester College. His complaint, however, gives an unbalanced
picture: the priory's obedientiary rolls indicate that in every year between
the early fifteenth century, when the names of monks studying at university began to be recorded, and the dissolution of the priory in 1538, except
1492, between one and four monks of the priory were at either Oxford or
Cambridge universities.

There are no comparable figures for the number of university graduates
at the four friaries in the city. For writers of the period *c.*1350 to 1530, John
Bale included in his catalogue of 'illustrious' British authors – *Scriptorum
illustrium maioris Brytannie catalogus* – four monks of the cathedral priory
in addition to Easton and Brinton, and one Dominican, three Augustinian, five Franciscan and 12 Carmelite friars – substantial numbers. Most of
them are known to have studied at Oxford or Cambridge. Bale had been a
member of the Carmelite friary in Norwich in the early sixteenth century
and so should have known the local scene – he modestly omitted himself
from the list. By contrast, the *Catalogus* included only one diocesan priest
from the city.

Not too much attention should be paid to the universities of Oxford and
Cambridge, especially regarding the friars' education. The *studium* within
each of the four friaries in Norwich is likely to have provided theological and philosophical education – mainly in preparation for the priesthood
– that was comparable to that provided by the two universities. Recent
scholarship points to this more optimistic assessment and, as a result, urges
caution against obsession with Oxford and Cambridge. Most is known
about the Franciscan friary. Adam Woodham (or Wodeham), the distinguished theologian and close friend of William of Ockham, was lecturer
there in the late 1320s. It was one of the order's seven friaries in England
that were officially established by Pope Benedict XII's ordinance of 1336 as
a *studium* where theology was to be taught to young friars. The notebook
of an Italian Franciscan, Nicholas of Assisi, containing notes on lectures

and disputations which he attended at the friary between 1337 and 1339, shows that it was fulfilling this function shortly afterwards and offering courses of a sufficiently high standard to attract a friar from Italy. Later in the fourteenth century Peter de Candia, the Franciscan friar who became Pope Alexander V, travelled from Italy to study at the friary before going on to Oxford. The *studium* was still attracting friars from abroad in the early fifteenth century: John 'of Westphalia', John 'of Austria' and Theodoric 'of Saxony' were among the student Franciscans 'of the Norwich convent' in 1406 and 1407.

Norwich contained three schools at which prospective priests and other boys (and maybe some girls) could get a rudimentary education: the Song School and the Almery School, which were attached to the cathedral priory, and the Grammar School. Some of the citizens' wills reveal their eagerness for a well-educated clergy. Robert Elys, for example, wanted his wife 'to keep little Reynold to the school, if he will abide with her, to the time she knows whether he will be a man of the church or not'. Walter Shane, too, was to be educated outside the universities: his master, in his will of 1496, 'gladly' dispensed Walter from his apprenticeship as a grocer so that he could study to become a priest with a certain John Russell, cleric. Philip Curson, an alderman of the city, left money in his will of 1502 for his son, if he 'will be a priest', to 'be found to Cambridge schools to learn that faculty that his mind is most disposed on, till he is bachelor in the law or of art'.

The libraries of the four friaries were dispersed or destroyed as a result of the dissolution of religious houses under Henry VIII. There is little evidence of their contents before that. The Benedictine cathedral priory was transformed at the Reformation into the dean and chapter of Norwich cathedral and the library substantially survived the change. It formed one of the finest libraries in medieval England. Cardinal Adam Easton, the former monk, bequeathed 228 books to it, which were transported from Rome to Norwich in six barrels in 1407. At the dissolution of the priory in 1538, the library contained at least 1,350 volumes.

For the parish clergy, the libraries of the cathedral priory and the four friaries may have been partly accessible to them. The fullest information about the books they read, in addition to the liturgical and service books that would have been available in their parish churches, comes from those mentioned in their wills and in the single surviving inventory. The inventory lists the goods at the time of death of John Baker, who was simultaneously rector of two parish churches in the city, Saint John Maddermarket and All Saints Berstreet, and who died, probably in middle age and still rector of both churches, in 1518. Probably he was not a university graduate but he lived at a time when printed books were becoming more available. The inventory gives details of 26 books and mentions generically 'twenty other small books'. Almost half the identified books were works of canon law, including the three basic textbooks of Western canon law (*Decrees*, *Decretals* and *Sext*), three commentaries on canon law by Continental scholars, namely the Italian Panormitanus (d.1445), the Spaniard Bernard of Compostella (d.1296) and the Frenchman William Durandus (d.1296), and *Provinciale*, the work on the canon law of the English Church by William Lyndwood (d.1446). Five collections of sermons were mentioned, two of them by Englishmen, the Carmelite friar Richard Maidstone (d.1396) and Bishop John Fisher (d.1535), one by the German Dominican friar John Herolt (d.1468), one by the French Dominican friar Vincent Ferrer (d.1419), and an anonymous collection. Among the other named books were *Legenda aurea*, the collection of saints' lives by the archbishop of Genoa, James de Voragine (d.1298), and a 'Bybill' – possibly an early English translation but more probably the Latin Vulgate version. The books indicate mainly conservative tastes and a keen interest in the law of the Church; the collections of sermons, especially, reveal a pastorally minded priest, and the number of works by foreigners indicate an outlook that was far from insular.

None of the books listed in John Baker's inventory was mentioned in his will. Accordingly, the books mentioned in other wills of the diocesan clergy (members of religious orders did not own personal property and therefore did not make wills), as bequests to individuals or institutions, are likely to represent but a fraction of the books they owned. For the most part they appear in ones or twos in any given will. They provide further evidence of the reading habits of the secular clergy. Most frequently mentioned were prayer books and other liturgical works – it is often unclear whether the testator was leaving his own book or wanted, rather, his executors to buy the book and give it to the beneficiary. Legal works and collections of sermons were much rarer, proportionally, than in Baker's will. Bibles appear in four wills, though it is unclear whether any of them was an English version. Commentaries on Scripture included works by the French scholars Anselm of Laon (d.1117), Peter Comestor (d.1179), Hugh of Saint-Cher (d.1263), Nicholas of Gorran (d.1295) and Nicholas of Lyra (d.1340), the fourteenth-century Italian Philip de Monte Calerio, and one by 'Acton', possibly Ralph Acton, the obscure fourteenth-century Englishman. A few works by Fathers of the Church were mentioned: Eusebius, probably Eusebius of Caesarea, Augustine, including his *Confessions*, and the *Dialogues* of Pope Gregory. Medieval theologians and spiritual writers were represented by Hugh of St Victor (d.1142), Hugh of Fouillou (d.1174), William of Auvergne (d.1249) and Peter of Limoges (d.1306) from France; Angelo da Chivasso (d.1495) and possibly Bonaventure (d.1274) from Italy; Werner Rolewinck (d.1502) from Germany; Alexander of Hales (d.1245), Robert Selk (early fourteenth century) and John Bromyard (d.1349) from England.

Very few works unconnected with Christianity, or by non-Christians, were mentioned in the wills, apart from some dictionaries and other academic aids. 'Cato' and 'Donatus' were probably works by the classical authors of those names and 'Bevis of Hampton' was a thirteenth-century romance of English provenance. *De planctu nature*, the dialogue with nature by Alan of Lille (d.1202), was mentioned in one will, and Petrarch's (d.1374) *De remediis utriusque fortune*, which was mentioned in another will, was the only clear evidence of the new Renaissance learning. Testators were unlikely to mention unorthodox works even if they owned them, and the only candidate of this kind was *Rosarium*, which may have been the Lollard treatise of that name and was owned by Geoffrey Chaumpneis (d.1472), vicar of St Stephen's parish church. Lollardy, indeed, appears to have made little headway among the clergy of late medieval Norwich, or indeed among the laity, even though it was quite strong in other parts of East Anglia. Notably absent were works by late medieval mystics, including those from England. The absence contrasts with the presence of such works in lay wills (see pp 121–2). Altogether, therefore, while the clergy's literary tastes appear traditional and mainstream, they were imaginative within this framework, and the number of works by Continental writers is impressive, indicating an outlook that was European and far from insular. Some development in book ownership is apparent during the period in question, as new books were written and came on to the market, but the overall continuity in taste and interest is more striking than the changes.

Lifestyles and morals

In terms of wealth and lifestyle, the secular clergy of late medieval Norwich fell into three broad categories. At the top of the first category, in a class of his own, was the bishop. He may have spent most of his time outside the city, elsewhere in the diocese and beyond it, but nevertheless he was its most important citizen, automatically a leading figure in East Anglia and in several cases prominent on the national scene. Norwich was among the middle-ranking English sees in terms of the income it gave the bishop. The bishops in question provided a mix of personalities that was characteristic of the late medieval English episcopate. The soldier-bishop Henry Despenser (1370–1406), who put down the Peasants' Revolt in East Anglia in 1381 and led a 'crusade' in Flanders, was balanced by John Salmon (1299–1325), whose reputation for holiness survived his death, and William Bateman (1344–55), the son of a bailiff of Norwich who became joint founder of Gonville Hall in Cambridge.

Within the same category, at a lower level, were various wealthy plural-ists who held at least one benefice within the city and who lived in Norwich for at least some of the time. Many of them held prebends at St Mary in the Fields, the largest of the three colleges of secular priests in the city. A classic example was Nicholas Goldwell, the younger brother of the Bishop of Norwich, James Goldwell. The latter appointed him dean of the College of St Mary in the Fields in 1498 and at the same time he was concur-rently archdeacon of Suffolk, master of St Mary Magdalen Hospital in the suburbs of Norwich, and, outside the city, rector of four or more parish churches and canon of a similar number of collegiate churches. He lived in Norwich at least part of the time: the only house mentioned in his will was his *mansio* in the city. He was a noted benefactor to many religious institu-tions in Norwich – often acting in association with his brother – as well as to All Souls College in Oxford.

The second category mainly comprised the beneficed parish clergy, that is to say, those who held tenured and normally lifetime benefices as rectors and vicars of the city's parish churches. A wide variety of means and life-styles existed within this category, yet all the men in question belonged to the upper clergy in terms of their status and responsibilities. Two exam-ples must suffice: John Baker, the rector whose library has been discussed, and Richard Caistor. Baker's inventory claimed to list 'all the moveable goods belonging to him' at his death and they were valued at just under £22 (multiply by several thousand for today's equivalent). They made him a man of comfortable means. Besides his books, he owned, according to the inventory, two feather-beds and plenty of bedclothes, a substantial ward-robe including six gowns, three tippets and three doublets, enough furni-ture and tableware to provide meals in comfort for several persons, and he must have owned one or more horses since his riding clothes, a bridle and two saddles were listed. Richard Caistor was vicar of St Stephen's parish church in Norwich from 1402 until his death in 1420. Margery Kempe, the holy woman of King's Lynn, valued his spiritual advice and he had a reputation for holiness. His brief will is very distinctive. It is unusual in containing no bequests for the saying of Masses and prayers for his soul and he wanted his wealth – apart from £10 that was to be spent on buying two antiphonaries for his parish church – to be given to the poor on the grounds that 'the good of the Church, according to canon law, belong to the poor'.

The third category comprised the other clergy, the majority of secular priests in the city: assistant parish priests, with temporary or less tenured posts, chantry priests and others. Within this category there was a wide range of material circumstances, yet the overall impression is of a decent standard of living. Lifestyles and expectations appear to have been quite attractive, both religiously and materially, and the work undertaken was appreciated. Thomas Oudolff presents an interesting case from the late fifteenth century. He belonged to a wealthy family in the city, of five or more children. His brother John was rector of a parish church in the city. Thomas, however, never had a benefice. Before his ordination he had been a married man – his deceased wife and a daughter were mentioned in his will. He was ordained priest probably quite late in life and died soon afterwards. He died comfortably well off, leaving in his will bequests worth £20 as well as a tenement and a farm. His will included imaginative instructions to his executors to hire two men to make pilgrimages to local shrines in atonement for his sins: one was to go barefoot to Our Lady of Walsingham, the other 'naked in his shirt' to the Holy Rood at Beccles. In Thomas we can detect a blending of clerical and lay lifestyles and piety.

Bequests in the wills of the laity, and other evidence, reinforce this sense of prevailing harmony between laity and clergy in the city. The overall impression is of strong support for the work and lifestyles of the secular clergy and members of religious orders. There are few hints of anti-clericalism. The laity appear almost more clerical than the clergy, urging them to perform better their priestly duties rather than to change the duties. Ninety-five per cent of the laity whose wills survive between 1370 and 1532 left bequests to one or more parish churches, including normally their own; there was no decline in this respect on the eve of the Reformation, indeed the percentage rose slightly after 1490. Nearly half of them left bequests to the friars – usually they gave to each of the four friaries in the city and occasionally to friaries elsewhere. Many bequests were small sums of money, perhaps conventional gestures suggested to the testator by the scribe who wrote the will, but many were substantial amounts, quite often very large sums. The gifts to parish churches may have been intended for the churches more than for the clergy, and it cannot be assumed that the attitudes of the upper ranks of Norwich society, to which most testators belonged, were shared by other inhabitants of the city. Despite these cautions, the evidence of wills, taken together, is impressive.

Another facet of the apparently cordial and constructive relations between clergy and laity was the clergy's important role in the religious activities of the many craft guilds and pious confraternities. Many of the activities were held in the churches and religious houses of the city. Priests were needed for religious services on the annual 'day' of the guild or confraternity, usually the patronal feast-day, to say Masses and prayers for deceased members, to take part in the various semi-religious processions of craft guilds and to help with the mystery plays which were performed annually by the guilds. The required work and cooperation formed an integral part of clerical life in late medieval Norwich. Indeed, in these respects, the city was following the norm for major towns in late medieval England and, for the most part, throughout Western Christendom.

Court records and records of ecclesiastical visitations provide further, fragmentary information. Among the charges brought against the clergy of the city, most related to sexual immorality, usually adultery or fornication. Agnes Saunder 'fosters sexual immorality among priests, women, members of religious orders, canons, and all sorts', lamented the lay people who were questioned during the bishop's visitation of the united parish of St Cuthbert and St Mary the Less in 1492. Other accusations of this nature were quite common. Regarding other charges, the laity's desire that the clergy improve on their duties and lifestyle, rather than radically alter them, is again prominent. Thus the five lay people questioned at the visitation of St Martin at the Palace Gates parish in 1416 made no sweeping requests; rather they complained that the rector failed to maintain the lamp (before the Sacrament) in the chancel and that the assistant priest spent his nights outside the parish. Large demands for radical change are unlikely to find their way into records of this kind, but even so the conservatism of the laity regarding the clergy is noticeable.

Assaults on the cathedral priory

Two assaults on the Benedictine cathedral priory, in 1272 and 1453, must be considered. The context, which was paralleled in many other towns in medieval England and elsewhere in Europe, was the growing power and ambitions of the city government, on the one hand, and the formidable position of the priory in the economic and political life of the city on the other. The priory was the largest employer in Norwich and by far the most extensive owner of land and property in the city and its suburbs, including spacious grazing lands for sheep and cattle that almost surrounded the city.

Simmering tensions between the citizens and the priory erupted in 1272 into an attack of exceptional violence. The spark appears to have been a scuffle between townsmen and servants of the priory at a quintain held just outside the priory gates. A large crowd from the city then gathered, including three of the city's four bailiffs and other prominent citizens. They entered the priory, burnt some of its buildings and part of the cathedral and killed at least 13 people – though, it appears, none of the monks perished. The reprisals were severe. The bishop of Norwich and later the pope excommunicated the attackers and laid the city under an interdict; some 30 citizens were hanged in punishment and the king confiscated the 'liberties' of the city and condemned it to pay the huge sum of £2,000 towards repairing the damage done to the cathedral.

Memory of the violence in 1272 remained vivid within Norwich throughout the later Middle Ages. Tension continued throughout the fourteenth
century, rooted in the exemption from the jurisdiction of the city government that the monks claimed for the priory and much of its property. It
flared up in a succession of lesser incidents and came to a head again in
1453 in the disturbance called 'Gladman's Insurrection'. There were striking
similarities between the assaults of 1272 and 1453, though in the latter case
no deaths occurred. Accounts differ regarding the details and the sequence
of events. Many of the citizens, it appears, led by a certain John Gladman (whose precise role remains obscure) and encouraged by the mayor
and other members of the city government, marched on the priory to
demand the surrender of various charters and other documents supporting
the exemptions and privileged status of the priory within the city and its
suburbs. They forced the prior 'by threats of burning, killing and plunder-
ing' to surrender the relevant records and then attacked and sacked the
priory. After a week or so of open resistance, the citizens eventually backed
down. Both the Church and the Crown struck back. The citizens involved
were excommunicated by the archbishop of Canterbury, and on the 'orders
of the king' the mayor was imprisoned in the Fleet prison in London for
over a month. Various rights and privileges of the city were declared forfeit
for several years and, among other penalties, the city was fined £2,000 and
individual rioters sums totalling a further £1,500.

Relations between the priory and the citizens gradually improved thereafter, while the Crown began to favour the citizens rather than the priory in
the dispute. A long-term settlement was reached in 1524, at the insistence of
Cardinal Wolsey as lord chancellor, in which the greater concessions came
from the priory. As a result, there was relative peace between the two parties
until the priory, along with other religious houses in England, was finally
dissolved in 1537. In a sense, therefore, from the point of view of the citizens
of Norwich, the dissolution of the cathedral priory was unnecessary rather
than the inevitable culmination of earlier grievances. Indeed it is important
to remember the measure of harmony and mutual dependence that existed
between the city and the priory throughout the late Middle Ages, not to
focus exclusively on conflicts. Interdependence came inevitably from the
priory's position as the largest economic institution in Norwich and from
the role of the cathedral – for which the monks had responsibility – as the
principal church in the city and the venue for various official religious functions of the city government. Cordial relations are glimpsed tantalizingly
in the account roles of the priory's cellarer, which list payments for the
annual banquet that the prior hosted for the city authorities – payments to

'minstrels of the city and other players performing before the lord prior, the major of the city and others on the day of the banquet at Christmas', as the account roll of 1421/22 recorded.

Conclusion

In any treatment of the clergy and religious orders of later medieval Norwich, consideration must be given to tensions between the citizens and the cathedral priory, including the disturbances of 1272 and 1453. But proper attention must also be paid to the wider picture. There is the evidence of better and more positive relations between city and priory, and also the fact that the conflicts touched economic and political issues more than religious matters. There were no conflicts, moreover, of comparable seriousness between the city and other religious institutions in the city. The apparent vitality of clergy and religious orders, in terms of both numbers and quality, has been outlined at some length. Why, nevertheless, the city of Norwich accepted the Protestant Reformation, indeed apparently embraced it with some enthusiasm, is a fascinating question that cannot be investigated properly here. In part, clearly, the Reformation was imposed on the city from outside and from above, notably by the Crown. In part, too, there is the paradox that the generally strong state of the clergy and religious orders in the late Middle Ages, at least in Norwich, actually led into the Reformation, that the latter was a development from within the late medieval Church as well as a reaction against it.

CHAPTER 3

Laity

Chapters 1 and 2 studied the more clerical and institutional aspects of the Church, that is, the papacy and Church councils, then the clergy and religious orders. It might be called a 'from above' approach, the advantage of which is that it provides a clear framework at the start, by treating of people (mostly men) and institutions about whom we are relatively well informed and whose roles and structures were, on the whole, clear. There is the danger, however, of giving the impression that movement and initiative in the late medieval Church came largely from above: from pope, bishops and priests, who then influenced the laity. Such an impression would be wide of the mark. The later Middle Ages was very much an 'age of the laity' in the Western Church (for the Eastern Church see Chapter 6). The laity, both men and women, provided much of the energy and creativity as well as constituting the overwhelming majority of the Christian population. The clergy, too, were products of the laity: born and brought up by and among lay people. Therefore this ambitious third chapter, which discusses the religion of the laity in the Western Church during the last two centuries of the Middle Ages, is central to the book.

Minimal obligations

Perhaps the best way to enter into the vast and complex topic of the religion of the laity in Western Christendom during the later Middle Ages is through their minimal religious obligations.

Those considered to be heretics, that is to say, men and women who were condemned by Church authorities even though they regarded themselves as Christians, indeed usually as better Christians than those who remained within the official Church, are discussed in Chapter 5. It would be wrong to exaggerate the importance and influence of such individuals, to place them centre-stage. They remained quite small in number and largely confined to particular areas and limited periods of time. Often they flourished because of special circumstances. The large majority of people seem to have been content to live and die within the framework of the Church. The reasons for this compliance are debated. Some historians have argued that people kept within the boundaries of orthodoxy out of fear of the punishments – ultimately the death penalty – that awaited them if they showed open dissent. No doubt this was true in some cases but it would be wrong, I think, to suggest that there were large numbers of such individuals, to propose that they came anywhere close to the majority of the population. It is crucial, in my opinion, to recognize that Christianity as taught and practised by the late medieval Church was popular and meaningful for the large majority of the population, that it had wide grassroots support. The Church remained, on the whole, remarkably in tune with the religious sentiments and aspirations of the people. This thesis is a frequent theme of the book. So it can be left here now for readers gradually to make up their own minds.

Alongside support for Christianity, Church authorities were normally reluctant to pry into the consciences of individuals. This reluctance was another reason why the large majority of the population lived and died within the Church. There were drives against heresy, but these were usually the result of open challenges on the part of dissident groups. Lollards in England and Hussites in Bohemia were the most obvious examples. Short of these challenges, Church authorities were largely content with quite a minimal level of religious knowledge and observance. It was recognized that the late medieval Church was a large ship sailing in turbulent waters – the image of a ship was often applied to the Church – and that it was unwise to rock the boat unnecessarily. Another consideration was the communal nature of life. The later Middle Ages is rightly considered a period of growing individualism, but this was relatively so in comparison with the earlier Middle Ages. Life was far more communal than today. People, as a result, normally and naturally followed the basic observances – including religious – of the community.

What were these minimal obligations of the laity regarding religious knowledge and practice? The thirteenth century formed an essential and largely still binding background to the later Middle Ages in this matter; hence a fair number of the examples that follow come from this earlier century.

Religious knowledge

The content of what the laity should know, and how this related to belief, had come under wide scrutiny in the twelfth and thirteenth centuries. Theologians of the time agreed that the laity could not be expected to have full knowledge of the faith, as might be desired of the clergy. Such an expectation was too cruel even to suggest, St Bonaventure said, since it implied that few would be saved. The tolerant attitude of most writers was based upon a distinction between implicit and explicit knowledge. Thus Peter Lombard wrote with approval of those who 'believe what they do not know', who could not elaborate the articles of the Creed yet 'believed' all that they contain. Pope Innocent IV gave clarity and authority to this distinction in knowledge, stating that 'the measure of faith to which the laity were bound' was to believe explicitly that God exists and rewards the good, and implicitly (that is, in accordance with the belief of the Church) the articles of the faith. He argued that intelligent lay people might seek to learn more, but there was no sin if they did not, since it was sufficient for them to devote themselves to good works. In a similar vein, Thomas Aquinas stated that intellectual study was not necessary for salvation, that the implicit faith of simple people was held in trust and guaranteed by the explicit faith of their betters (principally the clergy) and ultimately by the faith of the Church, which would never fail.

Writers of the later Middle Ages followed much the same approach. Duns Scotus was relatively exigent, arguing that those endowed with reason ought to know 'the more easily intelligible articles' of the faith. William Lyndwood, the English canonist writing in the early fifteenth century, stated that literate lay people, who ought to know the articles of the faith more explicitly than simple people, did not sin mortally if they failed in this respect, since the acquisition of such knowledge 'was not their profession'. Later this rather wide tolerance of ignorance and dependence upon the faith of the Church would incur sharp criticism from Reformers. Calvin, especially, argued that faith rests on knowledge – of God and of Christ – and not upon reverence for the Church.

Ecclesiastical legislation also took a tolerant approach insofar as it treated inquiry into the religious knowledge of the laity. Indeed the large amount of legislation requiring minimal knowledge on the part of the clergy highlights the paucity of similar legislation regarding the laity. The decrees of the later medieval general councils of the Western Church, from Vienne (1311–12) to Basel-Florence (1431–45), contain no such regulations enforcing inquiry of the laity (nor was there legislation of this kind surviving from earlier general councils); neither are they to be found in *Corpus iuris canonici*, the other great source of medieval ecclesiastical law. Aquinas held that uneducated (*simplices*) Christians should be examined in detail about their religion only if they were suspected of heresy, and even then they were not to be charged with heresy unless they persisted in clinging to error. Canon lawyers such as Henry of Segusio (Hostiensis) and John Andreas generally concurred with this tolerant approach.

Some sanctions were expressed locally through legislation exhorting parish priests to instruct their parishioners. Robert Grosseteste, Bishop of

Lincoln in the mid-thirteenth century, directed that the laity should know the Ten Commandments and the seven deadly sins and possess a 'rudimentary understanding' of the seven sacraments. Peter Quinel, Bishop of Exeter, required that lay people have knowledge of the seven sacraments and their effects, the Lord's Prayer, the articles of the Creed and the Hail Mary. In the fourteenth century Spanish clerics were instructed by the Council of Valladolid in 1322 to convey basic aspects of the faith to the laity; fifteenth-century visitations of Salisbury diocese in England confirmed that clergy were indeed instructing their parishioners on the articles of the faith, the Ten Commandments, the seven deadly sins, the four cardinal virtues and the seven beatitudes. Nevertheless, while ecclesiastical legislation might oblige the clergy to know the basics of the faith and to teach them, for the most part it refrained from ordering the laity either to listen or to attain a required level of knowledge.

The sacrament of confession offered the most regular opportunity to investigate the religious knowledge of the laity. Confessional manuals from the thirteenth century onwards increasingly urged priests to discover whether their penitents knew the Lord's Prayer and the Creed. While some manuals urged confessors to withhold absolution if the knowledge was not forthcoming, others regarded inquiry into the penitent's knowledge as optional. The widely used thirteenth-century (anonymous) manual *Confessionale* suggested that after the confessor had inquired about the seven deadly sins 'he may if he wishes' go on to inquire about the articles of the Creed, but even then it is belief in, rather than understanding of, the articles that was to be uncovered. In the fifteenth century, John Mirk's *Instructions for Parish Priests* urged the priest, when his parishioners came to confession, to teach them the articles of faith and the seven sacraments, and to use an elaborate exposition of the Ten Commandments, the seven deadly sins and the seven venial sins in order that they might profit from the sacrament. Robert Grosseteste seems to have been one of the few bishops to legislate that his parish clergy were to inquire in the confessional about the religious knowledge of their parishioners, yet even he did not attempt to impose sanctions on those whose knowledge was deficient.

Of lay men who addressed the issue, King Louis IX of France urged his courtiers that 'the Christian religion as defined in the creed is something in which we ought to believe implicitly, even though our belief in it might be founded on hearsay'. The devout king was exhorting rather than legislating, and relying on his courtiers' implicit belief in even so fundamental an aspect of faith as the Creed. Such unshakeable belief, Louis continued, would guard against the devil who 'tries all he can to make [the dying] die with some doubt in their minds on certain points of our religion'. Some recent historians have identified among the laity not merely lack of effort in religious education but scepticism and unbelief. Alexander Murray suggested that both unbelief and lack of knowledge were present in some thirteenth-century northern Italian cities (Murray 1984: 83–106). Unbelief and bizarre beliefs, in some cases coinciding with considerable knowledge, have been brought to light by Emmanuel Le Roy Ladurie in his study of late thirteenth- and early fourteenth-century Montaillou (Le Roy Ladurie 1978: 306–26), and by John Edwards for the late fifteenth-century diocese of Soria and Osma in northern Spain (Edwards 1988: 3–25). Susan Reynolds went further, suggesting quite widespread scepticism in medieval Europe (Reynolds 1991: 21–41). Such cases may have been exceptional rather than the norm, yet they suggest that the lower end of religious knowledge could be quite frail and that ecclesiastical authorities may have preferred not to pry into the situation too closely. The authorities' reluctance seems to have stemmed from practical considerations in administering such a large body as Western Christendom as well as the desire to protect the laity from both easy charges of heresy and impossibly high prerequisites for salvation.

Pockets of ignorance or eccentric opinion did not necessarily mean that people remained pagan and unconverted. Practice of the faith, as Pope Innocent IV remarked, was even more important than knowledge of it. Indeed such practice was a form of learning and it was in this sense that Bonaventure could speak of the faithful learning through 'the usage and custom of the Church ... and by means of its solemnities and priestly activities'. How far participation and practice were expected and compelled is, therefore, an essential question. It may be explored through observance of the sacraments and other areas of Christian life that were subject to ecclesiastical discipline.

Religious practice: the sacraments

Shortly before the beginning of our period, at the Second Council of Lyons in 1274, the Church had for the first time declared in a definitive manner that the sacraments numbered seven: baptism, confirmation, confession, Eucharist, marriage, orders and last anointing. The sacrament of orders concerned the ordination of deacons, priests and bishops. The other six sacraments were fundamental to the basic religious obligations of the laity.

Historians have generally assumed that baptism of infants was widely practised throughout the Middle Ages. Without baptismal registers, which survive in quantity only from the sixteenth century, it is impossible to verify the assumption with any conclusiveness for the later Middle Ages. There is, nevertheless, considerable indirect evidence in favour of the assumption, notably a sense that parents understood and desired the rite for their child's salvation. In the early Middle Ages there had been fierce legislation compelling baptism. The notorious laws of Charlemagne threatened with death anyone actively avoiding baptism and required all children to be baptized within a year of birth. Anglo-Saxon penitentials and law codes imposed penances and fines on parents who failed to have their children baptized. Such concern, and its implications that the rite was not universally observed, was mainly confined to this earlier, missionary period. By the twelfth century there is little evidence to suggest that people needed such compulsion, and observance of the duty to baptize was almost taken for granted. In the later Middle Ages, when failure to baptize appears as an infrequent charge at visitations of parishes, it usually concerned carelessness or a dispute about who was responsible for the baptism of a particular child rather than any resistance to the rite. Thus, at the extensive visitations of parishes in Lincoln and Hereford dioceses in England, the only complaints of failure were made by the laity against the clergy: that the baptistery was not kept locked or properly cared for or that the rector failed to baptize infants, in one case obliging parishioners to go elsewhere for the rite. Ecclesiastical texts were less concerned to exhort or explain the need for baptism than to ensure that the laity understood that anyone – including a Muslim midwife – could baptize an infant at risk of death and therefore it was important to know the words that would effect the rite. Baptism, the most compulsory of the sacraments, seems to have enjoyed widespread support and observance.

Confirmation remained perhaps the most enigmatic sacrament throughout the Middle Ages. With no clear precedent in the New Testament, it was not generally separated from baptism until the eighth century, and remained for long afterwards a subject of debate as to whether it was a sacrament and regarding the proper age of its reception. It seems likely that the majority of people never received the rite even in the later Middle Ages, though by then reception of it was becoming more common. Most theologians did not regard it as necessary for salvation, and therefore not compulsory. In the thirteenth century Aquinas wrote that confirmation contributes to the perfection of salvation but is not indispensable provided it is not refused out of contempt; Bonaventure drew a similar distinction, although he emphasized its importance more strongly. William of Pagula, writing in fourteenth-century England, urged that 'a priest ... should warn his parishioners and effectively persuade them to take care to have their children confirmed by a bishop within five years of birth, if they have the opportunity to see the bishop'. Since the sacrament was normally administered by the diocesan bishop or his suffragan, its conferral was logistically difficult, particularly in the large dioceses that were common north of the

Alps. There are few records to suggest that confirmations took place regularly. Bishop Grosseteste of Lincoln made it his practice to confirm all the children in his diocese, deanery by deanery, though he admitted this practice was unusual. There was a growing amount of legislation from the thirteenth century onwards insisting on the importance of confirmation, but it was local or directed at specific groups. The decree of the Second Council of Lyons in 1274, mentioned earlier, while declaring confirmation to be a sacrament, said nothing about the desired frequency of its conferral.

Acknowledging that the sacrament was in great neglect, the 1281 Canterbury synod sought to promote its reception and ordered that the unconfirmed should not be given the Eucharist unless they were in danger of death or had been 'reasonably prevented' from receiving confirmation. A roughly contemporary synod of Cologne ruled that confirmation was a prerequisite for becoming a cleric. While encouraged more, confirmation still appears to have been far from widespread and was not declared by the ecclesiastical authorities in the fourteenth and fifteenth centuries to be obligatory in any full sense. There is little evidence, too, of pressure from the laity to make the sacrament more widely available.

For the sacrament of confession (penance), the crucial legislation for enforcement was Canon 21 of the Fourth Lateran Council in 1215. The canon mandated all Christians – the text read 'persons of both sexes', *omnis utriusque sexus*, but the witty Richard Helmslay, a Dominican friar of Newcastle-on-Tyne, was roundly condemned when he argued that the decree applied only to hermaphrodites – who had reached 'the age of discretion' to confess their sins once a year to their parish priest or, with his permission, to another priest. Many theologians, including Duns Scotus, thought that annual confession was only necessary if a grave or 'mortal' sin had been committed, but grave sin was interpreted rather widely so that only the very devout were thought likely to pass a whole year without committing such a sin. How far the obligation of annual confession was fulfilled has been the subject of considerable debate among historians. Exhortation and legislation promoting the Lateran canon, especially from local councils, often admitted explicitly or implicitly a degree of non-compliance, and late medieval visitation records provide instances of alleged failure, although fewer than might be expected. Various heretical groups rejected the sacrament outright, and their attitude no doubt influenced some who remained within the bounds of orthodoxy. Nevertheless various recent local studies, some sceptical regarding other religious practices, have concluded that the large majority of people fulfilled the obligation of annual confession.

Attendance, however, did not necessarily mean an exhaustive confession. The event took place annually in the parish church, perhaps with others awaiting their own encounter with the priest, and in public, as the *Confessionale* (anonymous, though widely attributed to Bonaventure) suggested, 'in an open place where there will be no grounds for suspicion and where the priest can be seen by all but not heard'. Confessional boxes were uncommon before the second half of the sixteenth century. The Lateran IV requirement for the laity to confess created a mirror obligation: to teach parish priests how to elicit a confession and instruct the laity to recognize sin. This obligation upon the priest was the greater concern of Church authorities, and manuals were produced to instruct parish priests in the seven deadly sins and the art of confession. The manuals underlined a need for caution on the part of confessors: it was better to leave sins uncovered than to probe too hard or too imaginatively and so to educate the penitent in sin rather than salvation. Lest the confession foster intimacy, priests were enjoined to be especially wary with women and inquire with caution only into common or well-known sins. The degree of confession was thus more at the discretion of the penitent than the confessor, and discussion might often remain at a formal level if the penitent so wished. That such was often the case became a source of concern as contrition on the part of the penitent was increasingly seen as necessary for true confession and absolution. Remigio de' Girolami, a Dominican friar living in northern Italy in the late thirteenth century, lamented that confessions were frequently superficial, as 'many people confess with their mouths but not in their hearts'; his fellow friar Giordano of Pisa added that 'many men and women come to confession without giving any thought to it beforehand'. Some manuals instructed confessors to promote a fear of dying unconfessed before the penitent began his confession, suggesting that even those who went to confession had to be encouraged in the importance and extent of the act.

The Lateran IV canon threatened those who failed to confess annually with excommunication. How far the canon and other punitive legislation were enforced in the late Middle Ages is difficult to answer and surely varied. The findings of Jacques Toussaert regarding late medieval Flanders are instructive if tentative (Toussaert 1960: 109–10, 121, 435–6). He revealed an anonymous monk of the region, possibly of the abbey of Dunes, who wrote that excommunication was incurred if Easter duties, which included annual confession, were neglected for several successive years. The monk's statement is supported by diocesan statutes of the region, which prescribed that the names of those who had failed to fulfil their Easter duties were to be sent by the parish priest to the dean and from him to the bishop. If they had persisted in their recalcitrance for ten years, their names were to be cited before the provincial council. This lengthy and cumbersome procedure left many loopholes, not least that its enforcement required the cooperation of the very parish clergy among whom Toussaert detected some hostility to the Lateran canon. In northern Italy, Friar Remigio de Giro-lami complained that many people did not confess at all for ten or 20 years at a stretch, apparently without effective action being taken.

The importance of the Lateran IV canon cannot be dismissed since it established an obligation that generated some friction throughout the later Middle Ages. The encounter between penitent and priest in confession was delicate and potentially intrusive. Nevertheless the results were prob-ably less dramatic than has often been allowed: the annual rite could be fulfilled in a fairly perfunctory manner, and studies suggest that refusal had to be persistent or coupled with more serious forms of dissidence to warrant penalty.

The sacrament of the Eucharist, or the Mass, had two attendant obli-gations for the laity in the later Middle Ages: annual reception of the Eucharist (or communion) at Easter, and regular attendance at church. The same Lateran canon that mandated annual confession also required annual reception of the Eucharist during the Easter season, again under penalty of excommunication, though it permitted individuals not to receive communion if 'they think, for a good reason and on the advice of their own [parish] priest, that they should abstain from receiving it for a time'. In visi-tation records from late medieval England, accusations of failure to comply were relatively infrequent. When they were recorded, such as during the 1397 visitation of Hereford diocese, they were typically coupled with other charges, suggesting that enforcement was primarily an issue only when other obligations were already being ignored.

The contingent and more onerous duty was attendance at Mass on Sundays and feast-days. The main feast-days requiring attendance were the same throughout Western Christendom, but there were considerable regional variations regarding the others. In some legislation the duty was specified more precisely: that the entire Mass had to be heard or that it must be at the parish church, rather than in the churches of mendicant orders or in private chapels. How far the legislation was observed is unknown and probably varied considerably by region and in time, but available evidence suggests that non-attendance was common and fairly widespread. From calculations of money offerings at Mass, among other factors, Toussaert concluded that the obligation of attendance was far from universally observed in late mari-time Flanders. Contemporaries could be even more pessimistic. Humbert of Romans, prior-general of the Dominicans, accused substantial sections of late thirteenth-century society of hardly attending church at all, and in the fifteenth century Nicholas of Clamanges, admittedly an inveterate pessimist, reckoned that on feast-days 'few go to church and even fewer listen to the Mass'. Perhaps these laments and accusations should not be taken too literally, nor should they undermine as superstition the faith of medieval Christians. What the insights do suggest, however, was a broad spectrum of responses to the late medieval Church, from the intense and devout at one end, to the distracted, apathetic or dismissive at the other.

Lay people, too, showed concern when their fellow parishioners absented themselves from Mass. At the 1492 visitation of the parishes in Norwich, the lay inquisitors brought charges against nine people of not attending their parish church on Sundays and feast-days. Three others were accused of keeping open taverns during services and one woman was said to observe 'an evil custom with various people from neighbouring households, who sit with her and drink during the time of service'. In early fifteenth-century Salisbury, those accused of non-attendance were said to go to fairs and markets; some had not attended in two or even five years. Practicalities suggest that a level of non-attendance was tolerated and that to prosecute large numbers of offenders would have been almost impossible. Those charged at visitations were probably persistent rather than occasional offenders, as records from Norwich city and Lincoln diocese suggest. Failure to attend church was an accusation levelled at suspected heretics, notably Lollards, but usually in concert with other behaviours, such as proclaiming that Sunday was not a holy day or denying transubstantiation and the power of the priest at Mass. Moralists admitted, albeit grudgingly, that there existed many legitimate or semi-legitimate reasons to excuse attendance: Humbert of Romans, for example, acknowledged that domestic servants were often prevented by their masters or mistresses from attending church. That church offered a social as well as a religious inducement limited the burden of ecclesiastical enforcement, but elicited the common complaint of late medieval commentators that people went to church to socialize or be entertained rather than for religious reasons. One parish priest in fifteenth-century England lamented of his parishioners, 'they come not thrice in a year ... they jangle, they jape, they kiss women, and hear no word of the service, but scorn the priests, saying that he sleepeth in his Mass and tarries them from their breakfast'. Irregular attendance, for whatever purpose, was probably sufficient to ward off accusation and potential coercion, despite a few decrees such as those of the Council of Lavaur in 1368 which prescribed that the priest should threaten with excommunication those who missed Mass on two consecutive Sundays without good reason.

Marriage, the fifth sacrament, has been the focus of significant recent study. The twelfth and thirteenth centuries had seen some important clarifications on basic questions about how a marriage was created, whether it was a sacrament, and the role of local customs. Nevertheless among late medieval theologians and canonists there was considerable debate, and some ambivalence, about the balance of natural and ecclesiastical law with regard to both the sacrament and the relationship between the man and woman. Marriage was the only sacrament enacted by the parties themselves and whose routine performance did not require a priest or bishop; even after Canon 50 of Lateran IV decreed that a priest should be present at the marriage, the sacrament itself was still formed solely by the consent of the two parties. Aiming to reduce arguments over invalid or disputed marriages, late medieval authorities increasingly proclaimed that marriage should be public, 'in the presence of the church', and numerous warnings were issued against priests who officiated at clandestine weddings. Even so, clandestine marriages continued to be valid until the Council of Trent in the sixteenth century, and would even be upheld over subsequent church marriages. Parties testified that marriages frequently occurred where the moment might seize them. A variety of such places were mentioned in the course of litigation in later medieval England: 'under an ash tree, in a bed, in a garden, in a small storehouse, in a field ... in a blacksmith's shop, near a hedge, in a kitchen, by an oak tree, at a tavern ... near the king's highway', as various parties testified (Helmholz 1974: 29, 49).

The conversation between Christian ideals and day-to-day workability was dynamic among the laity themselves, who displayed a wide variety of responses to the catholic ideal. Arrangements regarding marriage were often informal, especially among the poor, and the laity did not always agree with the Church's definitions of sexual morality. Confessors' manuals repeatedly enjoined priests to remind penitents that fornication was indeed a sin. Visitation records reveal, nevertheless, that fornication and adultery might be both common and assertively defended: those for fourteenth-century Normandy suggest that fornication and adultery were only reported in extreme cases, such as a pregnancy of an unmarried woman, and that sexual activity was often viewed as an accepted part of courtship. In English Church courts, authorities tended to proceed against fornication only when it was public, scandalous and long-running. Especially in the fifteenth century, however, communities were keen to use visitations and Church courts to enforce a sexual morality more in accordance with that of Church teaching. Court records suggest that the laity recognized Church law as both proposing an ideal and providing a guide within the realities of life.

While many tried to follow the Church's directives, and indeed often demonstrated a complex understanding of their requirements, they were also willing to defy them when they proved too inconvenient. Some couples went to neighbouring parishes to marry when consanguinity or another known prohibition would prevent them marrying at their own church. Despite repeated proclamations that marriage must be formed 'in the presence of the church', many marriages continued to be formed with no intention of being solemnized. Numerous such marriages appear in court records, usually not because the Church was enforcing solemnization but because the concerned parties had brought a contested marriage to be decided by the ecclesiastical court. Clarification was generally the goal of the ecclesiastical authorities, but where correction was desired, penalties for fornication were usually fines, and efforts were made to regularize long-term living arrangements into marriage. If the partners proved unwilling to marry, they were abjured to separate, under the understanding that future sexual relations would themselves constitute marriage. In short, both ecclesiastics and laity generally sought to steer a judicial course through the difficulties of marriage, and while the Church tried to call attention to moral discipline, it primarily defined a role as arbiter of individual claims and of communal complaints against long-term or scandalous abuses.

The final sacrament pertaining to the laity was extreme unction, or anointing of the sick. It had emerged as a distinct sacrament only in the ninth century and although highly recommended by writers and councils it was never regarded as obligatory or as necessary for salvation. Some lack of understanding or regard for this sacrament is suggested by statutes that repeatedly exhort priests to impress on parishioners that they must pay reverence when the host is carried through the street (to be given to the sick or dying), and to explain its importance and purpose which, the statutes admit, was often misunderstood. Practice appears to have varied. The rite appears to have been almost unknown in upper Ariège in the early fourteenth century and there is evidence of resistance to it in some regions. On the other hand, Toussaert found no such evidence of hostility in late medieval Flanders. In England, from the mid-thirteenth century onwards, Church authorities are recorded as both urging the laity to act with reverence when the host was being carried in procession to the sick, and impressing upon priests the duty to attend, even in the middle of the night, when called to a sick person. While the Church tried to foster the call for extreme unction, its systems of enforcement were directed more at the clergy than at the laity, to ensure that when the sacrament was requested it would be forthcoming.

Religious practice: other obligations

Canon 54 of the Fourth Lateran Council stated that tithes took precedence over all other financial impositions, 'since the Lord has reserved tithes unto himself as a sign of his universal lordship'. Tithes – that is, payment normally to one's parish church of a tenth of income or produce – may have been the most intrusive and onerous non-sacramental obligation imposed by the Church on the laity. Mentioned frequently in various forms in the Old Testament, the payment of tithes had become an obligation for Christians during the early Middle Ages. The obligation was backed by severe penalties, both spiritual and civil. Evidence regarding the extent to which paying tithes was accepted or opposed by the laity is somewhat mixed. Many tithes had fallen into lay hands in the early Middle Ages, as lay people established themselves as patrons of parish churches, and despite the attempts of reform movements of the eleventh century onwards to wrest them back to the Church, in some regions of Europe – Italy, for example – the laity remained closely involved in the system in the later Middle Ages both as possessors of tithes and as collection agents for the Church. As a result, some of the opposition to the payment of tithes was to lay people profiting from the system. Tithes were often more closely associated with landholding than with parish membership inasmuch as they were paid according to the location of the income rather than the parish of the tithe-payer, in the case of someone who owned property outside the parish where he lived. Disputes, therefore, often concerned the rights to receive revenues, and how the sums of money and produce should be calculated, rather than to the principle of payment. As Richard Helmholz and William Pantin wrote succinctly, 'there was never a golden age of obedient tithing', and 'it must have required the tact of a saint to make the system run smoothly' (Helmholz 1974: 434; Pantin 1955: 204). Some compromise was required of all parties.

It is perhaps surprising, nevertheless, that tithes did not meet more resistance. A letter of Pope Innocent III (1198–1216) to the bishop of Vercelli, later included in the *Decretals*, outlined the many problems of collecting tithes that were to remain through the later Middle Ages: that some Christians paid only on net income (after expenses had been deducted); others paid their tithes to clerics or churches of their choice or gave them straight to the poor; some did not pay at all because they objected to the immoral conduct of the clergy, or claimed they had been exempted by the emperor; or drew a distinction between 'novel' and 'ancient' tithes. Canonists debated how tithes should be calculated and how far necessary expenses could be deducted before payment was calculated. There is some evidence that resistance to tithes was increasing towards the end of the Middle Ages. In Italy the towns of Parma, Bologna and Reggio openly revolted against their tithes, while other towns passed legislation that limited the powers of tithe-owners. Again, however, these do not seem to have been revolts about the concept or principle of tithes; they were usually directed against the local lay magnates who collected the tithes or against the wealth of cathedral chapters in receipt of them. Where there were clashes over payment, the laity were frequently arguing for a return to a stricter and more evangelical, less temporal, use of the tithe. The citizens of Bologna preferred to pay their tithes directly to the poor, while those of Reggio agreed that no one 'was to be compelled to pay tithes in the future except as his conscience dictated ... but that they were still binding upon believers as part of the divine law'. In England, of 140 parishes inspected during a visitation of Salisbury diocese, only seven produced cases of non-payment of tithes. In the same country, a degree of flexibility is indicated by testamentary bequests to parish churches 'for unpaid tithes', which became common in wills in the late Middle Ages. In late fifteenth-century Norwich, for example, prosecutions for non-payment of tithes were rare, yet testamentary bequests 'for unpaid tithes' were common, although the amount of money was usually nominal. The device suggests that citizens had practised in life a measure of freedom in calculating their payments. Importantly and more positively, many people surely appreciated that the parochial system, which they generally supported, depended upon the payment of tithes.

The obligation to abstain from work on Sundays and feast-days also developed from biblical precedent. The early Church had been cautious about transferring observance of the Old Testament Sabbath to the Christian Sunday, but the prescription was recognized gradually, finding its way into Justinian's *Code* (3.2), Gregory IX's *Decretals* (2.9.1) and other legislation. By the thirteenth century the obligation was far reaching, encompassing all Sundays and almost the same number of feast-days. The legislation prohibited 'servile' work, a category that was difficult to define. It had originally meant activities that made the doer a slave (*servus*) to sin and by extension it became work that was prone to involve sin, principally work for earthly gain, or was proper to slaves or servants, namely manual work. In a ruling subsequently incorporated into the *Decretals* (2.9.3), Pope Alexander III (1159–81) had exempted necessary labour – to protect crops, for example, or catch fish during a limited season – and the canonical interpretation of 'need' subsequently became relatively broad. Legislation not only allowed the purchase of necessary food and drink but was relatively indulgent towards recreation and amusements on Sundays and feast-days.

Failure to abstain from work on prescribed days appears as a charge at various parochial visitations in the late fourteenth and fifteenth centuries. In England it occurred in visitations in the diocese of Lincoln, and more prominently in the dioceses of Canterbury, where butchers were notable offenders, and Hereford. In Flanders, according to Toussaert, frivolity and licentiousness, not work, were the problem, and the obligation to abstain from work was a serious problem only when there were particularly inquisitive authorities (Toussaert 1960: 357–9). Feast-days, indeed, seem to have been generally welcomed by villeins and labourers who pushed for additional days and even celebration on the vigils of feasts; landlords and sometimes synodal legislation seem to have worked instead to limit the number of days applicable. Such holidays were welcome at least in part, and a certain laxity about definition probably meant that it was commonly only the most openly and repeatedly dissident who were prosecuted.

Lack of biblical precedent made the obligations of fasting and abstinence problematic. Christ had surpassed Old Testament prescriptions and declared all foods clean (Mark 7.14–19). Nevertheless fasting and abstinence assumed a major role in the asceticism of the early Church and this continued to be the case throughout the Middle Ages. The legislation appears formidable. There were considerable regional variations, but the basic minimum was fasting on the weekdays of Lent, the 12 Ember days and the vigils of major feasts, and abstaining from meat on these fast-days and on all Fridays except those falling on major feast-days. In theory, infringement might incur excommunication. There were, however, a wide range of official exemptions and, increasingly, a general relaxation in interpretation and practice. Fasting had originally meant only one meal a day, but this meal was brought forward from the evening to mid-day or the afternoon, and a light evening meal, or 'collation', was permitted. Many were exempted from even this legislation: the old and the infirm, those not yet adults and in cases of necessity. The last category might be interpreted quite widely to include travellers and possibly even all those who performed manual work.

The reception of this legislation remains a matter of debate. Toussaert considered that the obligation, at least in late medieval Flanders, was genuinely popular. He thought it fitted the popular mentality, particularly the idea that fasting was the wages of sin, and was appreciated both as healthy in balancing large-scale eating at other times and as enabling the conservation of meat and other foods in short supply (Toussaert 1960: 428–34). His assessment may be overly optimistic, and may be less applicable to the countryside than to towns. Even so, the legislation may not have been as disruptive as might initially appear. Records of parochial visitations in England suggest accusations in the matter were rare: no cases were mentioned at the extensive visitation of Hereford diocese in 1397, and only one case at the later visitations of Lincoln diocese, apparently due to the curate forgetting to remind his parishioners about an Ember day. Fast-breaking could be used to identify heretics and the charge was brought against suspected Lollards. Behaviour in these cases was allegedly more provocative: assertive attacks on fasting, sometimes in the form of shared ritual meals where meat was consumed, and active denials that fasting was an obligation. Flexibility

within the legislation regarding fasting and abstinence and some measure of sympathy for its aims probably rendered the obligations tolerable for
most people, and the indications are that Church authorities troubled to
prosecute only blatant or persistent offenders or those who were also suspect
on other grounds.

Enforcement and obligation

The medieval Church took care to establish and propagate minimum
expectations of Christian knowledge and behaviour. However, legislation
articulating the more binding of these goals must be viewed within the
context of recognized points of canon law: that laws of the Church were
to be interpreted restrictedly (that is, not imposing more obligations than
necessary) and that local customs and practice might influence the reception and comprehensiveness of legislation. The arms of the Church – its
laws, courts and writers – were keen both to engage with and respond to lay
understanding or scepticism and to address the more practical demands of
lay behaviour and community. There was also a fair measure of flexibility
within the legislation, a tendency for ecclesiastical authorities not to rock
the boat more than necessary and to keep prosecutions within the bounds
of the possible. These principles limit both the implications of some of the
more fierce-sounding legislation and the words of preachers and moralists, words that were often exaggerated for rhetorical and exhortatory effect.
These points are illustrated by ecclesiastical procedures for supervision and
penalty: visitation, the courts and excommunication.

Lists of questions for late medieval visitations of parishes suggest rather
invasive oversight by diocesan officials, extending from the lifestyle of
local clergy to reception of the sacraments, the status of church fabric and
possessions and the moral behaviour of parishioners. Surviving records,
however, suggest the practice of visitation was less intrusive of lay behaviour than the questions might suggest. Thus the returns resulting from the
visitations focus on the business of the church, its upkeep and possessions
and the priest. Most parishes brought no recorded accusations of lay moral
transgression; those that did focused on one or two particular topics (such
as fornication or adultery), suggesting that these not uncommon problems
were more the object of local lay preoccupation than the subject of system-
atic ecclesiastical investigation. In moral cases, Church courts were used
more as judges and arbiters of personal disputes than for official prosecution. The extensive records of lower ecclesiastical courts in late medieval
England suggest that many cases were *ad instantiam* (that is, brought by one
lay person against another) and that the overwhelming majority of cases
concerned sexual morality, debt and testamentary bequests. These were

issues of less practical concern to Church authorities than to the laity who, as the defrauded party, turned to the Church courts to resolve their disputes or, especially in the fifteenth century, to enforce communal sexual morality against prostitution, pimping and other public nuisances.

Punishment of those found guilty took the form of fines, penance or, most severely, excommunication, but the goal of the court was less to punish than to resolve controversy or put an end to offending behaviour. If a case of fornication was so notorious that it brought the couple to the court's attention, the court's primary concern was to put a stop to the wrongdoing, usually by eliciting an agreement from the couple either to separate or to marry. If a couple proved obdurate or incorrigible, they might also be fined. An act of penance might be assigned, often public in form, though such penances were increasingly commuted to monetary payments. Excommunication was the most severe sanction available to the Church and could be incurred for a range of offences: an anonymous late medieval monk of Flanders listed 38 excommunicable offences which required papal absolution and a further 54 requiring episcopal absolution.

Canonists underscored the seriousness of excommunication and warned that it must not be used lightly, stressing its medicinal use in healing a correctable problem rather than in punishing wrongdoing. In theory, excommunication was incurred for failure in almost all the obligations discussed above, but in practice it was used sparingly by courts for disciplinary cases. Canon 33 of the Fourth Lateran Council warned against abusive use of the sanction: authorities should 'carefully avoid proceeding to excommunicate anyone without manifest and reasonable cause'. Later general councils prescribed similar caution. Whole populations, such as the Venetians and Bolognese in the thirteenth century, and the Flemings, Scots and Florentines in the fourteenth century, were excommunicated during political struggles, usually to little effect.

The overuse of excommunication in the later Middle Ages severely threatened its power: parishioners from Toulon diocese in France could go so far as to tell their prelates, 'We don't care about your excommunication or set any store by it.' At an individual level, excommunication could be a routine accompaniment to commercial and other transactions, or even for failure to return a book, according to an edict of Bishop Sutton of Lincoln. A marginal note on a debtor in arrears said that 'he has been excommunicated; if he were a priest, it might make some difference'. Canonists themselves mitigated the impact, stressing that an unjust excommunication was effective in the world but not before God, warning that one should not submit to an excommunication if it was contrary to the health of one's conscience or to the Church in general, and upholding the basic rights of an excommunicate to interact with family, servants and serfs and to draw up valid contracts.

The sanction of excommunication, nevertheless, carried weight. It entailed exclusion from the services and ministries of the Church and from the Christian community, and might incur a range of civil penalties that were enacted when civil authorities were notified by the Church authorities through a process known as signification. Signification was a distinct step, taken if the person failed to respond to excommunication for at least 40 days, but there might be years of obduracy before signification was carried out. The effectiveness and cooperation of civil authorities might vary dramatically by region. In late medieval England, some 16,869 writs issued by the civil authorities for apprehending excommunicated persons (known technically as writs *De excommunicato capiendo*) have been counted for the years 1250 to 1534. This substantial figure testifies to the effectiveness of both the signification procedure and excommunication itself.

The register of the deanery of Oudenberg in Flanders points in a similar direction, revealing a remarkably high number of persons who were cited as excommunicates or subject to other serious canonical sanctions (the distinction is often unclear): a total of 1,667 citations are recorded from 44 parishes in the four years between 1450 and 1454, an impressive figure even allowing that most individuals were cited more than once. The Oudenberg register, which indicates that offenders had to be reported by parish priests to the local dean, shows that steps were taken to follow up and enforce the penalties. There were limits, however, to what ecclesiastical authorities could do, and at times even the deanery of Oudenberg seems to have preferred to turn a blind eye to offenders. Cumbersome procedures of excommunication mentioned by the anonymous Flemish monk, possibly of the abbey of Dunes, have been noted. In the diocese of Barcelona, priests were permitted to absolve parishioners who had been excommunicated for clandestine marriages and fine them instead; one rector was permitted to absolve excommunicates after they complained it was inconvenient to go to the dean for absolution. These cases suggest that the system did work to chasten wrongdoers but that it required a good measure of tolerance and flexibility.

The Church in the later Middle Ages was a wide umbrella. In addition to the devout and committed, it had to shelter the run-of-the-mill, the lax, the superstitious and the ignorant. Once baptized, a person was entrusted to, and became a member of, the Church. Baptism was itself an undertaking both by the Christian, who retained responsibility for his or her own salvation, and by the Church and its ministers, who now had an accountability to promote and foster that path. As a consequence, authorities recognized a right and duty to compel observance from those who had entered the Church through baptism. Yet they did so cautiously. Every obligation enjoined upon a Christian might help to define and promote the journey to salvation, but it also created an opportunity for that Christian to fail and thus endanger their salvation.

The later medieval Church deliberately retained a balance between the ideal and the possible. Theologians and pastoral authorities showed themselves concerned not simply to articulate the practicalities and ideals of lay Christianity, but to guard the salvation of those barely clinging to its lowest rung. The result was a complex, often subtle theology and legislation of pastoral care, which balanced notions of ideal, exhortation, education, oversight, punishment and protection. It was a system that expected much of lay Christians, but tolerated a much lower level, and which recognized considerable variety in the circumstances, perceptions and behaviour of individuals.

Popular religion

It may be reckoned that the minimal obligations outlined in the last section were accepted willingly by most Christians, often indeed enthusiastically. Certainly it would be misleading to think of them only as imposed from above by Church authorities against the wishes of the laity. In addition to these basic requirements, there existed a wide range of religious activities open to lay men and women, who enjoyed a good measure of choice regarding them. This section, accordingly, both retraces some of the material treated in the first part of the chapter, looking at the topics in terms of devotion and ideals rather than of minimal obligations, and focuses on the participation of the laity in a wide range of other religious activities and lifestyles that were open to and indeed in large measure created by them.

Such will be the approach, though it should be remembered that to begin by focusing on particular activities is somewhat misleading. Life was more in the round and integrated than today, so that religion was part of life rather than a compartment of it. In principle, therefore, it might be better to begin with life as a whole, which for most people was influenced by Christianity at almost every turn, and then to see particular religious activities as intensifications within this general context. The short third part of the chapter, 'Relaxation and enjoyment', will attempt this more holistic approach by looking at some areas of life that today would be considered largely separate from religion but in the Middle Ages were regarded as integral parts of it.

Eucharist

Two duties regarding the Eucharist – receiving communion at least once a
year and attending Mass on Sundays and feast-days – have been discussed
(see pp 79–80). Over and above these minimal obligations, focus on this
sacrament increased much in popular devotions in the later Middle Ages.
It is appropriate to begin this section on popular religion with it, inasmuch
as the Eucharist was central to the belief and practice of Christians and
pervaded many other activities and institutions – chantries and craft guilds,
for example – that will be discussed later in the section.

Receiving the Eucharist, or 'communion' as it was often called –
responding to Christ's invitation to his disciples at the Last Supper, 'Take
and eat, this is my body ... and drink, for this is my blood' – remained a
rare occurrence for most individuals in the later Middle Ages. Few of the
laity, it seems, received communion more than three or four times a year,
while only the very devout approached the sacrament weekly or in rare cases
– such as Catherine of Siena or Margery Kempe from England – daily.
Only much later, in the early twentieth century, did frequent and daily
communion become normal for large numbers of Catholics.

In the late Middle Ages, therefore, Eucharistic devotion lay largely
outside frequent communion. It centred, rather, on intense belief in Christ's
presence in the Eucharistic bread and a strong interpretation of the words
spoken by Christ over the bread, 'This is my body'. Two events in the thirteenth century had given momentum to the development. First, the Fourth
Lateran Council in 1215 had formulated the doctrine of 'transubstantiation':
that in the Mass the bread and wine are changed (Latin, *transubstantia-
tis*, changed in substance) into the body and blood of Christ. Secondly,
Pope Urban IV in 1265 ordered the feast of 'Corpus Christi' (Latin for 'the
body of Christ'), which celebrated Christ's presence in the Eucharist, to
be observed annually throughout the Western Church. Through these and
other official declarations, as well as much popular devotion, the Eucharistic bread, in which Christ was believed to be truly present, came to be
preserved in tabernacles and hanging pyxes in churches, for adoration and
prayer by the people, as well as to be carried in procession on the feast of
Corpus Christi and on other occasions.

There were perils in an exaggerated emphasis on Christ's physical presence, a preoccupation with the miraculous, when hosts were seen to bleed
or when Christ was reckoned to appear visibly in person to the priest and
others present at the Mass. There was the danger, too, of forgetting that it is
the risen and glorified Christ, rather than the earthly Jesus, who is believed
to be mysteriously present. For the most part the Church authorities were
well aware of the dangers and sought to avoid them. Protestant reformers

of the sixteenth century were fiercely critical of many aspects of medieval Eucharistic devotions. The Catholic Counter-Reformation, too, sought to purify practices and to bring them more into line with correct theology. Nevertheless it would be wrong to focus too much on the abuses and to forget the central and wholesome truths: Christ's promise to remain among his people, the offer of himself as food and drink – spiritual sustenance – in this life. Late medieval Eucharistic devotion represented intense gratitude for God's generosity to humanity.

Attendance at Mass, and having Masses offered for oneself and for others, especially those in purgatory, were popular forms of Eucharistic devotion in the late Middle Ages. Margery Kempe, whose presence at Mass is documented in her *Book*, represents the extreme end of emotional participation (see pp 95–6). Many other people were noted for their great devotion during Mass, even if the manifestations were less external and visible than those of Margery. At more normal levels of humanity and sanctity, participation at Mass on weekdays, when attendance was voluntary, was evidently a widespread and deeply meaningful practice for very many people throughout Western Christendom.

Chantries, the 'chanting' (singing) or at least 'saying' of Masses principally for those in purgatory, were a notable feature of the time. They were already a well-established institution by 1300 and grew in size and complexity in the later Middle Ages. They ranged from a single Mass to a sizeable college of priests whose principal function was to say Mass daily for the benefactor and usually for other people, such as family members and friends and other individuals to whom the founder felt indebted, often too for 'all the faithful departed' who were still detained in purgatory. Wills provide plenty of evidence of chantries at the lower end of the scale, with testators leaving money for priests to say a limited number of Masses. Wills, too, and more visibly the chantry chapels that survive inside many cathedrals and parish churches, attest to 'perpetual chantries', for which the benefactor left money for a succession of priests to be hired to say daily Mass 'in perpetuity'. At the grandest end of the scale came All Souls College in Oxford, which was founded by the archbishop of Canterbury in 1438 for 40 priests, with the principal object of their offering Mass and praying for the souls of King Henry V and the Englishmen who had died in the wars in France, as well as their forming an academic institution.

The multiplication of Masses, especially Masses for the dead, might give the impression that Christ's passion could be quantified and repeated. There was the danger, too, of suggesting that time in purgatory could be shortened, and thereby heaven could be 'bought' through the stipends offered to priests to say the Masses. Chantries encountered fierce criticism from

sixteenth-century Reformers as well as attempts at simplification and purification on the part of the Catholic Counter-Reformation. Yet medieval
people were generally aware of the abuses and knew that in no way could
God's judgement be manipulated by financial inducements. Masses for
the dead represented, positively, the solidarity of the living with the dead,
a rich sense of community. They showed, too, an intense appreciation of
Christ's passion and death, which were remembered in each Mass: 'Do this
in memory of me.' More materially, they formed an important source of
income for many priests, enabling them to live and, at best, to engage in a
variety of spiritual and pastoral works.

Eucharistic processions, in which people processed round the streets
and other public spaces of a parish or town, led by a priest carrying the
Eucharist (the consecrated host), were a notable feature of late medieval
piety. They followed directly from the establishment of the feast of Corpus
Christi in 1265 and were held principally on this feast-day, which was kept in
early summer (on the Thursday following Trinity Sunday). Sometimes the
procession was organized by the parish, sometimes by the local monastery
or friary, sometimes by a lay confraternity or craft guild. The support and
initiative of the laity was crucial to the event. The painting by Gentile Bellini (1429–1507) of the Corpus Christi procession around Piazza San Marco
in Venice, replete with both clergy and laity, brings to life this dimension of
Eucharistic devotion at the end of the Middle Ages.

Prayer

Prayer was practised in many ways, adapted to the different capacities and
temperaments of individuals. All prayer involved raising up mind and heart
to God; some prayer was also directed to the saints in heaven.

The central and most public form of prayer for both laity and clergy
was the Mass (or Eucharist). Closely linked to the Mass was the 'divine
office'. The singing or recitation of the 'hours' of the office was principally
the duty ('office' comes from the Latin word *officium*, meaning 'duty') of the
clergy and members of religious orders, but in the later Middle Ages more
laity were saying at least some of the 'hours'. In some cases the laity prayed
the hours individually; more frequently they did so in a group, with one
member, or a priest, reading aloud the psalms and prayers to the others.

The near-contemporary account of the life of Cicely, Duchess of York,
mother of kings Edward IV and Richard III of England, provides a vivid
description from the late fifteenth century of the daily order of this devout
lady that centred around prayer and spiritual reading:

> Me seemeth it is requisite to understand the order of her own person
> concerning God and the world. She used to arise at seven of the clock, and

had ready her chaplain to say with her Matins of the day and Matins of our Lady. And when she is full ready, she has a low Mass in her chamber. And after Mass she taketh somewhat to recreate nature; and so goes to the chapel, hearing the divine service and two low Masses. From thence to dinner, during the time whereof she has a reading of holy matter, either [Walter] Hilton of Active and Contemplative Life, Bonaventure *De infancia Salvatoris* [Infancy of our Saviour], the Golden Legend, St Maud, St Katherine of Siena, or the Revelations of St Brigit.

After dinner she gives audience to all such as have any matter to show unto her, by the space of one hour. And then she sleeps one quarter of an hour. And after she has slept, she continues in prayer unto the first peal of Evensong. Then she drinks wine or ale at her pleasure. Forthwith her chaplain is ready to say with her both evensongs, and after that she goes to the chapel and hears Evensong by note [sung]. From thence to supper, and in the time of supper she recites the reading that was had at dinner to those that be in her presence.

After dinner she disposes herself to be familiar with her gentle women, to the following of honest mirth. And one hour before her going to bed, she takes a cup of wine, and after that goes to her private closet and takes her leave of God for all night, making an end of her prayers for that day; and by eight of the clock is in bed. I trust to our Lord's mercy that this noble princess thus divides the hours to his high pleasure. (Pantin 1955: 254)

Mystical prayer was a notable feature of late medieval religion, though perhaps it receives more attention today, especially among scholars, than it did at the time. For the large majority of people, prayer meant the Mass, the divine office, other spoken prayers and meditative or contemplative prayer.

Mysticism was recognized as an exceptional gift, given by God to a few and in no way to be claimed or expected by everyone. It was recognized, moreover, as a largely hidden gift, known to God and the individual, and partially revealed to others through the somewhat chance communications of those who, for various motives and often through intermediaries, attempted to describe their experiences, feebly and very imperfectly, in written works. Mysticism is impossible to define but Jean Gerson, writing in the early fifteenth century, gave a neat description of it as 'knowledge of God by experience reached through the embrace of unifying love' (*Theologia mystica*, consid. 28).

Hildegard of Bingen (1098–1179), the brilliant German nun, had brought a new level to mystical experience through her writings, notably *Scivias* ('Know the ways'), in which she sought to describe her visions of the divine. The thirteenth century produced many notable mystics, some men and more especially women: Francis and Clare of Assisi; the Flemish beguines

Mary of Oignies, Hadewijch and Juliana of Liege; three German nuns, Mechtild of Magdeburg, Mechtild of Hackeborn and Gertrude 'the Great'; and others. The later Middle Ages continued and developed this tradition.

Some of the male mystics in the later Middle Ages who were priests or members of religious orders are treated more fully in Chapter 4: Meister Eckhart, Henry Suso and Johann Tauler, three German Dominican friars; the English priests Walter Hilton, Richard Rolle and the author (possibly a priest) of the anonymous *The Cloud of Unknowing*. Notable too was the Spanish layman Raymond Lull, who wrote mystical works and may have met a martyr's death in North Africa in 1315.

Women retained a strong presence in the mystical tradition. Almost all those concerned were lay women, many of them married, rather than nuns belonging to religious orders. While they made a major contribution to the development of lay piety, it would be misleading to consider their part in terms of anti-clericalism. Many of them had close links with the clergy, choosing them for their spiritual directors, and several of them were 'terti-aries' (lay associates) of religious orders or beguines.

Catherine of Siena was the best-known mystic, indeed the best-known saint, of her time. Born the third youngest of 25 children of a prosperous dyer of Siena, she was drawn to long hours of prayer as a child. At the age of 16 she joined the lay branch of the Dominican order as a 'tertiary' and there-after led an increasingly independent life, unmarried, becoming famous in Italy and beyond for her sanctity and wisdom. She intervened in the disputes between the city of Florence and the papacy, she met Pope Gregory XI and helped to persuade him to return from Avignon to Rome, and became an ardent supporter of Urban VI after the outbreak of the papal schism in 1378, even while she rebuked the pope for his poor behaviour and ill temper. She was surrounded by a devoted group of supporters, both lay and clerical, including the English priest William Flete. All the while she led a life of holiness and prayer, focused on God yet acutely aware of the needs of other people. Her prayer, both intercessory for others and mystical, is reflected in various publications: the letters written or dictated by her (almost 400 survive), the synthesis of her teaching called *Dialogo* ('Dialogue'), and vari-ous 'prayers' which were compiled by her followers from what she was heard to utter during her prayer and mystical experiences. She died at the young age of about 33 in 1380 and was canonized as a saint by Pope Pius II in 1461.

Also from Italy, at either ends of our period, were Angela of Foligno (d.1309) and Catherine of Genoa (1447–1510). Angela, after the death of her wealthy husband, converted to a life of austerity and prayer and later became a Franciscan tertiary. She dictated her visions to her confessor and these accounts were written up into *Liber visionum et instructionum* ('Book of Visions and Instructions'), a refined work of mysticism. Catherine married at the age of 16 and some ten years later underwent a religious conversion which led to prolonged mystical experiences, some of an almost pathological nature. An account of these experiences and the conclusions she drew from them were published in 1551 as *Vita et doctrina* ('Life and Teaching'), which is a mixture of the authentic Catherine and the work of editors. She devoted herself to the care of the sick in a hospital in Genoa and was joined in this work by her husband.

Later medieval England produced two remarkable women mystics of very different temperaments: Julian (or Juliana) of Norwich and Margery Kempe. They, alongside Richard Rolle, Walter Hilton and the author of *The Cloud of Unknowing*, gave England a major role in the development of mystical prayer in the Western world.

Little is known about Julian beyond that she lived as an anchoress in Norwich, attached to St Julian's parish church in Conisford ward, in the late fourteenth and early fifteenth centuries, and that she is the author of the remarkable mystical work, *Revelations of Divine Love*. A few casual references show that she was respected at the time as a holy woman, but the renown of her *Revelations* had to await a later age. The work survived precariously in a few manuscripts, in a longer and shorter version, and achieved widespread fame only with its publication in the twentieth century. Julian's emphasis on the love of God, her description of the motherhood and feminine nature of God and her optimistic tone, epitomized in the words revealed to her, 'All shall be well and all manner of things shall be well', which seem to offer the hope of salvation for all people, accord well with modern concerns. Christopher Abbott, in his recent book *Julian of Norwich*, has suggested further significant features in Julian's spirituality: heaven is becoming our true selves; how our deficiencies are transformed into good rather than destroyed; God as a 'playful lover'; Julian's concern for people living amidst the dangers and difficulties of the world (Abbott 1999: 22, 118–19, 164–78). Today the *Revelations*, translated into modern English and many other languages, is perhaps the most widely read of all medieval mystical treatises.

Margery Kempe was also rediscovered in the twentieth century, largely thanks to the publication of her autobiography. This work, which was written down by clerics at her dictation, was little known and only through extracts until the discovery of the complete manuscript around 1930; it was subsequently published under the title *The Book of Margery Kempe*. Almost all our knowledge of Margery comes from this single work. Like Julian, she came from East Anglia, the wife of a citizen of Lynn (now King's Lynn).

She was the mother of 14 children and eventually persuaded her husband to live in continence with her. Thereafter she engaged in extensive pilgrimages to various shrines in England, Norway, Danzig in modern Poland, Wilsnack in Germany, Santiago da Compostella in Spain, Rome and Jerusalem. She received many mystical gifts in prayer. These gifts, she tells us, were frequently accompanied by 'boisterous' groans and copious tears, especially when she was attending Mass, often to the annoyance of her companions, including those on pilgrimage with her. They found tiring, too, her almost exclusively religious conversation. She was courageous in rebuking the unworthy, even the Archbishop of Canterbury, Thomas Arundel, for the poor behaviour of the clerics and other members of his entourage. Margery has been dismissed by some as a hysterical eccentric, but such a description does not do justice to her. She was a remarkable woman, of extraordinary energy and religious creativity, who was granted exceptional gifts and insights in prayer and yet remained firmly attached to the framework of the institutional Church: one of the most colourful characters of later medieval Europe. She respected Julian of Norwich and recounted her visit to the city to consult with Julian.

Bridget of Sweden came from a wealthy family, married at the age of 13 and bore eight children. After the death of her devout husband, she received a series of visions and mystical experiences which drew her into ecclesiastical politics. She publicly urged the pope's return from Avignon to Rome and challenged the decay in the Church's spiritual life. She was the founder of a new religious order, the 'Bridgettines'. In 1349 she went to Rome where she remained for the rest of her life, except for occasional pilgrimages. The writings describing her mystical and other revelations were highly esteemed in the later Middle Ages. She was declared a saint by Pope Boniface IX in 1391. Her daughter Catherine, who entered her mother's Bridgettine order and became its first abbess, was also later canonized as a saint. Bridget, along with most of the other mystics, perhaps especially the women, shows how mystical and other gifts in prayer did not lead to retreat from the people and problems of this world, but rather to greater engagement with them.

Margaret Porete was one of two well-known mystics in the late Middle Ages who ran into mortal trouble with Church authorities. That Margaret was exceptional in this respect reveals the wide support of the late medieval Church for mysticism and prayer, which was not always accompanied by tolerance in other areas of life. Probably a native of Hainault in modern Belgium, Margaret became a beguine and was burnt at the stake in Paris in 1310 – after being condemned by the Inquisition, she was handed over to the secular authorities for punishment – for continuing to promote her mystical treatise, *The Mirror of Simple Souls*. Despite the beauty and depth of the work in many respects, there were the twin perils that its teaching led to pantheism – mystical union was so close that absorption in God led to loss of the individual's human identity – and the belief that the mystic was invulnerable to sin, so close was the resulting union with God.

The second woman to run into conflict with the Church was Joan of Arc (Jeanne d'Arc). She is best known for her warlike qualities, yet she was evidently a young woman closely in touch with God through prayer, and the divine 'voices' she claimed to hear were central to her life and mission. She was born around 1412 in the countryside of eastern France. As a teenager she began to hear God instructing her to meet with Charles VII of France in order that the English might be chased out of the country and the war and misery of France be ended. Finally she met Charles at Chinon in March 1429 and assured him of his legitimacy as king, which for various reasons he had doubted. Events then moved rapidly. Church authorities accepted her after an examination and she then led the French army to dramatic victory in May by relieving the city of Orléans, which was besieged by the English. In July Charles was consecrated and crowned king at Reims, with Joan at his side. Thereafter the Hundred Years' War gradually moved in France's favour. In May 1430 Joan was captured when attempting to relieve the city of Compiègne, which was besieged by French allies of the English. She was tried at Rouen by the court of the bishop of Beauvais, with English support, on charges of witchcraft and heresy – her wearing male dress, notably trousers, was also alleged against her. Her visions were declared 'false and diabolical', and she was burnt at the stake as a relapsed heretic in May 1431. Some years later, however, the verdict was reviewed at length by a court in France authorized by Pope Callistus III and in 1456 the earlier judgement was overturned and Joan was vindicated, though it was only in 1920 that she was formally canonized as a saint. The personality and career of Jeanne d'Arc are unique, yet any understanding of the late medieval Church has to come to terms with her life and with the reactions of contemporaries to her.

Pilgrimages

Any account of lay piety in the later Middle Ages must take into account the popularity of pilgrimages. They were a form of prayer. The origin of Christian pilgrimages may be found in the peace brought to the Church by the conversion of the Emperor Constantine to Christianity in the early fourth century. This peace made long journeys and public manifestations of religion relatively safe for Christians. Almost immediately, Egeria, Constantine's mother, made a pilgrimage to Jerusalem that was written up into what became a classic account of pilgrimage during the Middle Ages.

Jerusalem, the site of Christ's passion, death and resurrection, remained the archetypal focus for Christian pilgrimage. The crusades to reconquer Jerusalem and the Holy Land from Muslim occupation, which began in the late eleventh century, were considered to be a form of pilgrimage even though different in kind from the earlier journeys. The failure of the crusades to regain Jerusalem and the Holy Land for Christianity in the later Middle Ages will be discussed in Chapter 7. This failure led to a revival of the original form of pilgrimage to these holy places, though now within the much more difficult circumstances of journeys to places occupied by hostile people.

Geoffrey Chaucer immortalized pilgrimages to the shrine of Thomas Becket in *The Canterbury Tales*. Wills of the inhabitants of Norwich provide further evidence from England. The imaginative bequests of Thomas Oudolff, priest of the city, have been mentioned (see p 66). Robert Baxter, a former mayor of Norwich, bequeathed in 1429 the large sum of £40 to Richard Ferneys, who lived as a hermit in the city, 'to make a pilgrimage for me to Rome, going round there fifteen times in a great circle, and also to Jerusalem, doing in both places as a true pilgrim does'. Equally ambitious, Edmund Brown, a wealthy merchant of the city who made his will in 1446, instructed his executors to hire three men to make pilgrimages on his behalf. One was to go on foot to the shrine of Thomas Becket at Canterbury, another was to make a pilgrimage to Saint James of Compostella during the next 'year of grace' and the third was to travel 'to Zeeland or beyond, over the sea, to the pilgrimage of the blood of our Lord Jesus Christ, called the Holy Blood of Wihenhak', which was probably the shrine at Wilsnack in Germany to which Margery Kempe had travelled (*Norwich*: 62, 87).

Rome, Compostella and Jerusalem were the three preeminent destinations for pilgrims of the Western Church. The first ever 'jubilee' for Rome was declared for the year 1300 by Pope Boniface VIII. Huge numbers of pilgrims flocked to the city to gain the plenary indulgence offered by the pope to those who visited St Peter's and other principal churches in the city. Thereafter jubilee years were proclaimed at diminishing intervals of 50, 33 and 25 years, for which large numbers of pilgrims came, though never again quite on the scale of 1300. Even outside these special years, Rome was a major centre of pilgrimage. The surviving records of St Thomas's Hospice (now the Venerable English College), which gave lodging to English pilgrims in Rome, listed an average of some 200 pilgrims a year between 1479 and 1514 – substantial numbers for a medium-sized country distant from Rome. The shrine of the apostle St James at Compostella remained a major centre for pilgrimage throughout the later Middle Ages, though the Black Death and the long papal schism, as well as other difficulties both within and beyond the town of Compostella, adversely affected the number of pilgrims. Jerusalem was under Muslim control, yet many pilgrims still made the difficult journey to this supreme location for Christian devotion. Margery Kempe described her feelings thus, as well as the good treatment she received from the Muslim inhabitants:

> And so we proceeded into the Holy Land until we could see Jerusalem. And when I saw it – riding, as I was, on the back of an ass – I thanked God with all my heart; and I prayed that just as he had brought me to see this earthly city of Jerusalem so, of his mercy, he would give me the grace to see the city of Jerusalem on high, the city of heaven. ... I was full of holy thoughts and meditation, full of devout contemplation of our lord Jesus Christ's passion, full of the holy intimations that our lord Jesus Christ made to my soul – so much so that I could never put these things into words once they were over, for they were so high and holy. Great was the grace which our Lord showed towards me during my three weeks in Jerusalem. ... Afterwards I rode to Bethlehem on an ass, and when I came to the church of the Nativity I went inside to see the crib where our Lord was born. I was overcome with deep devotion and I received many words and intimations in my soul and a great sense of inner consolation. ...The Saracens also feted me, they escorted me and guided me to all the places I wanted to visit throughout the country, and I found everyone good and kind to me except my own countrymen. (Kempe 1940: chapters 28–30)

Pietro Casola, canon of Milan cathedral, wrote a detailed account of his pilgrimage to Jerusalem in 1494, when he was approaching 70 years of age. The warm send-off he received reveals the wide support for pilgrimage on the part of both laity and clergy:

> I begged his most Reverend Lordship [the archbishop of Milan] to bless the emblems of my pilgrimage – that is, the cross, the stick or pilgrim's staff, and the wallet – and to bestow his blessing on me, according to the order and the ancient institution to be found written in the Pastoral. ... When the benediction was over, his Lordship embraced me with no ordinary tears, and kissing me most affectionately, he left me with the peace of God, surrounded by a great crowd, from which I had some difficulty in separating myself, for everyone wanted to shake hands with me and kiss me. (Newett 1907: 117)

There was, however, the other side of the coin. Pilgrimages were widely condemned by English Lollards, and those to the shrine at Wilsnack in Germany were censured by Jan Hus. Many of the orthodox, too, had their reservations. Thomas à Kempis had these sharp words in *De imitatione Christi* ('The Imitation of Christ'): 'They that go much on pilgrimage seldom grow in sanctity' (Book 1, Chapter 23); 'Many run to sundry places to visit the shrines of the saints. ... Often such pilgrims are moved by human curiosity and the quest for novelty, and carry home with them small fruit of amendment, especially when they run so gaily from place to place without true contrition' (Book 4, Chapter 1).

Craft guilds and pious confraternities

Craft guilds and pious confraternities made an important and varied contribution to popular religion, especially in the towns. In their group activities, the communal aspect of late medieval religion was realized, as was the appeal to the senses. The members of each craft or trade in a town – especially in the larger towns – might organize themselves into a 'guild' (usually called a craft guild) which had a variety of responsibilities for the economic, social, political and religious arrangement of the craft or trade. Frequently, too, groups of like-minded people within a parish, or associated with a friary or other religious house, formed a confraternity for the purposes of prayer as well as for various religious and charitable activities that went beyond what the parish could normally offer. Both craft guilds and pious confraternities depended upon the clergy: they needed them for the conduct of their religious services, especially the Mass, and in other ways. Once again, therefore, it would be wrong to contrast sharply the religious interests and outlooks of laity and clergy. Guilds and confraternities, nevertheless, were essentially lay-driven. Control was largely in the hands of the laity and their concerns were paramount: the clergy were largely at their service.

A key event for each craft guild was the annual 'guild day'. It was normally held on the feast-day of the saint, or the day of an event in Christ's life (birth, resurrection, ascension etc), to which the guild was dedicated. Celebrations usually consisted of a mixture of religious activities, principally Mass for all the living and deceased members of the guild, and a meal together. In addition, all the guilds of a town might come together on one or more days in the year for a joint celebration, a mixture of religious and social activities: a procession through the town, with the members of each guild often dressed in the livery of the guild, followed by a Mass or other religious service and a communal meal. The distinction between 'religious' and 'social' was much less obvious than today – the two dimensions blended into each other. Guilds were normally responsible, too, for providing charitable assistance to members in need. Many of the larger and grander guilds owned their own guildhall – some still to be seen today, notably in the Low Countries – which provided a centre for the guild's social, religious and charitable activities.

Mystery plays were special features of craft guilds in late medieval

England. Cycles of between a dozen and 50 plays, based on the 'mysteries' of the Bible, from both the Old and New Testaments, survive for half
a dozen towns, including York, Coventry, Chester and Norwich. All the
plays were normally staged on a particular day, usually the feast of Corpus
Christi, each performed by members of one guild or several guilds together
and often staged on a cart or moveable float, so that the same play would
be performed in several places while making, as reported of the Norwich
cycle, 'a great circuit of the city'. Plays based on Christ's passion and on the
lives of saints survive for other countries, notably France, but organization-
ally they appear to have been linked with cathedrals or monasteries rather
than with craft guilds.

Pious confraternities were more immediately religious bodies than were
craft guilds, more private too, for the most part. They responded to the
particular needs of groups of people within a parish or a locality, rather than
being based on a craft or trade. Their purpose was more directly the religious
growth of their members and they reached out to others through prayer
and works of charity. They normally lacked the clear economic functions
of craft guilds, though some were socially conscious so that membership
was confined to a particular class or group in society. Some confraternities
were linked closely to the town government, with membership more or
less restricted to the governing body. Indeed the distinction between craft
guilds and pious confraternities was sometimes blurred, both as words and
in reality, so that there was a measure of overlap between the two.

Flagellant confraternities were specially popular in Italy. The flagellant
movement, in which groups of men, usually hooded and in procession, would
scourge themselves in public, came to the fore in central and northern Italy
in the second half of the thirteenth century as a penitential response, aimed
at averting divine anger, to wars and famines in the region as well as to the
prophecies of Joachim of Fiore regarding the imminent end of the world.
The movement spread across the Alps to France, Germany and the Low
Countries and received new impetus from the horrors of the Black Death.
Pope Clement VI in 1349 called for the suppression of the movement, but
in Italy and some other regions it was allowed to continue within the more
regulated framework of officially authorized flagellant confraternities.

Guilds and confraternities varied greatly in size and complexity. They
ranged from large, powerful and public institutions in major cities to small
confraternities attached to parish churches in the countryside. The key fact
remains, however, that these institutions, in their various forms, enjoyed
huge popularity in the later Middle Ages and were vigorous expressions
of lay Christianity. Significantly they were not abolished in the sixteenth
century. Many Protestant reformers recognized their importance and sought

to transform rather than to abolish them, while the Catholic Counter-Reformation valued them and endeavoured to order them more correctly.

Beguines, Beghards, Brethren of the Common Life

The origin of the words 'beguine', signifying the person, and 'beguinage', meaning the house or community in which beguines lived together, is unclear. The two words may derive from Lambert le Bègue, a priest and notable preacher in Liège in the 1170s who is sometimes regarded as the founder of the movement, or from the word *begayer*, meaning to stammer, as if the women could not speak properly, or maybe from *bégeule*, meaning prude or prim, or from *beguin*, on account of the 'hood' that some of them wore, or from *beige*, because their clothes were of simple cloth and natural colours. The words first appear, as applied to the movement, in the 1230s, possibly with a derogatory meaning, but the women, it seems, gradually came to accept them and they lost any negative connotations.

The movement in the thirteenth century had found many important patrons, including Pope Gregory IX and King Louis IX of France. Some beguines were well known, especially as mystics. They appear as women who wished to lead committed religious lives outside the framework of the traditional·religious orders. Precise information about their lifestyles is hard to come by, but it is clear that they usually lived together in houses in towns. The movement, therefore, was essentially an urban phenomenon and it was largely confined to the Low Countries, the Rhineland and northern France. Frequently a woman who wanted to become a beguine and who possessed a suitable house or apartment would invite other women to join her and form a beguinage; thus existing dwellings were used and no new buildings were necessary. The way of life was both religious and somewhat informal, without a written 'Rule'. Beguines engaged, it seems, in the works and occupations then common for women, while the beguinage afforded them a home and time for prayer. They were normally unmarried women or widows, though they insisted upon more flexibility than was allowed in religious orders, so that women could enter and leave the beguinage with some freedom.

Robert Grosseteste, as archdeacon of Oxford (before he became bishop of Lincoln), had praised the beguines in a provocative address to the Franciscan friars in Oxford. He told them there was a still higher form of poverty than theirs, to live by one's own labour, 'like the beguines'. Shortly after, Matthew Paris, in his Chronicle (*Chronica majora*) under the year 1243, gave this early description of the movement:

At this time and especially in Germany, certain people, especially women, have adopted a religious profession, though it is a light one. They call themselves 'religious' and they take a private vow of continence and simplicity of life, though they do not follow the Rule of any saint, nor are they as yet confined within a cloister They have so multiplied within a short time that two thousand have been reported in Cologne and the neighbouring cities.

Despite the early rapid expansion of the movement, it reached a crisis shortly after 1300. The condemnation of the beguine Margaret Porete in 1310 has been mentioned. Influenced by her case, the Council of Vienne two years later issued an extensive censure of the movement. Its decree stated:

> The women commonly known as beguines, since they promise obedience to nobody, nor renounce possessions, nor profess any approved rule, are not religious at all, although they wear the special dress of beguines and attach themselves to certain religious to whom they have a special attraction. We have heard from trustworthy sources that there are some beguines who seem to be led by a particular insanity. They argue and preach on the holy Trinity and the divine essence, and express opinions contrary to the catholic faith with regard to the articles of the faith and the sacraments of the Church. These beguines thus ensnare many simple people, leading them into various errors. They generate numerous other dangers to souls under the cloak of sanctity. We have frequently received unfavourable reports of their teaching and justly regard them with suspicion.

> With the approval of the sacred council, we [the pope] perpetually forbid their mode of life and remove it completely from the church of God. We expressly enjoin on these and other women, under pain of excommunication to be incurred automatically, that they no longer follow this way of life under any form, even if they adopted it long ago, or take it up anew. We strictly forbid, under the same penalty, the religious mentioned above, who are said to have favoured these women and persuaded them to adopt the beguinage way of life, to give in any way counsel, help or favour to women already following this way of life or taking it up anew. No privilege is to avail against the above.

> Of course we in no way intend by the foregoing to forbid any faithful women, whether they promise chastity or not, from living uprightly in their hospices, wishing to live a life of penance and serving the Lord of hosts in a spirit of humility. This they may do as the Lord inspires them. (*Decrees*: 374).

At first reading the decree appears to be an outright condemnation of the beguine movement and an order for its suppression. The final paragraph provided something of a way out, on two conditions. First, that beguines change their name; secondly, that they live in 'hospices' (Latin, *hospicia*). The two conditions were met, more or less. It seems that women who wished to follow this way of life stopped calling themselves beguines, for the most part, even though other people continued to use the word, at least sporadically, when referring to them. And they gradually moved from apartments and small town houses into larger and more convent-like buildings, which the visitor can see still today (though mainly as they came to be constructed from the sixteenth century onwards) in the Netherlands and Belgium. Usually the ecclesiastical authorities alone are blamed for the beguines' change of lifestyle, but it may be that many of the women themselves were happy with the new arrangements.

The beguine movement remained a significant force in lay piety in the Church during the rest of the later Middle Ages. Its public face and outstanding personalities, however, were less prominent than previously. The Council of Vienne's decree of 1312 was modified by a somewhat more permissive ruling issued by Pope John XXII in 1318 in the bull *Ratio recta non patitur*. At other times ecclesiastical authorities, including popes, continued with the more hostile approach of Vienne. Many of the clergy, especially Dominican and Franciscan friars, supported the beguines and assisted them as spiritual directors and through other priestly ministries. Precise numbers are difficult to estimate, partly on account of Vienne's prohibition against using the name 'beguine', yet it seems that the high numbers of the thirteenth century were substantially maintained for some time; modest declines may partly be explained by the drop in the overall population. In Cologne the evidence suggests some 1,170 beguines in 169 beguinages in the middle of the fourteenth century, and some 637 beguines in 93 beguinages in 1452; in Strasbourg, another centre of the early beguine movement, some 85 beguinages in the fourteenth century. In the Low Countries (modern Belgium and the Netherlands) foundations of new beguinages appear to have remained buoyant in the first half of the fourteenth century, with some 83 new foundations, followed by 27 in the next half century and 25 in the fifteenth century – though these figures must be balanced with the demise of some earlier foundations.

Beghards existed as the male counterpart to beguines, but in the later Middle Ages they were much less numerous than beguines and much less is known about them.

Another close male counterpart to beguines were Brethren of the Common Life. This association was founded by Gerard Groote (1330–84), a native of Deventer in the Netherlands, who studied at Paris university and taught at Cologne and elsewhere. In 1374 Groote underwent a religious conversion and began to lead a simpler and more devout life, spending three years at the monastery of Munnikhuizen. In 1379 he became a missionary preacher in the diocese of Utrecht, though he was not ordained a priest. His sermons condemning the clerical abuses of his time led to the withdrawal of his licence to preach. Towards the end of his life he gathered round him disciples who lived together a quasi-monastic life at Deventer. He demanded no vows of his followers but left them free, whether clerics or lay men, to continue in their previous vocations. The community at Deventer became the nucleus of the Brethren of the Common Life.

After Groote's death the movement spread widely and rapidly within the Low Countries and parts of Rhineland Germany. Its members developed a spirituality that urged a deeper and more Christocentric practice of Christian life and devotion, which came to be known as *Devotio Moderna*. They stressed the importance of teaching and founded schools all over the Netherlands and in parts of Germany, which provided excellent education without fees. Other educational works were the copying of manuscripts and, soon, the printing of books. Florentius Radewijns, a member of the original Deventer community, assumed the leadership after Groote's death. Under his influence the monastery at Windesheim near Zwolle was founded in 1387, which led to a more clerical branch of the movement, called the Windesheim Congregation. Famous among the Brethren as members or as pupils at their schools were Pope Hadrian VI, Cardinals Nicholas of Cusa and Gabriel Biel, and the humanist Rudolph Agricola. Most famous of all were Thomas à Kempis (see p 120), and Desiderius Erasmus (1469–1536), essentially a sixteenth-century figure who later remembered an unhappy time at the Brethren's school at Hertogenbosch. The movement, part lay and part clerical, exercised a profound influence upon the spirituality of the late medieval Church.

Conclusion

It should be obvious from what has been said above that, in Western Christendom, the later Middle Ages witnessed much energy and creativity in the religion of the laity. The period is rightly called an 'Age of the Laity'. There were tensions, certainly, but they should not be allowed to detract from the many positive features. Cooperation and mutual need between laity and clergy is evident at almost every turn. There appears, indeed, little support for the thesis of a profoundly decadent religion of the laity, which led inevitably into the reactions and corrections of Reformation and Counter-Reformation.

Relaxation and enjoyment

To understand religion in the late medieval West, it is essential to appreciate the attitudes of Christians of the time to relaxation and enjoyment. Much of the first two sections of this chapter have focused on particular religious activities and duties. But, as was made clear in the opening remarks of the second section (see p 89), these individual activities must be considered within the wider, more holistic context of life as a whole. Some relaxation and enjoyment were seen as an essential part of a well-balanced life and therefore both a religious duty and an integral part of Christianity. This short third section, accordingly, tries to look at various features of the broader context. It must be complemented by the discussion of art and music in Chapter 4. There were also aspects of relaxation and enjoyment, both individual and communitarian, in many of the religious activities already treated: prayer, as in both individual and community prayer as well as mystical prayer; singing, as in the liturgy; social gatherings, as at Sunday Mass and within religious communities; pilgrimages; various activities of craft guilds and pious confraternities; and others.

Thomas Aquinas, writing shortly before the beginning of the period, confronted recreation in his discussion of 'Good manners', which comes in *Summa theologiae*, 2.2, question 168. In article 2 of this question, he asks 'whether there can be virtue in the acts we do in play'. The argument of the early Christian writer John Chrysostom that 'the devil, not God, sends us to sport', Aquinas counters by asserting that it refers to people who play inordinately and especially those who make amusement their main purpose in life. Augustine of Hippo's counsel is quoted with more approval, 'Spare yourself I pray, for it befits a wise man to relax at times and soften the edge of attention.' Then speaking his own mind Aquinas says, 'Man must rest his body for physical refreshment because he cannot work without intermission.' He then proceeds to quote with approval from the *Conferences* of the Abbot Cassian, in which:

> It is related of blessed John the Evangelist that when people were scandalized at finding him at play with his disciples, he requested one of his questioners who carried a bow to shoot an arrow. When this had been done several times, the man, on being asked whether he could keep on doing so continuously, replied that the bow would break. Whereupon the blessed John pointed the moral that so, too, would the human spirit snap were it never unbent.

Aquinas's approval of relaxation, so far, may seem to be somewhat grudging, a concession to human weakness rather than approval, and to have in mind the intellectual kind more than the physical. The concessionary nature is emphasized in the next article (3), entitled 'Of the sin of playing too much', where the limits of lawful sport are pointed out. However, in the final article (4), entitled 'Of the sin of playing too little', a more positive note is struck:

> It is against reason for someone to be burdensome to others, by never showing himself agreeable to others or being a kill-joy or wet blanket on their enjoyment. And so Seneca says, 'Bear yourself with wit, lest you be regarded as sour or despised as dull.' Now those who lack playfulness are sinful, those

who never say anything to make you smile, or are grumpy with those who do, Aristotle speaks of them as rough and boorish.

An extensive and more theoretical treatment of enjoyment (Latin, *fruitio*) is to be found in Part 2.1, Question 11, of the *Summa*.

Some moral theologians of the later Middle Ages may appear excessively negative towards recreation and relaxation, the 'kill-joys' censured by Aquinas, harping on dangers rather than positive merits. But the reality may have been that people were so fond of sport that they needed some check, some direction to their energies, which the clergy tried to provide.

One area in which the clergy were stout advocates of relaxation was in their defence of Sundays and feast-days. Fifty-two Sundays and about the same number of feast-days each year were exempt from work, largely thanks to the legislation initiated by the Church. It is true that a primary purpose of the legislation was to provide people with the opportunity to attend Mass – indeed there was an obligation to do so – and much of the legislation concerned the prohibition of illicit forms of sport and recreation, such as drunkenness and immorality. Nevertheless even rigorists did not expect people to spend the whole day in church or at prayer, so the Church's protection of proper human rest and leisure should be acknowledged: a fight for justice, too, defending the vulnerable from exploitation of their work.

In the types of sports engaged in, attention was given to the whole person and thereby – usually more implicitly than explicitly – respect for the mysteries of creation and Incarnation. Teresa McLean gave the following titles to the eight chapters in her book on play in medieval England: Out of Doors; Animal Sports, Hunting and Fishing; Tournaments, Jousts and Tilts; Outdoor and House and Garden Games; Board, Table; Glee, Medieval Music, Singing and Dancing; Medieval Drama; Folk Games. The titles give some idea of the broad range of play and recreation. Much the same would have been true for the rest of late medieval Europe as for England, though certainly there were local and regional variations, depending on climate and temperament. Play and games were part of the fabric of life.

The violence involved in many of these activities may horrify us today, yet it was an essential dimension. Partly the activities were forms of semi-institutionalized violence, safety-valves for competitiveness and aggressive drives for which any society is wise to provide some outlets; partly they embraced some useful purpose. People ate meat and fish, so hunting, hawking and fishing made sense. War was part of the fabric of life – people had to defend themselves – so tournaments, jousts and tilts made sense. There was some gratuitous cruelty to animals, as in bear-baiting or cock-fighting, but people were generally tolerant of each other's views in these matters and reluctant to impose their own political correctness upon others.

Most people lived in close proximity with animals. Farm animals, as well as domestic pets, lived under the same roof, often in the same room, as humans. An I–Thou relationship, not of equality but still of some intimacy and understanding, was reached with them. A wide variety of animals – not just dogs and horses – seem to have understood human beings and their needs, in a sense to have loved them even sometimes to the extent of sacrificing themselves for them. Human beings did not reciprocate with the same tenderness and self-sacrifice, to be sure, but at least they gave many animals the pleasure of living with them and sharing in their life, as is well portrayed in much of late medieval art, perhaps most brilliantly by Pieter Bruegel, a little later in the sixteenth century, in 'The Hunters in the Snow'. Much of late medieval sport is intelligible only in terms of animals.

In many ways, therefore, sport and recreation pointed to fundamental mysteries of the Christian message: creation, including that of the animal kingdom; the fall of humankind; the Incarnation; the need for human endeavour as well as for relaxation and enjoyment; the mysteries of pain and suffering; the parousia.

The archetypal recreation, in the literal sense of re-creation, was sexual intercourse. Not only was sexual intercourse considered an eminent form of recreation, and in a sense sport, other forms of relaxation and recreation were seen in terms of it. The point would have been taken more or less for granted, without any embarrassment or prudishness, thus revealing a proper respect for both sex and sport. The point is underlined by the way in which the spiritual life, or relationship with God, was also seen in sexual terms. Many writers of the period expressed themselves in such categories, most notably the 'love mysticism' of Margaret Porete and the 'spiritual espousals' of Jan van Ruysbroec. This appreciation, too, helps to explain why celibacy was valued by the Church. For, however much married life was valued and enjoyed, celibacy gave a special entry into that still higher state, indeed was a foretaste of it, the very enjoyment (*fruitio*) of God, the Beatific Vision.

CHAPTER 4

Knowledge and Culture

Knowledge and culture lay at the centre of medieval religion. Many aspects of knowledge are touched on in other chapters of the book, including art, though less prominently. The present chapter, therefore, focuses more directly on the intellectual and artistic features of the time while relying on much of what is said elsewhere in the book.

Universities

The later Middle Ages witnessed a boom in European universities. The origins of these institutions of learning in the West, from the earliest in the twelfth century, most notably Bologna, Paris and Oxford, and the foundation of some 15 more in the following century, have been described in the previous volume of this History. Between 1300 and 1500 successful new foundations numbered some 23 in the fourteenth century and 34 in the fifteenth (the exact figures are debatable because of mergers, changes of location and other factors). In addition, several universities were projected but never realized. Almost all regions of Western Christendom were accounted for: ten new universities in Italy, adding to the 11 foundations of the twelfth and thirteenth centuries; 13 in France, adding to the five earlier; nine in Spain and Portugal; 16 in Germany and Central Europe; six in Hungary, Poland, Denmark and Sweden; three in Scotland, namely St Andrews, Glasgow and Aberdeen; but in England there were no additions to the earlier foundations of Oxford and Cambridge. Some of the early universities had emerged more or less spontaneously, without any clear founder, including those at Bologna, Paris and Oxford. But almost all the universities emerging in the later Middle Ages had definite founders, either churchmen, usually the pope or a bishop, or a king or prince or the city commune, or a combination of both ecclesiastics and lay authorities.

Institutions

The Latin word *universitas* means the 'whole body of people' or 'corporation'. During the Middle Ages it was applied to many institutions, such as guilds and the governing bodies of cities. Indeed it was only gradually in the thirteenth century that the word came to be applied regularly to institutions that we might recognize as universities, and then with the root meaning of 'the whole body of teachers and students'. Other descriptions continued to be used for the same institution, especially *studium generale*, meaning a place of study that drew students from a wide area (students in the larger universities were divided into 'nations'), or simply *studium*; both of these terms were, in turn, used for non-university institutions, notably the study-houses of the orders of friars. There are difficulties, therefore, in defining what constituted a medieval university.

There were also wide variations in size and fame. Many of the smaller institutions that are counted as universities numbered at most a hundred or so students. Bologna claimed a certain precedence by way of its early foundation, but its eminence was largely confined to canon law and its fame was in decline before 1300. Paris, with several thousand students, had been the largest and most famous university in the thirteenth century and it retained this preeminence during the later Middle Ages. Oxford, with perhaps 1,500 students in 1300, enjoyed a notably high reputation in the first half of the fourteenth century. The reputation of Cambridge was highest in the late fifteenth century, due in part to its early welcome of the Renaissance to England.

Universities in the later Middle Ages retained the framework of studies that had been established, principally by the university of Paris, during the previous two centuries. There were five traditional faculties: arts and the four higher faculties of theology, canon law, Roman or civil law, and medicine. All universities appear to have had a faculty of arts, which taught at the BA level what might be described as a 'general culture course' comprising – at least in theory, for in practice there appears to have been considerable variation – the *trivium* (three subjects) of grammar, rhetoric and dialectic, and the *quadrivium* (four subjects) of music, arithmetic, geometry and astronomy. For the faculty of theology, Peter Lombard's *Sententie* ('Sentences'), written in the twelfth century, remained the basic textbook. It was a skeleton outline of all theology which afforded the lecturer plenty of room to develop his own thoughts. Interest in Thomas Aquinas's *Summa theologiae* remained largely confined to the Dominican order and the work achieved much wider fame only towards the end of our period. The textbooks for canon law were the Decrees (*Decretum*) of Gratian and the Decretals (*Decretales*) promulgated by Pope Gregory IX, of the twelfth and thirteenth centuries respectively, supplemented by four shorter collections authorized by Boniface VIII (*Liber sextus*), Clement V (*Clementis Pape V constitutiones*), John XXII (*Extravagantes Pape Joannis XXII*) and Innocent VIII (*Extravagantes communes*). The six collections were subsequently promulgated together and known collectively as *Corpus iuris canonici*. For Roman or civil law, the textbook remained *Corpus iuris civilis*, which had been promulgated by the Emperor Justinian (527–63).

Regarding the normal age of entry into the university, there has been debate among scholars. It is clear that some students entered as boys of 13 or 14, a few even younger, so that the university would have seemed, in parts, like a modern secondary school. But entry at such a young age was exceptional, it seems, and the norm was probably between 16 and 20. The large majority of students were preparing for the priesthood or (among graduate students) had recently been ordained. Universities, therefore, were similar to modern seminaries or theological colleges. The curriculum was far from narrow. The breadth of subjects in the arts programme has been noted and in the other faculties debate and questioning were encouraged. In theology, for example, the young Bachelor, before being admitted to the Licence degree, had to undergo his 'Quodlibet' – a public examination in which teachers and select students could ask questions about any matter (Latin, *quodlibet*) they wished and the candidate had to reply more or less unprepared. Lay men were predominant among students of the faculty of medicine – though only a minority of universities possessed this faculty, notably Montpellier in France and Salerno in Italy – and they were to be found among the civil lawyers. In addition, a number of students of arts, which in most universities was the largest faculty, were lay men who did not intend to proceed to the priesthood – a number that was growing in the late fifteenth century. Some women were surely to be found among the students, following the example of Heloise who attended the lectures of Peter Abelard at Paris in the twelfth century. But essentially medieval universities were male institutions and had the priesthood in mind.

Personalities

Some of the most brilliant and influential thinkers of the later Middle Ages were university teachers.

Duns Scotus (1265–1308) came from the village of Duns in Scotland (hence his name), entered the Franciscan order at a young age and spent almost all his short life at the three universities of Oxford, Cambridge and Paris, first as student and then as teacher. His two main published works were *Reportationes*, which was based on his early lectures on Peter Lombard's *Sentences*, as 'reported' by his students and written up by them in polished form; and *Ordinatio*, which was the text of his later lectures on the *Sentences*, delivered at Oxford in 1303/4. The two works contained important theological developments. In them Scotus stressed that even more than intellect or knowledge, as Thomas Aquinas and most theologians in the twelfth and thirteenth centuries had taught, God is primarily love. The redemption of people by Jesus Christ, accordingly, was seen as the expression of God's love more than in terms of satisfaction – God accepting that Christ's work 'satisfied' or paid the price for people's sins – which had previously been the generally accepted explanation of how and why humans are 'redeemed'. Christ's birth and life were seen as constitutive of this redemption, not just as preparation for the redemption that was accomplished by Christ's death on the Cross: altogether a more attractive and rounded theology. Love, moreover, took precedence over knowledge in the response of individuals to God: loving God was even more important than knowing him. Among philosophers, Plato was preferred to the previously fashionable Aristotle; among theologians, Augustine to Aquinas. The writings of Scotus do not make for easy reading; nevertheless they exerted a fascination within and well beyond the universities and they have continued to do so.

William of Ockham (1285–1347) was an Englishman, originally from the village of Ockham in Surrey. He joined the Franciscan order and taught at both Oxford and Paris universities. On account of his teaching at Oxford, he was denounced by the chancellor of the university and was summoned to Avignon by Pope John XXII in 1323 to answer charges of heresy. Five years later he escaped from his detention in Avignon to southern Germany, where he spent the rest of his life under the protection of Duke Ludwig of Bavaria. During his time at Oxford, he lectured on Peter Lombard's *Sentences* and, after the manner of Scotus, his commentaries on them were published in two works, *Reportationes* and *Ordinatio*. Ockham was impatient with the complexity of philosophy and theology as they had developed at the universities in the thirteenth century and with what he saw as the attempts by theologians to reduce God to human categories of thought. He emphasized the transcendence of God and a certain philosophical asceticism. What may appear like common properties, called 'universals' (such as 'good' or 'man' or 'true'), are usually no more than common names or labels that we use to organize our thought but which have no basis in reality: hence 'nominalism', the school of philosophy of which Ockham was the most renowned adherent. He is famous for his 'razor', though he was not the first to cite the principle: that 'beings [including concepts and explanations] should not be multiplied unnecessarily' (Latin, *entia non sunt multiplicanda sine necessitate*). He drew sharp distinctions between God and humankind, as well as between faith and reason, stressing their dissimilarity rather than common ground.

Despite his positive intent, Ockham has been accused of radical scepticism, of destroying the synthesis of faith and reason that had been established in the thirteenth century, most notably by Thomas Aquinas, of introducing the intellectual disintegration of the later Middle Ages, also of paving the way for the sixteenth-century Reformation's exaltation of faith above reason. He was certainly a key figure of the age, probably the most influential thinker of the later Middle Ages within university circles. Many were fascinated by his tough logic and what seemed like his ability to get straight to the point, to reach the heart of complex issues. His influence may be compared to that of Ludwig Wittgenstein in the twentieth century. In later years, in Bavaria, the focus of his writing moved from philosophy and theology to political theory, in which field he also made a notable contribution.

John Wyclif was the third university teacher from the British Isles whose reputation was Europe-wide in the later Middle Ages and has endured until today. Jan Hus, professor of Prague university in Bohemia, achieved widespread and lasting fame in somewhat similar circumstances. Both men will be treated in Chapter 5.

The two best-known university academics in France were Pierre D'Ailly and Jean Gerson. They were friends, both had distinguished careers as teachers at the university of Paris, both were elected its chancellor and both were created cardinal by popes of the time. During his years at Paris university, D'Ailly, in addition to lecturing on the *Sentences* of Peter Lombard, wrote a variety of scientific, philosophical and theological works. Later he became bishop of Le Puy (briefly), then of Cambrai, and much of his energy was devoted to trying to find a solution to the papal schism and to bringing about reform in the Church. He played a prominent role at the Councils of Pisa (1409), Rome (1412) and Constance (1414–18). At Constance he supported the condemnation and execution of Jan Hus. He was an exponent of 'conciliarism', advocating the supremacy of a general council over the pope. A man of wide interests, he also wrote on astronomy and geography: his *Imago mundi*, in which he suggested the Indies could be reached from the West, was known to Christopher Columbus.

Jean Gerson entered the university of Paris in 1377 as a young student aged about 14. He studied under Pierre D'Ailly and eventually succeeded him as chancellor of the university. He wrote and worked for reform of the Church and the ending of the papal schism. He was a prominent figure at the Council of Constance, maintaining the superiority of the council over the pope and urging that doctors of theology have voting rights at the council along with the bishops. He took part in the council's condemnation of Jan Hus. The last years of his life were spent in seclusion, mostly at Lyons. Some of his writing focused on the nature of the Church (ecclesiology) and he promoted conciliarism alongside a moderate doctrine of papal primacy.

In moral theology he was much influenced by nominalism, particularly the view that no action is sinful in itself but rather the goodness or sinfulness of an act depends solely on the will of God. He wrote extensively on the spiritual life, including several treatises on mysticism. Altogether he was a man of wide academic and practical interests. Much respected in his time, Gerson, along with D'Ailly, influenced Luther and other sixteenth-century Reformers, as well as Gallicanism in seventeenth-century France. He continues to be read today.

Of other clerics of high intellectual repute in the later Middle Ages, most had studied at a university. It may be assumed that they profited from their university education, even though the balance between this education and other factors in their formation is difficult to assess. They were not long-term university academics after the manner of the six mentioned above. There is nothing surprising about this. Students normally went to university with a view to a career or ministry in the Church, so that after they had completed their studies, and often following a short spell of teaching at the university for the more able graduates, they were ready for a new way of life. In some cases, especially among the friars, men would return to university teaching after they had been engaged in other works, and then leave again for other occupations after a few years of teaching. Even for the professors, therefore, university teaching as a lifetime career was the exception rather than the norm.

Meister Eckhart (1260–1328), the German Dominican friar, is a good example of a 'temporary' university teacher whose writings received widespread acclaim. He entered the Dominican order at a young age and was sent to study at the university of Paris; probably he also studied at the Dominican *studium* in Cologne. He had two spells as teacher at Paris university. In between, he held several posts within his order in Germany, as prior and later provincial. After his second period of teaching at Paris, he lived in various friaries of the order in Germany. He was well known as a preacher and as a counsellor to nuns and beguines. As a university or 'scholastic' theologian he wrote the long work *Opus tripartitum* in Latin, only parts of which survive. He is most famous, however, for his writings on mysticism, most of which he wrote in German. He was a master of the German language, with a fine turn of phrase and rich vocabulary, and contributed notably to the development of the language. In his mystical writings, he taught that we should 'break through' the complexity of the particulars in this world to reach the simple 'ground' of all reality, where God and the soul are inseparably one. There was the danger of stressing too closely our union with God in this life and indeed he was censured for this by both the archbishop of Cologne and Pope John XXII (see p 6). Eckhart has often been interpreted as reacting against the intellectual 'scholastic' theology prevalent in the universities, towards the more intimate and personal union with God proposed in his mystical writings. Such a sharp contrast may oversimplify the reality. He cannot be understood apart from his time at university; nevertheless he was the product of many other influences, both intellectual and personal. In a sense he represents the late medieval university at its best: an institution that made a major contribution to Christianity, as well as to knowledge and life more widely, without being restrictive or oppressive.

Nicholas of Cusa (1401–64) was another distinguished German who spent considerable time at university without becoming a long-term professor. A native of Cues (hence 'Cusa'), he studied at the universities of Heidelberg and Cologne in his own country and at Padua in Italy where he became a doctor of canon law. He was ordained priest in 1426. Thereafter he led a varied life, remaining a scholar but largely outside university circles. As a humanist he was specially noted for his scholarship on the manuscripts of the classical writers of ancient Greece and Rome. He took part in the Council of Basel, worked for reconciliation with the Hussites in Bohemia and wrote *De concordantia catholica*, which outlines a programme for reform of the Church. In 1437 he abandoned the Council of Basel in favour of Pope Eugenius IV. Thereafter he was active in papal service, visiting Constantinople in the cause of reunion with the Orthodox Church and undertaking a number of other papal missions. He was created a cardinal by Nicholas V in 1448 and spent his last years in Rome. He remained a prolific and versatile writer until the end of his life, providing something of a synthesis of classical and humanist learning, medieval scholasticism and mysticism. *De docta ignorantia* ('On Learned Ignorance'), perhaps his best-known work, published in 1440, draws the distinction between truth and knowledge. The former, which is one and absolute, is unreachable for us in this life; knowledge, on the other hand, is relative, complex and approximate; the road to truth, therefore, leads beyond reason, and intuition is needed for the discovery of God. Cusa, while very much a man of his time, pointed both backwards and forwards, to the world of Antiquity and into the sixteenth century

Gabriel Biel (1420–95) studied at three universities in his native Germany: Heidelberg, Erfurt and Cologne. He joined the new religious movement 'Brethren of the Common Life' and served as prior (or provost) of two of its houses. Much later he became professor of theology at the new university of Tübingen in 1484 and rector of the same university in the following year. As a 'scholastic' theologian, for which he is best known, he was a nominalist, much influenced by William of Ockham. His interests and writings extended to other areas, notably economics: he held that the 'just price' was determined by supply and demand rather than by theological principles and he praised the merchant as an important and useful member of society. Biel is another example of the lively and broadminded intellectual climate of the later Middle Ages.

The English mystics Richard Rolle (1300–49) and Walter Hilton (1343–96) probably studied at university but never taught there. Rolle, according to an early account of his life, studied at Oxford and possibly later at Paris university, but broke off his studies at Oxford when aged 18 in order to become a hermit. His spiritual and mystical writings are very personal and above all seem to spring out of his life and prayer as a hermit. He was a versatile author, with works written both in Latin – of which *Incendium amoris* (later translated into English with the title 'Spark of Love') is the best known – and in English, including a number of poems. Alongside his eremitical lifestyle, he maintained a wide circle of friends of both sexes and of varying positions in life. He was sought out as a counsellor. Much respected in his lifetime, interest in him remains strong today. Walter Hilton probably studied canon law at Cambridge university. After a period as a hermit, he became an Augustinian canon at Thurgarton priory in Nottinghamshire. His best-known work, written in English, is entitled *Scale of Perfection*. The treatise contains a mixture of practical teaching, of a moral and ascetic nature, with insights into higher levels of prayer and of the love of God. Hilton, like Rolle, was influenced by his university studies, it may be assumed, but was quite ready to go beyond them.

The author of *The Cloud of Unknowing* remains anonymous, though usually thought to be male and possibly a priest. This fourteenth-century English masterpiece seeks to help those who experience God, especially in prayer, as mysterious and cloudy. Whether or not the author studied at a university remains unclear.

From Ireland, the best-known scholar of the period was Richard Fitzralph (1300–60). Born in Dundalk, he grew up in Ireland and moved to Oxford for his studies, where he proceeded to doctor of theology in 1331. The following year he was elected chancellor of the university. While at Oxford, he wrote a commentary on the *Sentences* of Peter Lombard that received considerable attention, especially his attempts to find a middle way between free will and predestination. He resigned as chancellor in 1334 and went to Avignon to defend the university at the Curia. There he found favour with the newly elected Pope Benedict XII and was drawn into papal service. Benedict appointed him to the commission he established to judge the orthodoxy of his predecessor, John XXII. While at Avignon he also became involved in discussions with emissaries of the Armenian Church, which led to the eventual publication in 1352 of his best-known work, *Summa de questionibus Armenorum*. In this work he treated of issues disputed between Catholics and Armenians but also many others. One such other issue was the much debated question of authority in Church and state: whether the authority of an office holder depends solely on his legitimate appointment or rather, as Fitzralph urged, on his state of 'grace', that is, his good standing before God. Another issue was the relationship between the Bible and philosophy: Fitzralph insisted on the primacy of the Bible and criticized reliance upon 'Aristotleian dogmas' – an implicit criticism of the universities. He returned to Ireland in 1346 as archbishop of Armagh and spent much of the rest of his life there, engaged in both writing and pastoral ministry. He became a fierce critic of the friars, especially of the Franciscans' practice of begging, which he regarded as contrary to the teaching of Christ. Eventually he was summoned back to Avignon to answer various charges regarding his orthodoxy, but he died there before any definitive judgment had been made. Fitzralph exercised considerable influence on John Wyclif and Jan Hus and, largely through them, on the sixteenth-century Reformation, especially in the British Isles. He possessed a remarkably versatile and enquiring mind.

Conclusions

A key question asked of the late medieval Church is whether it was in a state of serious crisis, even of terminal decline. The question is central to this book. Some of the historiographical reasons for such a gloomy conclusion have been outlined in the Introduction, especially the underlying thesis that the late medieval Church was in such a state of crisis that it needed the Reformation. However, the individuals who have been highlighted above argue, for the most part, against such a negative assessment. They reveal lively, questioning minds, ready to think and write about a broad range of issues and to find connections between them. In this sense they may be seen in continuity with their predecessors – especially from the time of Anselm in the late eleventh century through to Thomas Aquinas – rather than in contrast to them. To exaggerate the intellectual harmony achieved in the thirteenth century – principally between faith and reason – and then to view this synthesis as blown apart by the destructive questioning of the late Middle Ages, would be unbalanced. The later age was, intellectually, a development from within the period that went before, more than a reaction against it.

It is important to see the intellectual interests of the main personalities in the round, not to separate them too quickly into the academic categories and disciplines that are accepted today. We have seen how life and study went together, how gifted students were ready to leave university for the wider world while continuing to pursue their academic interests in a variety of ways. But even within these academic and intellectual interests, there was much more unity than would be the case today. An individual could expect to have some grasp of all the available knowledge of his time. There would have been nothing surprising, therefore, in the fact that Richard Fitzralph's academic interests ranged between Armenian studies, politics and the Bible, or Pierre D'Ailly's between philosophy, theology, ecclesiology, geography, science and astronomy. The *trivium* and *quadrivium* of the arts faculty prepared students for this 'universal' knowledge and to know its inter-connectedness. More particularly, it is important not to exaggerate the distinction between philosophy and theology. Today they are taught in two separate faculties at most universities and, largely as a result, modern publications tend to assume they were separate in the Middle Ages. But this was not really the case at the time; rather they were seen as complementary approaches to the one Truth.

This section has concentrated on the more famous intellectual products of the universities. It is essential to remember the many other men, mostly clerics, who went to university and whose life and studies there must have influenced their subsequent careers and, as a result, the wider Christian community. Glimpses of this influence are scattered throughout this book, most concretely in the section on Norwich (see pp 60–1).

Other learning

This short section returns to various topics regarding education and learning that have already been visited and looks at some new issues and personalities.

Institutions

Universities formed the institutional pinnacle of learning in the late Middle Ages and still today their distinguished individuals and surviving buildings command attention. It may be, nevertheless, that their importance has been exaggerated and the many other sources of learning have been underestimated. Most historians today are university graduates and so tend to assume the importance of universities in a past age. We are, moreover, relatively well informed about medieval universities, so that they and their students have become obvious subjects for historical study, whereas other institutions and sources of learning are less well documented and, as a result, less fully studied by historians.

Schools, in a variety of forms below the level of universities, are one such area of partial neglect by historians. Those who studied at university had already attended one or more schools, it may be assumed. The importance given to such schools by the Fourth Lateran Council in the early thirteenth century has already been noted (see p 41). The council's legislation referred primarily to youths who had the priesthood in mind, but other evidence shows that throughout the late Middle Ages many lay students attended schools of various kinds: parochial schools, cathedral schools, those conducted by religious orders, and others. The number of such schools rose significantly during the late Middle Ages. The educational arrangements in the city of Norwich (see pp 60–4) may be seen as typical of a major city and many of the facilities would have been found, with due local modifications, in smaller towns and in the countryside. While universities were for a relatively small number of people and were non-existent in some regions, schools catered for a much larger number of people and were more evenly spread throughout Europe.

Religious orders formed a major source of education outside the universities, primarily for their own members but also for lay students. Life in a religious order was meant to be learning in the widest sense, education of the whole person, so that while the 'school' for the younger members was an important part of a monastery or friary, it must be seen within the wider context of the overall education and formation provided by the religious community. In this respect, it is remarkable that two of the three best-known Dominican mystics of the period had (probably) not studied at a university, but received their adult formation largely within the framework of the order: John Tauler (1300–61) and Henry Suso (1295–1366) – the third was Meister Eckhart (see pp 114–15). Together they formed a trio, all from Germany, and were aware of each other, with the two younger men much influenced by Eckhart.

Some personalities: clerics

John Tauler probably studied at the Dominican *studium* in Cologne and lived in various friaries mainly in Germany and Switzerland. He was famous as a preacher and director of nuns. His teaching comes to us principally through his surviving sermons. He balanced the inner gifts of mystical prayer with the importance of virtuous living and good works, and he stressed the importance of accepting the sufferings that come to us in life both in imitation of Christ and as helping to open our souls to receive God's gifts. His writings achieved widespread popularity and had a lasting influence on both Catholic and Protestant piety.

Henry Suso entered the Dominican friary in Constance aged 13 or so. He studied at the order's *studium* in Cologne, taught at the *studium* in Constance and lived in various friaries in Germany and Switzerland. Like Tauler, he was much appreciated both as preacher and as director of nuns. His teaching survives through his letters and his widely read book, *Das Büchlein der Wahrheit* ('The Little Book of Truth'), which clarifies and develops the sometimes controversial teaching of Eckhart.

Both Tauler and Suso were major intellectual and spiritual figures in their own time and have retained their stature ever since, very much products of the German-speaking world and of the Dominican order. They are good examples (assuming they had not attended university) of the fruits of a non-university education. Both men, through their writings and sermons, made an important contribution to the development of the German language.

Thomas Hemerken, better known as Thomas à Kempis (1380–1471), is probably the most famous spiritual writer of the age apart from Dante Alighieri. He, too, never studied at a university. Born at Kempen in the Netherlands, he attended the school run by the Brothers of the Common Life at nearby Deventer. He joined the community of the Windesheim branch of the Brothers at Agnietenberg, near Zwolle, taking the habit as a novice in 1406. Thomas was ordained priest in 1413/14 and remained a member of the Agnietenberg community for the rest of his life. He was appreciated by his companions, as evidenced by his election as procurator, sub-prior (twice) and novice master of the community, and by many other people as a religious counsellor. He was a prolific writer on spiritual topics as well as a copyist of manuscripts. His best-known work by far is *De imitatione Christi* ('The Imitation of Christ'). There is some debate regarding his role in the work, but the likelihood is that he was responsible at least for its final redaction. The work achieved fame in his lifetime and enormous popularity thereafter – one of the most frequently reprinted books (including translations into vernacular languages) of all time. The mood of the work favours inner devotion rather than learning, as expressed in the often quoted sentence, 'I would rather feel compunction (Latin, *compunctio*) than know its definition' (1.1.20). Some hostility to university learning of the age seems implicit, but to say the work is anti-intellectual would be going too far.

Laity

For the laity, minimal levels of religious knowledge have been discussed in Chapter 3. Some knowledge, moreover, was integral to the various devotions that were treated later in the same chapter. In terms of institutions and verifiable criteria, the religious knowledge of the laity is much more difficult to ascertain than that of the clergy. As mentioned, some lay men attended schools and universities and a few women attended schools. Religious knowledge came to the laity principally through the clergy. At least this was the prevalent theory in the drive for education that characterized the thirteenth-century Church, as revealed most clearly in the decrees of the Fourth Lateran Council in 1215. In the later Middle Ages, however, the laity were increasingly taking religious education into their own hands. The period has been described as the age of lay piety, of the devout and educated lay person, and this meant women as much as men, perhaps more so.

Women

Of women, we have already looked at the mystics of the period. Most of them would, no doubt, have said that their knowledge of God resulting from mystical experience was an outright gift of God, knowledge 'infused' by God according to the terminology of some writers. Looking at the lives of mystics more in the round, we can detect a variety of influences on their learning. All of them came from Christian backgrounds, so that religious knowledge was imparted to them through many channels: church services, the sacraments, sermons, conversations with other people and prayer. Their brilliant writings show the exceptionally high level of understanding – both theoretical and intuitive – to which all these sources could lead. At a more ordinary level, one important reason why women became nuns or beguines was likely to have been the possibilities for growing in religious knowledge: convents and beguinages offered many opportunities of this kind.

The spiritual reading of Duchess Cicely of York has been mentioned (see pp 92–3). Lady Margaret Beaufort (1443–1509), mother of King Henry VII of England, provides another aristocratic example. A devout yet ruthless person herself, she was a great patron of religious learning. She founded the Lady Margaret professorships in divinity at Oxford and Cambridge universities as well as two colleges at Cambridge, Christ's and St John's. She promoted the publication of religious books and translated two works into English, *The Mirror of God for the Sinful Soul*, from the French original, and the fourth part of Thomas à Kempis's *De imitatione Christi*. She was also a patron of humanist and Renaissance scholars of whose religious dispositions she approved, most notably John Fisher, Lady Margaret professor at Cambridge and subsequently chancellor of the university, bishop of Rochester and martyr.

At the bourgeois level, the wills of several women of Norwich provide further evidence of a highly religious city. Three wills from the late fifteenth century stand out, in microcosm, inasmuch as they mention the only works by or about late medieval mystics that are known to have been in private ownership in the city. Women, therefore, in this respect, appear more adventurous than the clerics and lay men of Norwich. Catherine Kerr left

in 1497 'the book of St Catherine' (probably Catherine of Siena); Isabel
Liston left in 1491 'my English book of Saint Margaret's life' as well as 'an
English book called *Partonope*', which was presumably a translation of the
twelfth-century French romance *Partenopeus de Blois*. Margery Purdans left
in 1481 an 'English psalter' and a 'small psalter'; 'Le doctrine of the Herte',
which was probably a translation of *De doctrina cordis*, the treatise addressed
to a woman on how to lead a devout life which was usually ascribed to
the thirteenth-century bishop of Lincoln, Robert Grosseteste; an 'English
book of Saint Bridget' (probably the fourteenth-century mystic, Bridget
of Sweden); and 'a book called Hylton', which was presumably a work by
Walter Hilton, the fourteenth-century English mystic (*Norwich*: 112).

Christine de Pizan (1364–1430) was probably the most learned and
certainly the most prolific writer among women of later medieval Europe.
Born in Italy, she came to France at the age of four with her father, a celebrated Bolognese doctor and astronomer who entered the service of King
Charles V of France. She lived the rest of her life in France. Widowed at
the age of 25, she devoted herself thereafter to writing, enjoying patronage
principally from King Charles and the French nobility. Her works reveal
a very wide range of knowledge and interests, touching on many modern
concerns. She wrote on political theory, which was perhaps the central
theme of her writings, she cited copiously from classical Greek and Roman
authors, wrote poems of courtly love, books in defence of the rights and
dignity of women, an autobiography, *La Vision de Christine*, a sympathetic
life of Charles V, and *Livre de Paix*, a passionate plea for peace in her war-
torn country. After the disastrous (for the French) Battle of Agincourt in
1415, she retired to a convent for the rest of her life, taking up her pen again
in the year before her death to write *Ditié de Jehanne d'Arc*, in celebration of
Joan of Arc's relief of the siege of Orléans. A moralist in the broad sense,
Christine reveals the complexity of late medieval thought and behaviour,
and the impossibility of drawing a sharp distinction between Christianity
and religion on the one hand, and the secular or profane on the other.

Lay men

Among lay men, Raymond Lull (1233–1315) was an exceptionally learned
and imaginative scholar, who just comes into the beginning of our period.
He was born in Majorca soon after it had been conquered by the king of
Aragon, following several centuries of Muslim rule. His early life was spent
as an official at the royal court of Aragon; he was married with two children. He returned to Majorca in his early 30s and spent nine years there
studying Arabic and Christian thought. During this time he wrote the
Book of Contemplation, which was written in Arabic and translated into

Catalan. Much of the rest of his life was taken up with various projects to promote the conversion of Islam. He persuaded the king of Aragon to establish a place of studies in Majorca where Franciscans could learn oriental languages, and he was instrumental in the decree of the Council of Vienne (1311–12) proposing the establishment of professorships in oriental languages at various universities (see pp 173–4). He travelled widely, visiting the courts of France, Aragon and the pope to gather support for his plans for the conversion of Islam, and wrote many books and tracts mainly with the same purpose in mind. On at least three occasions he spent time in North Africa. The place and date of his death are obscure, but the widely held belief that he died a martyr, stoned to death at Bougie in North Africa, is discounted by most modern scholars. Lull worked also for the conversion of Jews. He hoped that 'in the whole world there may not be more than one language, one belief, one faith' (*Blacquerna*, 16) and sought to convince both Muslims and Jews by rational argument rather than recourse to the Bible and by appealing to the monotheism common to them and to Christians. He had no training in the 'scholastic' learning of the universities and he was something of a lone figure in his lifetime. A committed Christian, he was a man of deep prayer and the recipient of mystical experiences from the age of 30, which he described in his work *Art of Finding Truth*. Lull remains today one of the most fascinating personalities of the late medieval Church.

The four literary giants of the later Middle Ages, Dante Alighieri (1265–1321), Francesco Petrarch (1304–74) and Giovanni Boccaccio (1313–75) from Italy, and Geoffrey Chaucer (1343–1400) from England, may be considered lay men, though probably two of them (Petrarch and Boccaccio) were ordained to minor orders and therefore technically were clerics. They are essentially non-university figures, though Boccaccio studied for a time at Naples university.

Dante was born in Florence and suffered a disturbed upbringing, losing both parents before the age of 18. He was betrothed when he was 12 and eventually married, but meanwhile he met his true love, Beatrice, who died young. Beatrice became the inspiration for his masterpiece, *Divina Commedia*, which he completed towards the end of his life. In this lengthy poem, written in Italian, Dante describes the three realms of the world to come, hell, purgatory and heaven, in that ascending order, with close reference to real persons and events in this life. The profound reflections that are intertwined in the narrative represent both philosophy and theology, yet they surpass in expression and vividness the scholasticism characteristic of universities. The outlook is deeply Christian and generally loyal to the institutional Church while at the same time fiercely critical of individual churchmen including some popes, whom he places in hell. The work established itself as a major European classic soon after his death, both for its contents and on account of its influence on the development of the Italian language. For a time Dante was active in Florentine politics, but twice chose the losing party and, as a result, was twice exiled, surely fortunately inasmuch as it gave him time for writing. Besides *Divina Commedia*, he wrote works of philosophy and political theory. *De Monarchia*, his best-known work of political theory, urged the independence of secular authorities – having in mind especially the city government of Florence and the Emperor Henry VII – against the claims to universal sovereignty in temporal as well as spiritual matters that were advanced by the popes of his time, especially Boniface VIII. A man of wide learning and varied experiences of life, Dante's lasting reputation depends on *Divina Commedia*, with its elegant and compelling language, vivid and topical imagery and profound reflections on human life in this and the next world.

Francesco Petrarch was also a deeply religious man, a prolific writer and of wide experience. He was fascinated with the ancient classical world of Greece and Rome, especially its literature, yet sought to reconcile it with Christianity. He hoped an updated Christianity could be combined with the more secular aspirations of Renaissance Italy. He was probably ordained to minor orders as a young man, thus enabling him to enjoy the income of various benefices, but he remained at heart a layman. His wide circle of friends included both laity and clerics, notably his patron Cardinal Giovanni Colonna. He was a critic of many aspects of the Church of his day and fervently supported Cola di Rienzo's establishment of a republic in Rome in 1347, which briefly supplanted papal rule. Yet to label him an anti-clerical would be simplistic. His *Secretum*, also known as *De contemptu mundi*, which consists of dialogues between himself and Augustine of Hippo, and *Il Canzoniere*, written in Italian, which is a collection of poems revolving around themes of life and death, reflect a man struggling with his humanity and eternal destiny, with mysteries that are central to Christianity.

The careers of Giovanni Boccaccio and Geoffrey Chaucer have many similarities. Both of them admired the writings of Dante and Petrarch, while Boccaccio was Petrarch's intimate friend for many years. As well as being prolific writers, both were active in public life, Chaucer mainly in the king's service and Boccaccio in a variety of occupations. Chaucer visited Italy on at least two occasions and became an avid reader of Boccaccio. In style and structure his *The Canterbury Tales* owes much to Boccaccio's *Decameron*. Neither of the two masterpieces gives much serious consideration to Christianity. The focus is, rather, on men and women in all their diversity and complexity in this life. Even in *The Canterbury Tales*, which has a pilgrimage for its setting and features a number of Church personalities – monk, friar, two nuns, parish priest – Christianity and the Church are treated in a rather superficial way and the tone for the most part – the treatment of the parish priest being an exception – is somewhat anti-clerical and hostile. Both men underwent religious conversions towards the end of their lives. As a result, Boccaccio was ordained to minor orders and dedicated himself to giving spiritual counsel to others, while not abandoning his literary activities; Chaucer pledged his allegiance to the Church and traditional Christian doctrine, and inserted into *The Canterbury Tales*, at a late stage, the sympathetic personality and tale of the parish priest. In their sophistication and inner struggles, their wide experience and readiness to change, the two men are symptomatic of the energy, creativity and doubts of late medieval Europe.

Humanism

The word 'humanism' derives from interest in 'human letters', understood as the literature of classical Greek and Rome. Thus 'human letters' were distinguished from 'sacred letters' (*sacra pagina*), the Bible. By extension, the word 'humanism' came to mean interest in, even exaltation of, the human person, including the body, as distinct from, or in reaction against, the negative or gloomy attitude towards humanity that was alleged to have characterized late medieval religion and particularly scholastic theology. Essentially, therefore, it was a literary movement, centred on interest in classical literature. It came to be closely associated with Renaissance art because of a shared interest in the classical world and in the human person. Sometimes, indeed, humanism and the Renaissance were treated as almost synonymous.

The topic of humanism intertwines much of this book. Renaissance art is treated systematically in the next section of this chapter and it features on many other pages. Interest in classical literature and concern for its preservation characterized some of the Renaissance popes, notably Nicholas V and Pius II, as well as various other clergy treated in Chapters 1 and 2. The career of Francesco Petrarch, who is often regarded as the first humanist scholar of the Renaissance, has just been outlined. He illustrates well that humanism and Christian studies were intimately linked in the later Middle Ages. For the most part humanism developed outside the universities, much of it within the courts and entourages of kings, nobles and prominent ecclesiastics. Indeed Renaissance humanism developed in good measure as a criticism of the 'scholastic' philosophy and theology prevalent in universities. There were some exceptions. Humanist scholarship at Cambridge university in the late fifteenth century, partly under the patronage of Lady Margaret Beaufort, has been mentioned (see p 121). Pavia university in Italy provided similar opportunities through the fifteenth century.

Lorenzo Valla (1406–57) was perhaps the most eminent humanist scholar of the fifteenth century. Initially he studied in Rome and held the chair of Eloquence at Pavia university for a short time. After spells in Naples and Florence, he returned to Rome for the final stage of his life. He received papal patronage in Rome, even though his scholarship had been decisive in proving that the Donation of Constantine – the document by which the Emperor Constantine (312–37) had allegedly bestowed much property and his temporal authority in the West on the papacy – was a forgery. Like Petrarch, he combined enthusiasm for classical authors with important studies on theological and Christian topics. Poggio Bracciolini (1380–1459) was another humanist scholar who received papal patronage, though his enduring patron was Duke Cosimo de Medici of Florence. His academic interests focused largely on the classical world. Interest in Plato was promoted most eminently by Marsiglio Ficino (1433–99), through the Platonic Academy in Florence, of which he was the head, and his translations of Plato's works (into Latin). Ficino was a devout Christian, a priest and canon of Florence cathedral, who sought to harmonize Christianity and Platonism, most notably in his work *De religione Christiana* ('On the Christian Religion'). Through these and other scholars, Italy was the undoubted centre of Renaissance humanism until 1500. Thereafter, principally through Desiderius Erasmus, other countries would come to share in the movement's leadership. In the later Middle Ages, humanism constituted both an academic movement in its own right, largely outside the scope of the present book, and a significant reform movement within the Church.

Arts, architecture and music

Regarding culture – that broad concept – the fourteenth and fifteenth centuries are known above all for the paintings of the early Renaissance. Renaissance art is one of the most popular and well studied of all academic topics and it is widely considered to have contributed to the birth of modern, secular humanity in the Western world. There is some truth in the latter proposition as regards results, but in terms of origins and development it is essential to understand the art of the early Renaissance as emerging from the late medieval world and to note its predominantly religious character. Renaissance art must be viewed from its point of departure, not just in terms of how later historians have come to interpret it.

In addition to painting, the present section surveys other fine arts – including sculpture – as well as architecture and music. All these cultural forms played significant roles in the Church and society in the later Middle Ages, and there were important developments in them during the period.

Painting

The initial and crucial role of Ambrogiotto di Bondone (1267–1337), commonly known as Giotto, in the history of Renaissance art was quickly recognized. The exceptional quality of the Florentine painter's work was acknowledged by his contemporaries, including both Dante and Petrarch, and he was regarded as a seminal figure by Giorgio Vasari, whose *Lives of the Artists*, written in the mid-sixteenth century, dominated the interpretation of Renaissance art for several centuries. The details of Giotto's life are sketchy, but a remarkable amount of his art survives, all of it painted in Italy and almost all of it of a religious nature. He moved beyond the somewhat rigid formality and stereotypical formulae prevalent in the art of the time – which was influenced by Byzantine art – to a new sense of dramatic realism. Whether he designed the frescoes in the basilica dedicated to St Francis at Assisi, which depict scenes from the saint's life, is disputed, but he was certainly responsible for the paintings in the family chapels of the Arena (or Scrovegni) in Padua and of the Peruzzi and Bardi families in Santa Croce church in Florence. In Rome he designed the huge mosaic in St Peter's basilica depicting the Church as a ship, with Christ walking on the water. His work reveals his genius for naturalism and characterization, whereby persons and scenes come vividly alive – qualities best seen today in the cycle of paintings of the life of Christ in the Arena chapel in Padua. Giotto played an important role in promoting the status of painters. Significant in this respect was his appointment in 1334 as head of the Florence cathedral workshop, an honour and responsibility that had hitherto been reserved for architects and sculptors.

Giotto was not succeeded immediately by artists of comparable talent. Regarding popular religion, however, it is misleading to concentrate too much on the greatest artists and to forget the wealth of paintings of more ordinary quality. An example of the latter is the cycle of frescoes of the life of Christ in the main parish church of San Gimignano in northern Italy, which were painted by Barna da Siena around 1380. They are of good artistic quality and are both educational and devotional. Inasmuch as they were to be found in the parish church at the centre of the town, they could be appreciated by many people, whereas much of Giotto's work was for the chapels of the aristocracy and thus less immediately accessible. The contrast in those who saw their works highlights fundamental problems of interpretation. The invention of photography in the late nineteenth century has meant that we have far more access to late medieval art than had people of the time. Subsequently, illustrated histories of art have focused on the great works of art and those considered to have contributed to developments in artistic styles, at the expense of works of more ordinary quality, which may nevertheless have been seen and appreciated by many more people. We must strain to evaluate the actual impact of art upon popular religion of the time. There is also the problem that much medieval religious art, especially that of more ordinary quality, was later destroyed during both Reformation and Counter-Reformation.

The fourteenth century produced the *danse macabre* (or 'Triumph of Death') genre of paintings. The genre, in which the reality of death is accentuated in various ways, developed especially after the horrors of the Black Death of 1347–50 and its recurrences. Most typically, living individuals are placed alongside skeletons or decomposing bodies, thus reminding the living of the fate soon to come to them. Vivid examples in Italy are the frescoes by Francesco Traini in the 'Camposanto' cemetery building next to the cathedral in Pisa, or those in the Sacro Speco church within the Benedictine monastery at Subiaco. There are numerous surviving examples in northern Europe. It was a pan-European phenomenon and was employed in miniature pictures in books, in sculpture and in wall-paintings. Evidently it was a popular format, one that appealed to the hearts and minds of many people. It contrasts, in both style and content, with the more optimistic tones normally associated with Renaissance art, as well as with more traditional 'late Gothic' painting, and reminds us of the pluralism of taste that existed within later medieval art and, indeed, within the Church and society of the time.

In the early fifteenth century painters from Flanders (north Belgium today) took the lead in new developments. Most notable among them were the so-called Master of Flémalle, who is probably to be identified with Robert Campin (d.1444), the brothers Hubert (d.1426) and Jan (1390–1441) van Eyck, and Roger van der Weyden (1399–1464). Their paintings combine religious devotion and attention to the divine with warm sympathy for the trials and triumphs of men and women. They are characterized, too, by their attention to details and to symbolism. Altogether there is a northern European air about them. The 'Merode Altarpiece' by the Master of Flémalle, with its three panels focusing on the Annunciation to Mary, and the altarpiece in St Bavo church in Ghent, painted by both Hubert and Jan van Eyck, with its many panels centring on the triumph of Christ as the 'Lamb of God', are their best-known works. A very important technical development, first introduced for large-scale paintings by the Master of Flémalle and followed by other Flemish artists, was the abandonment of 'tempera' (finely ground colour pigments 'tempered'/mixed with diluted egg yolk), which had hitherto been the prevalent medium, in favour of combining the pigments with oil – a combination that allowed for richer and brighter tones as well as finer attention to detail. The second half of the fifteenth century saw the sensitive work of Hugo van der Goes and Hans Memling, both painting in Flanders, and the imaginative creations of the Dutchman Hieronymus Bosch, most notably his 'Garden of Delights', which is now in the Prado Museum in Madrid; and many other distinguished though less famous artists. After about 1430, the new realism of Flemish painters spread into France and Germany and gradually exercised a profound influence throughout Western Europe. It was fundamental also to the development of Flemish and Dutch art in the sixteenth and seventeenth centuries.

Flemish painters appear to have developed largely within their own tradition, taking little notice of Italian artists at least until the late fifteenth century. Italian painters, on the other hand, knew about and were much impressed by developments in Flanders. Antonello da Messina (1430–79) was an important link between the two schools. He knew Flemish artists, certainly through personal contacts and possibly also by visits north, and he combined both schools well in his own works, including fine portraits of St Mary and St Sebastian. Equally important, he was the first Italian artist of note to paint in oils, having learnt the new technique through his Flemish contacts, and so ushered in a revolution as other Italian artists followed his example.

Fifteenth-century Italy was rich in distinguished artists. Most notable were Masaccio, who died aged 27 in 1428, and, in roughly chronological order of activity, the Dominican friar Fra Angelico (1387–1455), Filippo Lippi (1406–69), Paolo Uccello (1400–75), Piero della Francesca (1416–92), Andrea Mantegna (1431–1506), Giovanni Bellini (1430–1516), Sandro Botticelli (1444–1510), Domenico Ghirlandaio (1449–94) and Pietro Perugino (1445–1523). Most of them painted both religious and secular scenes and portraits, normally following the instructions of their patrons. Many of the religious paintings are of very high quality both technically and in terms of content. Masaccio's portraits of Adam and Eve in his 'Expulsion from Paradise', painted as part of a series of frescoes for the Brancacci family chapel within Santa Maria del Carmine church in Florence, is one example; another is Fra Angelico's intense and lyrical 'Annunciation', depicting Mary and the angel Gabriel, which he painted for his Dominican friary in Florence. Botticelli's 'Birth of Venus', another masterpiece, reminds us of the abiding interest in pagan mythology and warns against an overly Christian interpretation of late medieval Europe.

The full flowering of Italian Renaissance art, which is usually associated with the sixteenth century, was well under way by 1500. The walls of the Sistine Chapel in Rome were painted in the early 1480s, principally by Botticelli, Ghirlandaio and Perugino. Leonardo da Vinci had painted many of his best-known religious works before the end of the century, including 'Adoration of the Magi', 'Virgin of the Rocks' and 'The Last Supper'. Michelangelo, born in 1475, was still focusing on sculpture; Raphael, born in 1483, was still in his youth.

For late medieval art, Italy and Flanders were the two most famous countries. The brilliance and depth of the work produced there helps to explain why the two countries remained Catholic thereafter: such fine and evidently Catholic art had to be appreciated. Painting flourished in the rest of Western Christendom, even if with lesser acclaim. In Germany, three great artists were born in the 1470s: Albrecht Dürer, who had produced some notable works before 1500, Matthias Grünewald and Lucas Cranach.

For England, a fine example of the period is the 'Wilton Diptych', which portrays King Richard II accompanied by three patron saints kneeling before Mary and the child Jesus and a company of angels. The work, late Gothic rather than Renaissance in style, may have been painted in France. Another example from the late fourteenth century is the 'Norwich retable' with five scenes from the life of Christ, which was probably made for the refurbished sanctuary of Norwich cathedral (it is now kept in St Luke's chapel in the cathedral) and was almost certainly the work of local artists. Wall-paintings have recently been revealed in many English churches, as whitewash dating back to the Reformation is removed. Those in St Peter's parish church in South Leigh in Oxfordshire, and in various churches in East Anglia, are among many examples. In some cases the art is poor in quality and oppressive, so one can understand why parishioners at the time of the Reformation – and no doubt some in the later Middle Ages – wanted a simplified interior for their parish church.

It is important to remember all the art of an earlier age that remained and influenced people, not to focus exclusively on the works produced in the later Middle Ages. A good example of an earlier work is the remarkable large-scale 'Last Judgement', which was discovered after the removal of whitewash in Chaldon parish church in Surrey, southern England. It was probably painted around 1200 and reveals Byzantine influences. With its emphasis on hell, the picture conveys a powerful and haunting message, though it is situated, with some discretion, on the back wall of the church rather than in a more imposing position.

Other fine arts

Closely linked to pictorial art, but traditionally considered to constitute a separate genre, were illuminations and miniature paintings in manuscripts. The genre was highly developed long before 1300, principally for prayer books and liturgical works, but the artistic advances of the later Middle Ages had some influence on it. A high point was reached in the early fifteenth century with the exquisite illustrations in the *Très Riches Heures du Duc de Berry*, which were executed by three Flemish brothers, Pol, Jean and Armand de Limbourg. The brothers had trained in Paris, also perhaps in Italy, and were active at the court of Duke Jean de Berry in Bourges, France. For this liturgical prayer book, they produced a series of panoramas of human life within the setting of nature, following the seasons of the year. The result is both secular and religious – perhaps 'incarnational' would be a better description. It was a work for a member of the high aristocracy, the uncle of the young king of France, and may have been seen during the duke's lifetime by few outside his immediate circle. The duke was the most lavish patron of religious art of his day in France, yet, paradoxically, a man of far from admirable character. Perhaps he should not be judged too harshly.

Among individuals, illustrated prayer books could be afforded only by the wealthy, but these works could be appreciated by a wider public by means of those on more open display in parish churches and in the churches of religious orders.

The invention of printing in the middle of the fifteenth century, and the accompanying replacement of parchment with paper, soon brought an end to miniature paintings in manuscripts. They were replaced in printed books by pictures made by wood-cuts and copper plates. Certainly there was a drop in artistic quality, especially regarding colours. On the other hand, the drawings could be sophisticated and educative and, of course, they reached a much wider public through the multiple copies of each printed book. This story belongs principally to the sixteenth century and later.

Stained glass was similar to painting in its effect, though quite different in technique. Pieces of glass were 'fired' with various colour pigments and then the pieces were composed into a picture within a window, which brought it light and vitality. This art had reached a high point in the twelfth and thirteenth centuries and plenty of it survived, still fresh and creative, to influence late medieval Christianity. The fourteenth and fifteenth centuries saw a healthy continuation and some development of a well-established tradition rather than notable changes. Much stained glass was destroyed through the 'purification' of churches during the Reformation, the Baroque rebuilding and reordering of churches in Catholic countries, and the ravages of wars and revolutions. It is remarkable, nevertheless, how much survives, giving us some idea of its impact on late medieval religion. The most sublime work is to be found in various French cathedrals, most notably Chartres, all dating from the twelfth and thirteenth centuries. England illustrates well the continuing vitality of stained-glass artists in the later Middle Ages. The period produced most of the splendid designs in the windows of York cathedral, some fine work in the college chapels and other churches of Oxford and Cambridge, and a fair amount of surviving work in parish churches, notably in East Anglia.

Developments in sculpture were almost as dramatic as those in painting, but they were confined largely to Italy, principally Florence, and to the fifteenth century. The twelfth and thirteenth centuries had been a golden age in Europe for religious sculpture, as can be seen today especially in the many surviving statues in cathedrals – most notably Chartres – and other churches, both inside and outside the buildings. These achievements remained largely intact to influence late medieval religion. This well-established tradition continued to develop, moreover, through the later Middle Ages, still fresh and creative – for which period it is commonly called 'late Gothic'. This style was well represented in Italy, for example in the early fourteenth-century carvings by Lorenzo Maitani on the façade of Orvieto cathedral.

But alongside this tradition, in Italy, the more realistic style of Renaissance painting was accompanied by similar developments in sculpture. An early masterpiece came with the scenes from the Old and New Testaments on the bronze doors of the baptistery next to the cathedral in Florence, which were carved by Lorenzo Ghiberti. The influence of earlier French sculpture is evident, yet the work is uniquely Ghiberti's. Donatello learned the technique of bronze sculpture as a youth while working under Ghiberti on the Florence baptistery, but in the 1420s he branched out on his own. 'The Feast of Herod', which he carved in bronze for the baptismal font of Siena cathedral, reveals both technical mastery and remarkable expressive power in the gruesome scene that portrays John the Baptist's head being brought to King Herod. Donatello was a prolific sculptor both in Florence and for patrons elsewhere in north Italy. His bronze 'David', which he made for an unknown patron, revealed an exaltation of the human body that had not been seen in Western art since classical times. The nude adolescent exults in his body as much as in his conquest of Goliath and the onlooker is invited to do the same. For many years it remained the only work of its kind. Exaltation of the nude body reappeared in Michelangelo's majestic statue of the young David, which he carved in marble between 1501 and 1504, and it remained a basic theme of Renaissance art thereafter. Many thought it took the 'incarnational' aspect of Christianity too far, yet the religious motivation in this more positive approach to the human body, in reaction to what was seen as the prevalent over-wary approach, needs to be appreciated. Both Donatello and Michelangelo sculpted their statues of David while they were living in Florence and the city remained the undisputed centre of Renaissance sculpture during the fifteenth century. Other artists of high quality working in the city were Luca della Robbia (1400–82), whose best-known work, the marble reliefs for the Singers' Pulpit in Florence cathedral, combines charm and gravity; Bernardo Rossellino (1409–64); the prolific and versatile Antonio del Verrocchio (1433–88), who worked in marble, terracotta, silver and bronze; and Antonio Pollaiuolo (1431–98).

Architecture

The late medieval Church received an impressive architectural inheritance. The twelfth and thirteenth centuries had seen the construction of magnificent cathedrals, large monasteries, especially those of the Benedictine, Cistercian and Carthusian orders, buildings of the new orders of friars, and the rebuilding of many parish churches. The contribution of the later medieval Church was, for the most part, to develop further this inheritance. The construction of cathedrals and other large churches, either building new ones or expanding and modifying those that already existed, continued throughout the period. Much of this work still survives today. Among many fine examples: for Italy, there are the cathedrals of Orvieto and Milan, begun around 1310 and 1386 respectively; in Germany, the choir of St Sebald church in Nuremberg, constructed between 1361 and 1372; in England, the choir of Gloucester abbey church (now Gloucester cathedral), constructed between 1332 and 1357, and, just after the end of our period, the chapel of King Henry VII in Westminster Abbey. Appreciation of the buildings of religious orders is more difficult because so much of the work was destroyed later. The visitor to Cluny abbey in France, or in England to the ruins of the Benedictine monasteries at St Albans and Bury St Edmunds and of several Cistercian abbeys in Yorkshire, can still gain some idea of the colossal size of the buildings and the impression they must have made on contemporaries.

The rebuilding of parish churches in the fourteenth and fifteenth centuries was on such a scale, in many countries, as to constitute new work. The results can be seen well in England and some other predominantly Protestant countries of northern Europe, which were relatively untouched by Baroque architecture and the resulting redesigning of churches. In Norwich, for example, the large majority of the approximately 50 parish churches in the city were extensively rebuilt on a grander scale between the fourteenth and early sixteenth centuries. As the visitor to the city can still see, the surviving churches are, for the most part, pleasing to the eye and elegantly religious: capacious but functional too and not overpowering. Although parish churches are somewhat overshadowed in the modern imagination by cathedrals, they must surely constitute a principal glory of the late medieval Church and a basic dimension of popular religion of the time.

University buildings formed another area of architectural innovation. Some of them existed before 1300, though in this early period the newly founded universities were, for the most part, using existing buildings rather than constructing new ones. In the fourteenth and fifteenth centuries, both well-established universities and many of the new foundations were taking pride in their new buildings. This can best be seen today in the colleges and other buildings of Oxford and Cambridge, and appreciated in individual works of some other universities, such as the splendid original college of the Jagellonian university in Cracow, Poland, some buildings of Salamanca university in Spain, and St Magnus church of Aberdeen university in Scotland. Sadly, almost nothing survives of the medieval buildings of Bologna university, and almost all those of the university of Paris that survived into the nineteenth century were pulled down in the course of Baron Haussmann's remodelling of the city.

It is important to recognize the other side of the coin: the distaste for architectural grandeur that existed within some quarters of late medieval Christendom. Hostility seems to have focused principally on the huge buildings of some religious orders and was often linked to disgust at the extensive lands and other property that they owned. It helps to explain why the dissolution of religious orders, and the confiscation or destruction of their property, incurred relatively little opposition in those countries that accepted the Reformation. In the later Middle Ages, wealthy religious houses and their large buildings were sometimes singled out for attack. During the Peasants' Revolt in England in 1381, for example, the buildings of St Albans and Bury St Edmunds monasteries were targeted; Norwich cathedral priory was assaulted in 1272 and 1453 (see pp 67–9). Sometimes opposition extended more widely and on principle to church buildings, especially to their ornamentation. At the Lollard trials held in the diocese of Norwich in England between 1428 and 1431, the accusation was made against several individuals, and admitted, that 'material churches be but of little avail and ought to be of little reputation, for every man's prayer said in the field is as good as the prayer said in the church'. Bell towers in churches, too, came in for attack at the same trials, on the grounds that the only purpose of ringing the bells was to 'enable priests to collect money'. Even among the orthodox, a certain puritanism regarding churches may be noted. In Thomas à Kempis's *De imitatione Christi*, for example, there is very little attention to church buildings or to services in church; the focus rather is upon interior devotion. On architectural issues, as on so many others, there was considerable diversity of outlook among Christians of the time.

Any discussion of religious architecture in the later Middle Ages must address the developments more closely associated with the Renaissance. Nevertheless it is right to place these advances alongside the lively and creative developments within late Gothic architecture, as outlined above, to avoid regarding the Renaissance in isolation or too exclusively as a break with the past. Often, indeed, it is difficult to distinguish between late Gothic and Renaissance architecture.

Before 1500 Renaissance architecture, as traditionally defined, was largely confined to fifteenth-century Italy. Much of it related to secular buildings: city halls and family homes. Filippo Brunelleschi was the undisputed initiator of the movement. Having been beaten by Lorenzo Ghiberti in the competition to design the bronze doors for the baptistery next to Florence cathedral, he (probably) went to Rome and moved from sculpture to architecture. In Rome, it seems, he studied the architectural monuments of the ancient city. Back in Florence around 1417, he was again in competition with Ghiberti, this time for designing the dome of the cathedral. Brunelleschi won the competition and designed a masterpiece that clearly broke with the late Gothic style. He was responsible for designing various other church buildings in Florence, all clearly in the new style, notably the churches of St Lorenzo, Santo Spirito and Sta Maria degli Angeli, and the chapel of the Pazzi family. Brunelleschi's death in 1449 brought to the fore Leone Battista Alberti (1404–72), who had studied the monuments of ancient Rome and wrote treatises on sculpture and painting as well as on architecture. He turned, in middle age, to the practice of architecture. Perhaps his best-known work was for a secular building, the palace of the Rucellai family in Florence, but he also designed churches in the new style, most notably San Francesco in Rimini and Sant'Andrea in Mantua. Leonardo da Vinci was interested in architecture as a theorist rather than a practitioner. His presence and the numerous designs for possible buildings that he drew, with their interest in the problems of structure and design, influenced other Renaissance architects, most notably his friend Donato Bramante. With Bramante and Michelangelo, Renaissance architecture enters the sixteenth century and its centre moves to Rome. The foundations, however, had been laid in the fifteenth century, principally in Florence.

Music

It will be obvious from the previous chapters of this book that the late medieval Church was very musical. Singing the 'office' was central to the life of members of most religious orders. Indeed this duty was called *opus Dei* (God's work) in the monastic orders because it was such an integral part of their vocation. Despite all the failings of religious orders in the later Middle Ages, this basic duty was largely observed, it seems. Monks and friars normally sang the office in the church of their monastery or friary, in the 'choir' of the church, so the laity could participate at least through hearing and sometimes more directly. Sometimes the laity organized their own singing of the office, such as Duchess Cicely who heard 'Evensong by note' before supper (see p 93).

Chantries represented an important development for church music, though one that has not yet been properly studied. They were specially popular in the later Middle Ages. The Mass (for the dead) was commonly 'chanted' by the priest, not just said. The laity could participate through hearing the Mass and perhaps by joining in the singing. It is possible to visualize a liturgical concert in a large church, with several chantry masses being sung one after the other or even simultaneously.

Some singing by the congregation in a parish church during Sunday Mass was probably normal, though this aspect of late medieval music also needs further investigation. Plenty of fine hymns for singing in church survive from the Middle Ages, such as 'O Crux fidelis', 'Pange lingua' and 'O victima pasquale' for Holy Week and Easter, or 'Veni Sancte Spiritus' for Pentecost. Although communities of religious orders formed the primary context for these hymns, and they were composed in Latin, it seems likely that there was some use and adaptation of them for the laity, for Masses in parish churches on Sundays and other days. Latin, moreover, was not wholly foreign to the laity. Singing, indeed, was an integral part of prayer.

The most important developments in religious music came in an area centred on the Low Countries and northern France. During the fourteenth and fifteenth centuries this region produced a remarkable group of talented composers and musicians, the majority of them born and trained in the counties of Hainault, Artois, Flanders and Brabant. An important factor was the court of the duke of Burgundy, who was the dominant noble within the region during the late fourteenth and much of the fifteenth century. Successive dukes promoted an elaborate style of court life, within which music was greatly encouraged. Composers associated with the Burgundian court included Johannes Tapissier, Gilles Binchois, Anthony Busnois and Hayne van Ghizeghem. The musical reputation of the Low Countries was widely recognized and many of its composers and musicians were attracted to work elsewhere. Around 1350 the Liégeois composer Johannes Chiwagne – better known as Ciconia – entered the service of Pope Clement VI in Avignon and subsequently worked in many cities in northern Italy. In the fifteenth century, Guillaume Dufay, from Cambrai in northern France, perhaps the most acclaimed composer of the century, worked in Italy and at the court of the duke of Savoy as well as in his native Cambrai; Johannes Ockeghem worked as a composer almost exclusively for the French royal chapel; Josquin des Prez, also from northern France, spent a long period in Milan, first as singer in the cathedral and then as composer at the court of the duke of Milan. As well as the high quality of their music, the musicians in question brought a number of technical improvements that were to have a profound influence on the development of religious music in the West: elegant counterpoint; compositions that reflected geometric or arithmetic proportions, including significant numbers from Christian theology, thus adding a mystical or symbolic dimension; music to stimulate the intellect as well as the ear; the development of polyphony – most notably in Josquin des Prez's *Missa Pange Lingua* – and motet as musical forms.

Conclusion

From the brief outline above, the high quality of artistic culture in the late medieval Church should be evident. Much attention was given to various artistic forms, and the results were lively and successful, in terms of both quality and their effect on popular religion. Arts, architecture and music were integral to Christianity of the time.

The later Middle Ages was a period of cultural transition. The two centuries were heir to the rich traditions of the twelfth and thirteenth centuries. They also produced the developments of the early Renaissance, which both looked back to classical Antiquity and pointed forward to the sixteenth-century Renaissance. The two terms 'late Gothic' and 'Renaissance' are helpful, yet the differences between them should not be exaggerated. 'Late Gothic' certainly cannot be categorized simply as decadent: its vivacity and creativity in various forms should be obvious from the present brief exposition.

In terms of theology, Church membership and much else, a great divide in Church history comes with the Reformation in the early sixteenth century. As regards religious art and culture, the major divide begins around the year 1400. The difference in starting dates means that Renaissance and Reformation cannot be associated too closely. There was no easy association between those countries responsible for the early Renaissance and those that welcomed the Reformation. In some respect, indeed, the contrary appears to be the case: notably in that the two principal regions of the early Renaissance in art – Italy and Flanders – remained Catholic.

Arts in the later Middle Ages formed something of a continuum. They were much less divided into separate categories than they later became and, partly as a result, than they have been treated by most cultural historians. Michelangelo began as a sculptor and moved to painting, Brunelleschi began as a sculptor and moved to architecture, Pollaiuolo was engraver and sculptor as well as painter, Roger van der Weyden was both painter and engraver, Leonardo da Vinci was extraordinarily versatile in the range of his artistic and other talents. Such diversity was common, almost normal. In 1300 the artist was essentially an artisan who painted and decorated rooms. By 1500 he was well on the way to becoming an admired professional, thanks especially to Giotto and later artists whose genius was widely recognized and appreciated. The transformation in status was completed in the sixteenth century, principally through Michelangelo's insistence upon this improved status and Giorgio Vasari's recognition of the new situation in his *Lives of the Artists*.

CHAPTER 5

Heresy and Dissent

This chapter focuses on dissenting and heretical movements within the Western Church. That is to say, it looks at people who considered themselves to be Christians, indeed usually considered themselves better Christians than those within the Church, at least in terms of doctrine, but whom the Church authorities and most other Christians regarded as dissenters or heretics. The chapter also looks at the attitudes of Church authorities and other Christians towards those considered to be unorthodox.

It will be clear from previous chapters that there was quite a wide pluralism of outlooks within the late medieval Church, and that Church authorities were normally hesitant to intervene except when dissent reached the level of public challenges to the status quo. To put the matter in another way, the line between orthodoxy and semi-legitimate dissent was none too precise; indeed there existed a zone in the middle that overlapped with both, and often the definition of dissent depended as much upon the somewhat variable decisions and approaches of prosecuting authorities as upon the beliefs and behaviour of individuals Christians. The medieval Church was lively and creative. It encouraged new initiatives to an extent that is remarkable for a large and well-established institution, even though it was somewhat less encouraging in this respect in the later Middle Ages than it had been in the twelfth and thirteenth centuries. Some tension between conservation and innovation, within this fundamentally healthy climate, was inevitable.

Later historiography, starting with the Reformation, has tended to place dissent and heresy more centre-stage than is warranted. Protestant writers, from the sixteenth century onwards, have looked for signs of discontent in the late medieval Church that led to the Reformation. For somewhat different reasons, recent concerns for the rights of minorities and for freedom of expression have resulted in much interest in minority groups of past times, including those who lived in the Middle Ages. Here, too, there is the danger of anachronism, of looking at earlier generations too much in terms of recent categories of interest and study, and thereby of exaggerating the influence of medieval heresy. These cautions notwithstanding, some consideration of heresy and dissent is essential to a proper understanding of the later medieval Church.

Some of the material has already been covered in previous chapters. Chapter 1 covered various individuals and groups who were accused of heresy or schism: Pope John XXII, whose dubious views on the Beatific Vision were corrected by his successor, and the many people who were charged with heresy during the long and tense period of the papal schism and the Councils of Constance, Basel and Florence. Chapter 2 mentioned various clergy and members of religious orders who incurred ecclesiastical censures. The first part of Chapter 3 discussed at some length the laity who lived on the borders between orthodoxy and dissent; and the second part treated of several lay men and women who were investigated by Church authorities, including Margaret Porete and other beguines, and Joan of Arc. Chapter 4 covered some more intellectual cases of possible heresy, including William of Ockham. The present chapter examines groups and individuals who belonged more clearly to institutionalized forms of heresy and dissent.

Cathars and Waldensians

Cathars

The word 'Cathar' comes from the Greek *katharos*, meaning 'pure'. Thus Cathars (in France they were often called Albigensians) sought for purity, for the spiritual principle, and therefore freedom from the material world, which they regarded as belonging to the evil principle. This dualist teaching, which has obvious similarities with Manichaeism and other heresies in the early Church and quite probably more direct links with them through the Bogomil movement in the Balkans, came to prominence in Western Europe in the middle of the twelfth century: in northern Italy and German-speaking countries, in France and the Rhineland, even briefly in England. Many of its outward forms and practices were similar to those of Catholicism, yet the central tenets of the teaching, with its radical rejection of the material world and therefore of Christ's Incarnation, placed it outside rather than alongside orthodox Christianity. The Church reacted to the movement with vigour, through the Inquisition and crusades, and through various internal developments – most notably the success of the Franciscan order – which cut much of the ground from under the Cathars' criticism of worldliness and other failures in the Church.

Catharism survived into the later Middle Ages in a somewhat fragmentary manner, principally in southern France. Jacques Fournier, Bishop of Pamiers, who later became Pope Benedict XII, recorded in minute detail his investigations into Catharism in the parts of his diocese that lay within the French Pyrenees, principally the village of Montaillou and surrounding districts, between 1318 and 1325. His findings, which Emmanuel Le Roy Ladurie summarized in his study *Montaillou*, make fascinating reading. They reveal a mixture of bizarre beliefs, serious theology and a harassed and threatened community. By this date Catharism as an organized movement appears to be in terminal decline, accelerated too by bitter internal divisions, though its memory and teachings continued to exercise some influence on religion in the West, for the most part in an indirect and diffuse way, throughout the later Middle Ages.

Waldensians

Waldensianism was both similar to and different from Catharism. The movement emerged later than Catharism and with a definite founder. It survived through the later Middle Ages, to resurface more openly during the sixteenth-century Reformation, though the extent of this continuity is debated among historians. It shared some of the puritanism and austerity of Catharism but was much less extreme regarding the dualism of spirit and matter. Waldensians saw themselves, for the most part, as a reform movement within the Church rather than an alternative to it.

Valdes, or Peter Waldo as he came to be known, was a rich citizen of Lyons who converted around the year 1170 to a life of poverty, good works and preaching. He soon attracted a following among like-minded people, first in Lyons and then further afield. While some of his ideas met with approval from Church authorities, these authorities refused to recognize the right of lay people to preach. As a result, Valdes and his followers were excommunicated and the movement moved into schism. It always remained a minority grouping. Many of their proposals, especially regarding poverty and preaching, were taken over by the new orders of friars, principally the Franciscans and Dominicans, and adapted to forms that were acceptable to the papacy and most bishops.

Jacques Fournier, the prosecutor of the Cathars of Montaillou, investigated the Waldensian leader Raymond de Sainte Foy (or de Costa) at Carcassonne in southern France during several months in 1319 and 1320. During the trial, which was recorded in fine detail, Fournier sat alongside the Dominican representative of the Inquisition at Carcassonne. Raymond appeared as a deacon of the moderate 'Lyonist' wing of the movement, who had studied at the Franciscan school in Montpellier and who had a good grasp of theology, especially the Bible. He maintained on Scriptural grounds that as a cleric he should not work with his hands, he refused to take the oath demanded by the court, citing Matthew 5.34, 'Do not swear at all', and argued that purgatory had no warrant in the Bible. On the articles of the faith and the sacraments he declared his orthodoxy. There were three orders of clergy, he said, which were similar to those in the Catholic Church: *majoralis* (equivalent of bishop), priest and deacon. Priests heard the confessions of the laity, and exhorted them therein, though without granting absolution, but celebrating the Eucharist was reserved to the *majoralis*. Deacons and other clergy, he said, maintained vows of poverty, chastity and obedience, recited a version of the breviary and observed the Church's liturgical calendar. He gave some further information about organization and personnel, but refused to name individuals for fear that they would be arrested and prosecuted. He distinguished clearly his beliefs from those of Cathars, who, he accepted, could legitimately be put to death if unrepentant. Notwithstanding the moderate nature of his beliefs, Raymond was condemned and burnt to death along with his nurse and two companions.

Waldensian communities in the later Middle Ages were to be found principally in southern France, northern Italy and various German-speaking countries. There were divisions within the movement, dating back to the thirteenth century, principally between 'moderates', often called 'Poor men of Lyons', who kept more or less to the teachings of Peter Waldo, and the more extreme wing, based in northern Italy and frequently called 'Poor Lombards', who went further in denying the validity of the sacraments and on other issues. Divisions within the movement appear, however, to have been less bitter than those among the Cathars. As with most persecuted groups, information about Waldensians remains shadowy and comes to a large extent from the prosecution.

The *Liber electorum*, which was probably written by an Italian Waldensian towards the middle of the fourteenth century and survives in Latin and Languedocian French, endeavours to bring comfort to the persecuted. It seeks a return to the poverty of the Church that had existed before the 'Donation' of the Emperor Constantine in the fourth century had started the process of endowing the Church with property. This Donation, the *Liber* urges, had ushered in a period of 800 years of darkness for the Church, with only a minority, the Elect, remaining faithful. Valdes had then appeared and restored the light for a while, only to be followed by the present darkness and persecution. The moon signified the Church, with its waxing and waning, and a brighter future was assured. An anonymous Waldensian work, *Nobla leycon*, was a popular poem composed around 1400. It surveyed the whole Bible under the headings of the three laws of God: the law of nature, the law of Moses in the Old Testament and the law of Christ in the New Testament. Throughout the poem, at its centre, lies the little flock, those who remain faithful in adversity.

Numbers in heretical groups are notoriously difficult to calculate.

Nevertheless it seems safe to say that the number of Waldensians, according to their various groupings, certainly ran into tens of thousands. Many of them, it seems, were willing to attend Mass and other religious services with Catholics in the parish church of the locality. In some investigations, Catholic witnesses, including priests, testified to the good life of Waldensians and their observance of the fasts and liturgical feasts of Catholicism. Evidently there was plenty of social mixing between them and Catholics, at least in some areas, as well as an overlap in terms of religious beliefs and practices. Many of them probably considered themselves to be both Waldensian and Catholic, or perhaps better 'Waldensian Catholics', though there also existed the more extreme wing of the movement. In the thirteenth century groups of Waldensians had converted back to Catholicism; so it was in the later Middle Ages. A list dating from the 1390s named 19 Waldensian teachers who converted to Catholicism, five of whom were later ordained Catholic priests and one became a monk. Such conversions may indicate the closeness of Waldensianism to Catholicism, but the other side of the coin appeared when four of the 19 converts were murdered, apparently by their former co-religionists.

Despite these aspects of proximity to Catholicism and of *convivencia* (living together), Waldensians continued to encounter sporadic and sometimes fierce persecutions from both secular and Church authorities. The city of Berne in Switzerland investigated its Waldensians in 1399 and expelled more than 130 of them. In the early fifteenth century many Waldensians sought to escape persecution by moving to Bohemia, where they found safe havens among Hussite communities. A crusade was launched in 1487–88, with papal support, against Waldensians living on both the Italian and French sides of the Alps and some 160 of them are known to have been killed.

The contribution of Waldensians to late medieval Christendom was significant in itself and the movement was taken seriously by the Church authorities.

John Wyclif and the Lollards

John Wyclif (or Wycliffe) provided the most formidable intellectual challenge to the Western Church in the later Middle Ages. He anticipated most of the teachings of the Protestant Reformation in the sixteenth century, so that with reason he quickly came to be called in English circles 'the morning star of the Reformation'. Wyclif was born around the year 1330, probably in Yorkshire. He studied at Oxford university, was ordained priest and spent most of the rest of his life as a teacher at the university. There he was widely recognized as the most brilliant teacher of his time in both philosophy and theology. He was a prolific writer. His teaching, crucially on the doctrine of transubstantiation (see p 90) but also on a range of other issues, gradually came in for censure on the part of various ecclesiastical authorities: those of his own university of Oxford, Pope Gregory XI through five papal bulls in 1377, and the archbishop of Canterbury presiding over two synods held at the Dominican friary in London in 1382. Wyclif had powerful friends, most prominently the king's uncle, John of Gaunt. Because of them and the relatively free atmosphere prevalent in English academic circles at the time, as well as out of respect for his age and status, Wyclif escaped mortal punishment. In 1381 he was obliged to retire from Oxford to Lutterworth in Leicestershire, where he held the benefice of rector of the parish church. He died there three years later, following a stroke.

Wyclif's teachings are difficult to outline or analyse. He wrote much and spoke in public frequently, through his university lectures and on various other occasions. He was constantly developing his thoughts and he was a man of varying moods, from the vigorous and vitriolic to the more subdued and reflective. It is unsurprising, therefore, that his recorded statements on many topics varied considerably, from quite extreme to more moderate tones.

His teachings received their most solemn condemnation some 30 years after his death, at the Council of Constance in May 1415. The condemnation both follows and significantly expands on the text of Archbishop Courtenay's censure of his teachings at the second of the London synods in 1382. Its articles do not provide citations in Wyclif's works for the offending beliefs and it is quite possible they were considered to come from his oral teaching as well as from his written works. They appear to represent Wyclif at his more extreme, sometimes indeed going beyond that: there seems no good justification for Article 6, for example, even allowing for his views of predestination. Even so, the articles give a good idea of the wide range and often radical nature of Wyclif's teaching: on the Eucharist (1–5), other sacraments (4, 7, 28), predestination (8, 26–7), prayer (19, 25–6), preaching (13–14), indulgences (42), oaths (43), tithes (18), clergy, religious orders and Church property (4, 10–12, 15–16, 20–4, 28, 30–6, 39, 44–5), papacy and the Roman Church (8–9, 28, 33, 36–7, 40–2, 44), universities and learning (29), and secular authorities (8, 12, 15–17, 29). The condemnation is revealing, too, of the mentality and fears of Church authorities regarding Wyclif and of how they defined heresy. It merits quotation in full:

> John Wyclif stubbornly asserted and taught many articles against the Christian religion and the catholic faith while he was alive. We have decided that forty-five of the articles should be set out as follows:

1. The material substance of bread, and similarly the material substance of wine, remain in the sacrament of the altar.

2. The accidents of bread do not remain without their subject in the said sacrament.

3. Christ is not identically and really present in the said sacrament in his own bodily person.

4. If a bishop or a priest is in mortal sin, he does not ordain or confect or consecrate or baptize.

5. That Christ instituted the Mass has no basis in the Gospel.

6. God ought to obey the devil.

7. If a person is duly contrite, all exterior confession is superfluous and useless for him.

8. If a pope is foreknown as damned and is evil, and is therefore a limb of the devil, he does not have authority over the faithful given to him by anyone, except perhaps by the emperor.

9. Nobody should be considered as pope after Urban VI. Rather people should live like the Greeks, under their own laws.

10. It is against sacred scripture for ecclesiastics to have possessions.

11. No prelate should excommunicate anyone unless he first knows that the person has been excommunicated by God; he who does so thereby becomes a heretic and an excommunicated person.

12. A prelate excommunicating a cleric who has appealed to the king or the king's council is thereby a traitor to the king and the kingdom.

13. Those who stop preaching or hearing the word of God on account of an excommunication issued by men are themselves excommunicated and will be regarded as traitors of Christ on the Day of Judgement.

14. It is lawful for any deacon or priest to preach the word of God without authorization from the apostolic see or from a catholic bishop.

15. Nobody is a civil lord or a prelate or a bishop while he is in mortal sin.

16. Secular lords can confiscate temporal goods from the Church at their discretion when those who possess them are sinning habitually, that is to say, sinning from habit and not just in particular acts.

17. The people can correct sinful lords at their discretion.

18. Tithes are purely alms and parishioners can withhold them at will on account of their prelates' sins.

19. Special prayers applied by prelates or religious to a particular person avail him or her no more than general prayers, if other things are equal.

20. Whoever gives alms to friars is thereby excommunicated.

21. Whoever enters any religious order whatsoever, whether it be of the possessioners (monks) or of the mendicants (friars), makes him less apt and suitable for the observance of God's commands.

22. Saints who have founded religious orders have sinned in so doing.

23. Members of religious orders are not members of the Christian people.

24. Friars are bound to obtain their food by manual work and not by

begging.

25. All are simoniacs who bind themselves to pray for people who help them in temporal matters.

26. The prayer of someone foreknown as damned profits nobody.

27. All things happen from absolute necessity.

28. Confirming the young, ordaining clerics and consecrating places have been reserved to the pope and bishops because of their greed for temporal gain and honour.

29. Universities, places of study, colleges, degrees and academic exercises in these institutions were introduced by a vain pagan spirit and benefit the Church as little as does the devil.

30. Excommunication by a pope or any prelate is not to be feared since it is a censure of antichrist.

31. Those who found religious houses sin, and those who enter them belong to the devil.

32. It is against Christ's command to enrich the clergy.

33. Pope Silvester and the Emperor Constantine erred in endowing the Church.

34. All the members of mendicant orders are heretics, and those who give them alms are excommunicated.

35. Those who enter a religious or other order thereby become incapable of observing God's commands, and consequently of reaching the kingdom, unless they leave them.

36. The pope with all his clerics who have property are heretics, for the very reason that they have property; and so are all who abet them, namely all secular lords and other laity.

37. The Roman Church is Satan's synagogue; and the pope is not the immediate and proximate vicar of Christ and the Apostles.

38. The decretal letters [canon law] are apocryphal and seduce people from Christ's faith, and clerics who study them are fools.

39. The emperor and secular lords were seduced by the devil to endow the Church with temporal goods.

40. The election of a pope by the cardinals was introduced by the devil.

41. It is not necessary for salvation to believe that the Roman Church is supreme among the other churches.

42. It is ridiculous to believe in the indulgences of popes and bishops.

43. Oaths taken to confirm civil commerce and contracts between people are unlawful.

44. Augustine, Benedict and Bernard are damned, unless they repented of having owned property and of having founded and entered religious orders; and thus they are all heretics from the pope down to the lowest religious.

45. All religious orders were introduced by the devil. (*Decrees*: 411–13)

The word 'Lollard' appears to come from the Dutch *lollen*, 'to mumble', and to signify a vagabond or religious eccentric. It was a term of abuse that the orthodox applied to those they regarded as disciples of Wyclif. The relevant individuals avoided the term and preferred to call themselves – so far as we can tell – 'true followers of Christ' or 'true followers of the Gospel' or perhaps Wycliffites. The words 'Lollard' and 'Lollardy' are retained in the present account in keeping with common usage, but their hostile derivation should be remembered.

The closeness of links between John Wyclif and the Lollards is debated among historians. During his lifetime Wyclif had some close associates, mostly at Oxford university, as well as a much wider audience. Within a decade or so of his death, the first ever English translation of the whole Bible – subsequently known as the 'Lollard Bible' – appeared (in two versions). Wyclif had advocated such a vernacular translation and so acted as an inspiration, but scholars seem agreed that at least most of the work was done after his death by a group of translators, possibly under the separate directions of Nicholas Hereford and John Purvey. This English Bible enjoyed notable success until the new translations of the sixteenth century, as evidenced by the many manuscript copies that survive; some of them, indeed, were owned by individuals otherwise known for their orthodoxy. In 1407 the archbishop of Canterbury, Thomas Arundel, prohibited the use of any translation of the Bible made 'in the time of John Wyclif or since' and forbade the making of any fresh translation without ecclesiastical approval. No such approval was given and the Lollard (or Wycliffite) Bible remained the only available, albeit prohibited, English translation of the whole Bible.

The rebellion in 1414 led by Sir John Oldcastle (also styled Lord Cobham), and its failure, proved damaging for the reputation of Lollardy. Born in 1378, Oldcastle became a close friend of the future King Henry V, mainly through their fighting together in wars. At the same time he maintained contacts with Lollards as well as with Hussites in Bohemia. Within the court and noble milieu within which early Lollardy drew some support, Oldcastle was a leading figure. In 1413 some Wycliffite tracts were discovered in his possession and, as a result, he was tried and condemned to death. However, he escaped from the Tower of London and began to plot a rebellion with the aim, according to later confessions, that one group would seize the royal family and another would take London. A small uprising took place in January 1414, but the project was discovered beforehand by the authorities and the revolt was easily suppressed. Oldcastle escaped but eventually he was captured in 1417 and executed. The resulting identification of Lollardy with insurrection – however unjustified among most of its supporters – damaged the credibility of the movement and appears to have lost it support, especially among the upper classes.

Despite this failure, recent research has indicated that Lollardy remained a significant force in England during the fifteenth century, its adherents coming mainly from the artisan and middle ranks of society. Most of our information comes from the records of their trials, and so presents the prosecution's picture of them rather than their own. Even so, the picture is of lively and knowledgeable individuals who formed Lollard communities mostly in the south, east and middle of England. William Sawtry, a priest from East Anglia, was the movement's first martyr. He was burnt at the stake as a relapsed heretic – on the grounds that he had been convicted twice – in London in 1401. Over a hundred more Lollards were executed during the fifteenth and early sixteenth centuries. In the repression, ecclesiastical and secular authorities cooperated closely, for heresy was seen as a threat to both Church and state.

The majority of known Lollards were men, as were most leaders of the movement, yet a number of women played significant roles. Whether Lollardy offered more religious opportunities to women than did orthodox Christianity, and was therefore attractive to them, is debated. Women, for example, numbered nine out of the 63 individuals who were prosecuted for heresy during the bishop of Norwich's extensive purge of his diocese in the years 1428–31. Several of them played important roles within the Lollard community. Margery Baxter of Martham was particularly remarkable. The articles to which she confessed are notable for their radical nature and social content: only the person who keeps God's commandments may be considered a Christian; the sacrament of confession is to be shunned because it implies lack of hope in God's mercy; pilgrimages should be made only to poor people; capital punishment and all other killing of humans is wrong; every good person is a priest; oaths are permissible only in a law court. Margery was also a vigorous proselytizer, who taught people sometimes alone and sometimes with her husband, both in their houses – while 'sitting and sewing by the fire' in midwinter, according to one witness, she put and answered many questions – and in her own home, preferably at night, it seems, or just as she met them.

The *Chronicon* ('Chronicle') of Henry Knighton, under the year 1391, mentions an intriguing half-case of an ordained woman, possibly a Lollard priest:

> There was a certain matron of the city of London who had an only daughter whom she instructed to celebrate Mass. She set up an altar with its furnishings in her secret chamber and got her daughter for many days to dress as a priest and go to the altar to celebrate Mass after her manner. But when she reached

the sacramental words, she prostrated herself before the altar and did not consecrate the sacrament, but rising completed all the rest of the Mass to the end with her mother assisting and attending her devotion.

News of the happenings leaked out through a neighbour who attended the service and the case came to the ears of the bishop of London. The daughter was discovered, her priestly tonsure was exposed and she was ordered to do penance. There were a few similar suggestions of the ordination of women, within a Lollard context, during the fifteenth century.

After the extensive Norwich trials of 1428–31, there was something of a lull in recorded prosecutions of Lollards through the middle decades of the fifteenth century. It is hard to say whether the gap represents a genuine decline in Lollard activity or, rather, inactivity – for whatever motive – on the part of the ecclesiastical authorities. It seems clear, however, that some of the ground was cut from under Lollardy by the 'orthodox' revival within the English Church during the fifteenth century, which involved both institutional reforms and encouragement given of various popular devotions. Prosecutions became more numerous again around 1490 and into the early sixteenth century. How far Wyclif and Lollardy led into and caused the English Reformation are questions that await the next volume of this History.

Jan Hus and the Hussites

Jan (or John) Hus was born of a peasant family at Husinec (hence his name 'Hus') in Bohemia (approximately the Czech Republic today) around 1372. He was a student and then a popular teacher at the university of Prague, which had been founded in 1348. Ordained priest in 1400, he was elected dean of the philosophy faculty in the following year. Alongside his university teaching, Hus soon became well known as a preacher at the Bethlehem Chapel, which was a large church with close links to the university. There he preached in the Czech language rather than in Latin or German. Some knowledge of John Wyclif's works had infiltrated from England into Bohemia at an early date – Nicholas Biceps, a Prague professor, for example, was arguing against Wyclif's Eucharistic beliefs already in 1381, while Wyclif was still alive – and it was promoted by links between the two countries partly resulting from the marriage in 1382 of King Richard II of England with Anne of Bohemia, sister of King Wenceslas IV of Bohemia. Hus was attracted to the teachings of Wyclif – especially those of a more moderate nature – regarding his criticisms of the excessive wealth and hierarchical structures of the Church as well as his emphasis on predestination and the Church of the elect. At first Hus received encouragement from the archbishop of Prague, Sbynek (or Sbinko) von Hasenberg, who appointed

him preacher at the archdiocesan synod in 1403 and supported his criticisms of pilgrimages to the popular shrine at Wilsnack in Germany, which
preserved three 'bleeding' hosts that had survived a fire in the local parish
church in 1383. Despite the university's condemnation in 1403 of various
propositions of Wyclif, Hus translated Wyclif's major work *Trialogus* into
Czech. Conflicts within the university partly reflected tensions between
the German professors, who had been in a majority and spoke and wrote
mainly in German and Latin, and younger professors, championed by Hus,
who promoted the Czech language. The rise of Czech nationalism from
around 1350 onwards, and the resulting distancing from German culture,
formed an integral part of the Hussite movement.

Hus's powerful sermons, especially those criticizing the low morals of
the clergy, most of which were preached in the Bethlehem Chapel, aroused
hostility. In 1407 he was denounced to Rome and Archbishop Sbynek,
following the orders of Pope Innocent VII, forbade him to preach. Hus
replied with a pamphlet justifying his criticisms. When the Council of Pisa
in 1409 deposed the two papal claimants, Gregory XII and Benedict XIII,
and elected Alexander V in their place, the university of Prague was divided
between Czechs who supported Alexander and Germans who continued
to support Gregory XII. In this division King Wenceslas of Bohemia
supported the Czechs, handing the university over to their control, with
Hus becoming its rector. Archbishop Sbynek, together with Alexander V
and his successor John XXIII, moved against Hus, condemning his propa-
gation of Wyclif's teachings. He was forbidden to teach or preach and was
eventually excommunicated. Wenceslas removed him from Prague for his
safety and he found refuge with his supporters among the Czech nobility in the countryside. In this semi-exile Hus wrote his major work *De
ecclesia* ('On the church'), which borrowed heavily from Wyclif. Eventually
he appealed to the forthcoming Council of Constance and arrived there,
with a safe-conduct, in November 1414. The safe-conduct, however, was
ignored by the council, and Hus was imprisoned, tried and condemned as
a Wycliffite, despite his protestations that his beliefs were not being fairly
represented. He was burnt at the stake, suffering the ordeal with great courage in July 1415. His close colleague, Jerome of Prague, met the same fate at
the council ten months later.

Jan Hus emerged within a context. Prague in the second half of the fourteenth century had seen several famous preachers who denounced abuses of
the clergy and religious orders as well as popular devotions that bordered on
the superstitious, and who emphasized Scripture as the norm for orthodox
belief and practice. Notable among them were Conrad Waldhauser – whose
German background warns against a simplistic Czech *versus* German expla-

nation of the Hussite movement – Jan Milic and Matthias of Janov. Other Germans, led by Nicholas of Dresden, had settled in Prague around 1411 and reinforced the radical party. Waldensian influences, too, were intermingled. Interest in Wyclif's teachings was shared by many others at Prague university besides Hus and predated Hus's arrival there as a student. Jerome of Prague had visited Oxford around 1398 and brought back to Bohemia copies of Wyclif's works *Dialogus* and *Trialogus*. Nevertheless it was Hus who provided the crucial catalyst for the movement, through his reputation in life and even more through his death.

When news of his death reached Bohemia, Hus quickly became a national hero. In a remarkable document that still survives, 452 of the nobility of Bohemia and neighbouring Moravia affixed their seals to a protest to the Council of Constance against his execution. The university of Prague declared him a martyr and soon his feast was fixed on the day of his death. Social and political grievances among the Czechs, especially regarding the wealth and alleged corruption of the clergy in Bohemia, and the dominant position of Germans in the country, overflowed into a widespread and partly violent movement of protest. The Four Articles of Prague were proclaimed in 1420 in which the Hussites, as they were now called, laid down a programme involving, first, secularization of Church lands and property; secondly, Utraquism (the word derives from the Latin *uterque*, meaning 'both'), whereby the laity would receive communion from the chalice as well as with the bread; thirdly, the use of the Czech language in the liturgy; fourthly, various elements of Church reform.

The Hussite movement was more united in opposition than in success. A basic division soon emerged between Utraquists (as the moderate party was called), that is, those who were largely satisfied with the Four Articles of 1420, together with greater autonomy from Rome, and those who wanted, in addition, more radical changes. The latter sought a form of Christianity that followed a more literal interpretation of the New Testament, as they saw it: there was no place for purgatory, for Masses and prayers for the dead, or for saints' relics; the Mass was to be transformed into a service of communion and scriptural preaching; the Bible was to replace Church authorities; various social and political doctrines were advocated, such as pacifism and common ownership of property, though on these issues there was less unanimity. A hill in southern Bohemia, which was renamed Mount Tabor, in memory of Mount Tabor in Galilee where Jesus was 'transfigured' in the presence of his disciples, became the focal point for the radical wing. On this and adjacent hills, meetings, sermons and services were held on a regular basis by the 'Taborites', as members of the radical wing came to be known.

The Taborites found in Jan Zizka a military leader of genius. Zizka, who had earlier been a professional solider in the royal service, managed to defeat various armies sent against the Taborites by the Emperor Sigismund (who had succeeded Wenceslas as king of Bohemia in 1419). Even after Zizka's death in 1424, the Taborites halted a succession of 'crusades' launched against them by Sigismund and other Catholic leaders. However, the balance of parties changed in 1433 when the Council of Basel reached agreement with the Utraquists in the 'Compactata of Prague': the chalice was permitted to the laity at communion and the confiscations of Church property that had taken place in the earlier stages of the Hussite movement were accepted. In the following year, an alliance of moderate Hussites and Catholic nobility, supported by the Emperor Sigismund, defeated the Taborites and other radicals at the Battle of Lipany. Thereafter the Taborites were militarily and politically a spent force and they finally surrendered in 1452 to George of Podebrady, the leading noble in Bohemia who was to succeed as king of Bohemia in 1458.

Despite this outward defeat, many of the ideas and concerns of the Taborites survived. Through them, as well as through the concessions made to the Utraquists by the Compactata of Prague, Bohemia remained a centre for theological debate and proposals for Church reform. Peter Chelcicky, (probably) a yeoman farmer in origin, who was at first attracted to the Taborites, emerged as the inspiration and leader of the Unitas Fratrum (Unity of the Brethren) movement in Bohemian and neighbouring Moravia in the second half of the fifteenth century. He was a pacifist, strongly opposed to the shedding of human blood, he urged manual work and shunned urban life and he encouraged the use of the vernacular language. He was a fierce critic of the evils of both Church and state, believing that poison had entered the Church when it was endowed by the Emperor Constantine. Property was to be held in common, at least for priests and lay preachers in the movement; the use of oaths was rejected, even in judicial proceedings; and the sufficiency of Scripture was emphasized. The likelihood of Waldensian influence upon his thought seems clear. Chelcicky was a prolific writer and maintained contacts with many individuals – dissenters and orthodox alike – who generally respected him even while not sharing his beliefs. George of Podebrady protected him. The movement attracted a sizeable following, especially in the countryside. However, when the Utraquists and Catholics reached another accord in 1484/85, accepting mutual toleration, the Unitas Fratrum was excluded from it.

The Hussite movement was intimately linked to events in Bohemia and Moravia. In these lands Hussitism, in its various forms, more or less achieved the status of being the majority religion, the only areas in late medieval Western Christendom where dissent from orthodoxy achieved this status. Some attempts were made by Hussites to evangelize in neighbouring Slavic lands as well as in Germany, but they met with relatively little success. When the Reformation began in Germany in the sixteenth century, it came as no surprise that the teachings of Martin Luther, as well as those of Anabaptists and other more radical groups, soon found receptive ears in Hussite lands, where many of the new teachings and practices had already been anticipated.

Inquisition and the prosecution of heresy

The Inquisition with a capital 'I' must be distinguished from inquisition. Inquiry (Latin, *inquisitio*) into religion, notably through the enforcement of emperor worship, was a feature of the Roman Empire into which Christianity was born and within which it lived for several centuries. Indeed it has been a feature of most societies, more or less pronounced. Christianity took over many features of the Roman Empire's procedures of religious inquiry when it emerged as the official religion of the empire in the early fourth century, enshrining them most notably in Book 16 of the Theodosian Code (438/39). In the following centuries uniformity of religion, including inquiry and coercion, were features, with varying degrees of intensity, of most communities that became predominantly Christian.

The beginning of the Inquisition (with a capital 'I') is usually dated to the reign of Pope Gregory IX, particularly to bulls issued by him in 1231, though his pontificate saw a crystallization of existing trends rather than a sudden change of policy. In a series of measures, the pope reserved the investigation of heresy in certain regions to officials appointed by him, thereby withdrawing the matter from the authority of both secular rulers and the bishops of the locality. Part of the context was the growing threat of the Cathar heresy in southern Europe. Dominican and Franciscan friars were usually appointed as the inquisitors, and gradually a body of recognized procedures and penalties grew up. To what extent the Inquisition was a permanent institution, rather than merely *ad hoc* commissions to individuals, is debated among historians. The commissions, from the thirteenth to the fifteenth century, were confined to certain countries, notably France, Germany and northern Italy. In many other countries, including England, the Inquisition never functioned and the prosecution of heresy remained in the hands of the local Church, principally the bishops but often including the secular authorities. In Spain a separate Inquisition, known as the Spanish Inquisition, was established at the end of our period, in 1478, approved by the pope but under royal control. It was only in the sixteenth century, during the reign of Paul III (1534–49), that the Inquisition became a clearly defined institution, centralized in Rome and with supreme authority (under the pope) in doctrinal matters throughout (Western) Christendom (with the partial exception of Spain and its colonies).

The use of torture by the Inquisition, to extract information and confessions, was authorized by Pope Innocent IV in 1252, albeit with restrictions. Penalties for those found guilty of heresy ranged, during the Middle Ages, from mild penances to imprisonment, beating, and the ultimate sanction, normally reserved for relapsed or obstinate offenders, of being handed over to the secular authorities, which usually meant death by burning at the stake. Church and state normally cooperated closely in the matter. While there was a genuine desire for the conversion of the sinner and mercy was often exercised – indeed the Inquisition protected many individuals from false accusations, especially women accused of witchcraft – nevertheless corporal punishment was frequent and many people were put to death. Partly there was a desire to protect other members of the Christian community from what was regarded as the infection of heresy, partly there was a sense that the Christian Gospel is self-evidently true, so that anyone who has seen the light and then rejects it must be gravely at fault.

The Inquisition was less active in the later Middle Ages, at least after about 1330, than it had been in the thirteenth century. The decline must be credited, in part, to the Inquisition's early success. The threat posed by Catharism was on the wane; so too, therefore, the need for inquiry and prosecution. Other authorities were also taking on the responsibilities. As mentioned, Jacques Fournier investigated the Cathars of Montaillou as bishop of Pamiers, not as an official of the Inquisition. It was in the same capacity as bishop that he examined the Waldensian leader Raymond de Sainte Foy at Carcassonne, though in this case he sat alongside a Dominican inquisitor. Waldensians continued to be brought before the Inquisition during the later Middle Ages, though often it was some other authority, such as the city government in Berne in 1399 (see p 143), that took the lead.

England and Bohemia were the most significant countries in terms of heresy in the later Middle Ages, yet it was authorities other than the Inquisition that tackled the matter in these countries, wholly so in England and for the most part in Bohemia (see pp 143–53). Several factors explain the situation in England. The country was largely untouched by Cathars and Waldensians, so there was little reason for the Inquisition to intervene in the thirteenth century. In addition, hostile feelings towards the French-dominated Avignon papacy would have made papal intervention through the Inquisition difficult in the early and mid-fourteenth century. The English bishops were capable and well organized, so when Wyclif and the Lollards appeared in the late fourteenth century, they were able to deal with the situation themselves, supported by the Crown and other secular authorities, without the need of outside assistance. The threat posed by Wyclif and the early Lollards, moreover, coincided with the papal schism and the conciliar movement, during which time a divided and weakened papacy had less authority to insist on its right to intervene. Even so, in the condemnation of John Wyclif's teaching, national and central authorities worked in harmony rather than in opposition: major contributions to the prosecution in England came, as we have seen, from both Pope Gregory XI – directly rather than through the Inquisition – and the Council of Constance.

The prosecution of heresy was the responsibility of a network of authorities and institutions, mostly working in cooperation with each other. The complexity within this network will be evident from the many instances of prosecution scattered through this book and briefly summarized in the introduction at the beginning of this chapter. Within this framework the Inquisition had some kind of an institutional role, though one that is difficult to define. For the most part it was called on to intervene when and where the traditional authorities proved deficient.

CHAPTER 6

Eastern Churches

The Orthodox Church

The Orthodox Church was the largest Church outside Western Christendom. With its capital city and patriarchal see in Constantinople (modern Istanbul), the Orthodox Church comprised various individual churches and Christian communities – stretching principally from Turkey in the south and various islands in the eastern Mediterranean, through Greece and the Balkans, and north to Russia and Lithuania – which were in communion with the patriarch of Constantinople and recognized his primacy (or seniority) among them. The background of the schism between the Orthodox and Catholic Churches, and various attempts to heal the schism, especially at the Council of Florence in 1439, have been mentioned (see pp xix, 23–5). The present chapter looks at institutional developments and spiritual life within Orthodoxy during the fourteenth and fifteenth centuries.

Geographical and political framework

The continuing advance of Islam into the Byzantine Empire and the fall of Constantinople in 1453 were crucial events for the Orthodox Church in the later Middle Ages. Already by 1300 the Byzantine Empire, which had once comprised the entire Eastern half of the Roman Empire, had been reduced to little more than western Turkey, the southern Balkans and parts of Greece. In the fourteenth century Muslim Turks advanced across the Bosphorus Sea and the eastern Mediterranean to capture the southern Balkans and most of Greece. Thereafter the Byzantine Empire was reduced to Constantinople and a small surrounding enclave of territory. The siege of Constantinople by Turkish forces in 1453 lasted almost two months and the eventual capture of the great city in May sealed the course of events that had been taking place over the preceding two centuries and more. Throughout the later Middle Ages, therefore, the Orthodox Church, in its original heartlands, was largely a community living under foreign occupation.

Several countries in south-east Europe that formed part of the Orthodox communion and lay wholly or partly outside the Byzantine Empire were conquered by the Turks in the fourteenth and fifteenth centuries: Bulgaria, Serbia, where the decisive battle was fought at Kosovo in 1389, and Romania. In these countries, too, the Orthodox Church came to live under foreign domination.

In Russia, the course of events moved in the opposite direction. In the principality of Muscovy/Moscow, which lay at the heart of the vast country that was to emerge as Russia, the suzerainty of the Mongol Tartars – who converted to Islam in the fourteenth century – lasted from 1237 to 1480. After the Battle of Kulikovo in 1380, when the grand-duke of Muscovy led the Russians to victory over the Tartars, this suzerainty was much weakened and by the middle of the fifteenth century it had become largely nominal. Russia had converted to Christianity between the ninth and eleventh centuries, principally through missionaries from the Byzantine Church, and the country continued to form an integral part of the Orthodox communion. However, due in part to its new-found freedom from Tartar domination, and in part to the capture of Constantinople by the Muslim Turks in 1453, the Russian Church was beginning to assume the role of leadership within Orthodoxy in the second half of the fifteenth century. Moscow would soon claim to be the 'third Rome', the centre of the Christian Church, following the schism of ancient Rome in 1054 and the fall of Constantinople, second Rome, in 1453.

Russia and its neighbour Lithuania, together with their capitals Moscow and Kiev, had struggled for leadership of the Orthodox Church within that region in the fourteenth century. In 1386 Jagiello, son of the pagan ruler of Lithuania, converted to Christianity and married the young Queen Jadwiga of Catholic Poland. For a time the two countries, Lithuania and Poland, were united. As a result of this union and other factors, Lithuania began to look west rather than east, and most parts of the country transferred their allegiance from the Orthodox to the Catholic Church.

Institutional developments

The Orthodox Church was, then, a federation of semi-independent Christian communities, or, to put the matter in more ecclesiastical language, a communion of autocephalous (autonomous) Churches. Not surprisingly, institutional developments within the various Churches of this communion varied considerably during the period, much influenced for many of them by the necessity of confronting Muslim conquest and occupation.

The most fraught situation occurred within Constantinople and the remnants of the Byzantine Empire. The Arsenite schism arose from conflicting appreciations of the patriarch Arsenius Autorianus (d.1273), who had clashed with the Byzantine Emperor Michael Palaeologus VIII.

The schism continued to fester during the two terms of office of the saintly patriarch Athanasius I (1289–93 and 1303–9), who abdicated as patriarch in 1293 in order to devote himself to the monastic life, and returned for a second term ten years later. The schism was eventually healed in 1310. In a startling ceremony, the new patriarch Niphon took from the hands of the dead Arsenius, whose skeleton had been disinterred and dressed up in patriarchal robes, a document, which had been composed for the purpose, absolving from excommunication and other censures all whom Arsenius had previously anathematized. Niphon was soon forced to abdicate and his talented successor John XIII Glykys (1315–19) had to resign on account of ill health. Thereafter, during the fourteenth and early fifteenth centuries, imperial interventions in patriarchal affairs, and many other tensions, meant that most patriarchs had difficult tenures of office. The Church was also disturbed internally by the Palamite controversy (see pp 160–1) and by different views on the advisability of reunion with Rome.

The fall of Constantinople in 1453 brought the trials of Muslim influence upon the Church. Sultan Mohammed II, the conqueror of the city, was generous and imaginative. On hearing that the patriarchate was vacant, he summoned the learned monk Gennadius (George Scholarios) and installed him on the patriarchal throne, investing him with the pastoral staff, just as Byzantine emperors had done formerly. Gennadius was a capable patriarch, though firmly opposed to reunion with Rome. Thereafter, Turkish protection and patronage of the patriarchs became a source of corruption and weakness more than of benefit. Following the good principles of the Koran, Christians were protected from physical persecution, but gradually they were reduced to second-class citizens. They paid heavy taxes, wore distinctive dress, were not allowed to serve in the army and were forbidden to marry Muslim women; they were not allowed to undertake missionary work and it was a crime to convert a Muslim to the Christian faith. There were many inducements for Christians to embrace Islam and already by 1500 the process of conversion was well under way.

The loss of freedom for Christians was experienced by other Orthodox countries that passed under Muslim rule. In Russia, on the other hand, the Church's freedom grew as the yoke of the Mongol Tartars was gradually thrown off. Archbishop Isidore, Metropolitan of Moscow, attended the Council of Florence in 1439 and was a strong supporter of the decree *Laetentur Caeli* proclaiming reunion between the Catholic and Orthodox Churches (see pp 23–4), but his church refused to accept his advice and firmly rejected the reunion. When he died in 1448 and a successor as metropolitan was sought, confirmation of the man chosen would normally have been sought from the patriarch in Constantinople. At the time, however, the patriarchal throne was vacant and officially the Church of Constantinople was still supporting *Laetentur Caeli*. As a result, the Russian bishops proceeded to elect a successor to Isidore without reference to Constantinople. Communion between the two Churches was restored in 1453 when Gennadius, the new patriarch in Constantinople, formally rejected the decree of reunion with Rome. But never again did the Russian Church seek confirmation from Constantinople when a new metropolitan of Moscow was elected. The change was indicative of the changed relationship between the two Churches, resulting from Russia's relative freedom from the Tartars and Constantinople's subjection to the Turks. Even so, relations remained cordial, symbolized in 1472 when Archduke Ivan III of Muscovy married Sophia, niece of the last Byzantine emperor.

Theology and spirituality

Despite – and no doubt partly because of – these many and varied trials, which arose principally from the advance of Islam, the Orthodox Church remained theologically and spiritually creative during the later Middle Ages.

Gregory Palamas and the hesychast controversy. The most lively theological controversy within the Byzantine Empire concerned hesychasm. The dispute concerned primarily the role of quietness and passivity in prayer: 'hesychasm' comes from the Greek word *hesychia*, meaning quietness or inner stillness. In the Eastern Church inner mystical prayer had a long tradition, which was associated especially with the monks of Mount Athos. Teaching in this form of prayer came to full expression in three writers of the fourteenth century: Gregory of Sinai, Nicephorus of Mount Athos and Gregory Palamas. Hesychasts, as they were called, attached great importance to the prayer of silence – to prayer that is stripped, as far as possible, of all images, words and discursive thinking. Words would be reduced to brief mantras, notably the short Jesus prayer, 'Lord Jesus Christ, Son of God, have mercy upon me (a sinner)', which is first found in the sixth- or seventh-century *Life of Abba Philemon*. Exponents of hesychasm attached much importance to bodily posture in prayer. Recommendations included that the head be bowed, eyes fixed on the heart, and breathing be controlled so as to keep time with the recitation of a short prayer. Through this union of mind and heart, they argued, prayer truly of the heart and therefore of one's whole being – lips, intellect, emotions, will and body – would result. Such prayer would eventually lead, in those specially chosen by God, to the vision of the Divine Light. This Light, it was believed, may be seen – even in the present life – with the eyes of the body, though it was first necessary for a person's physical faculties to be purified by God's grace and so rendered spiritual. Hesychasts believed the Divine Light to be identical with the Light that surrounded Jesus Christ at his 'Transfiguration' on Mount Tabor and to be, indeed, God's own eternal and uncreated 'energy'. They considered this Light and energy, rather than God's essence (as believed in Western theology), to be the object of the Beatific Vision – the 'vision' that the blessed in heaven will behold for all eternity.

Hesychast prayer found a fierce critic in Barlaam the Calabrian, a learned Orthodox monk originally from Italy. He ridiculed the claim that human eyes could behold the Divine Light and criticized the hesychast distinction between the 'energies' and 'essence' of God, arguing that it impaired the unity and simplicity of God. He propounded the otherness and unknowability of God in an extreme form. Gregory Palamas, a monk of Mount Athos, countered Barlaam's criticisms with skill and passion, principally in his work *Triads in Defence of the Holy Hesychasts*, which was published around 1338. He argued that the Incarnation demonstrates both the importance of our bodies (in prayer) and that God is not wholly unknowable. He emphasized the distinction – first drawn, as he noted, by Basil of Caesarea in the fourth century – between the 'energies' of God, principally his Light, which we can experience, and the essence of God, which remains wholly beyond and unknowable to us. Through experience of this Light, we share in God's life and indeed become fully redeemed and deified. Palamas's fellow monks on Mount Athos issued a statement in his support, known as the *Hagioritic Tome*. In 1341 the council of the patriarchate of Constantinople likewise took his side and condemned Barlaam. Three years later the opponents of Palamas gained the upper hand and secured his conviction for heresy and his excommunication, but the orthodoxy of his teaching was finally reaffirmed by two councils of Constantinople in 1347 and 1351. Thereafter hesychast teaching on prayer formed an integral part of the spirituality of the Orthodox Church.

Gregory Palamas was the most notable figure in the Orthodox Church of his time. Besides the *Triads*, he wrote a succinct exposition of theology, *One Hundred and Fifty Chapters*. He was consecrated archbishop of Thessalonica in 1347, though he was able to take possession of his see only in 1350. He was captured by Turks while travelling to Constantinople in 1354 and was held in captivity for more than a year. He died in 1359 and nine years later was declared a saint by the Orthodox Church.

Among moderate hesychasts, mention should be made of Nicholas Cabasilas (active 1345–65). It seems he remained a layman throughout his life and was on friendly terms with Gregory Palamas and defended him in a short work against Nicephoras Gregoras. While he valued mystical prayer, he emphasized the importance of the Church's liturgy and sacraments. His work *Life in Jesus Christ* explained how union with Christ was to be achieved principally through the sacraments of baptism, confirmation and Eucharist. His *Commentary on the Divine Liturgy* achieved classic status in the Orthodox Church as a study of the liturgy. Cabasilas showed how closely mysticism was linked to the liturgy and the sacraments, how mystical prayer does not bypass the normal institutional life of the Church. Mysticism for him always remained sacramental and ecclesial as well as centred on Christ. He was declared a saint by the Orthodox Church in 1983.

Matthew Blastares and canon law. Continuing interest in canon law in the Orthodox Church is best illustrated by the *Syntagma* of Matthew Blastares, a monk of Mount Athos who settled in Thessalonica. This large work, produced in 1335, provided a handbook of laws concerning the Church and the behaviour of Christians. Both concise and convenient, with topics arranged in alphabetical order, it achieved wide popularity particularly in the Balkans and Russia. The versatile Blastares wrote, in addition, treatises against the Western Church and against Jews and was (probably) the author of a collection of hymns. Another noted canonist, also from Thessalonica, was the judge Constantine Harmenopoulus, who compiled two works wholly or partly dedicated to canon law, *Hexabiblos* and a much used *Epitome* of canons.

Translations of Augustine, Boethius and Aquinas. Late medieval Byzantium was notable for translations into Greek of the two giants of Western theology, both of whom wrote in Latin: Augustine of Hippo and Thomas Aquinas. Selections from the works of Augustine, and possibly whole books, had been translated into Greek during his lifetime or soon afterwards. Thereafter his writings suffered a long period of benign neglect in the East. Then, around 1280, his most sublime theological work, *De trinitate*, was translated into Greek by Maximos Planudes. Planudes was born in Nicomedia and his father belonged to the court of Emperor Michael VIII. His translation may be seen as the fruit of improved relations between the Churches of East and West, resulting in part from the temporary reunion between the two Churches that was negotiated by Emperor Michael and Pope Gregory X at the Second Council of Lyons in 1274. The translation, which reached quite a wide readership in the Eastern Church, put Augustine on the map of Byzantine theology, even though he remained a controversial figure for Orthodoxy. It seems likely that Planudes' translation was known to Gregory Palamas and influenced him in his teaching on hesychast prayer.

Prochoros Kydones was another monk of Mount Athos who translated Augustine into Greek. In his case it was parts of three early works of Augustine, *De vera religione* ('True Religion'), *De beata vita* ('The Blessed Life'), and *De libero arbitrio* ('Free Will'), and a collection of eight letters. Kydones met a notably different fate in comparison with Gregory Palamas and Maximos Planudes. Partly because of his perceived infatuation with Augustine, he was put on trial, condemned and excommunicated by his fellow monks of Mount Athos, as well as by the patriarch of Constantinople, Philotheos Kokkinos, and his teachings were anathematized.

In addition, fourteenth-century Byzantium saw translations into Greek of Boethius's *De trinitate*, which was translated by Manuel Calecas, and of Thomas Aquinas's *Summa contra gentiles* and a large part of his *Summa theologiae*, which were translated by Demetrios Kydones (1324–97). The latter was a distinguished scholar in his own right and the younger brother of Prochoros Kydones, the translator of Augustine. Demetrios was a confidant of the Byzantine emperors John V and John VI. He converted to Catholicism in 1357 and seems to have been partly responsible for the conversion of Emperor John V, who converted to Catholicism while in exile in Rome in 1369.

Differing attitudes towards reunion with Rome. We have seen how the reunion between the Churches of East and West, which was proclaimed at the Council of Florence in 1439, failed to materialize (see p 25). There was, nevertheless, significant support for reunion with Rome within the Byzantine Empire in the century or so before the council. It would be wrong to see all the efforts at reunion between the two Churches during the later Middle Ages as doomed to failure from the outset: at least, the probability or inevitability of the failure was not obvious to people at the time. Within Byzantium there existed a wide range of attitudes. Pro-unionists were led by the Emperor Michael VIII at the Second Council of Lyons 1274 and by Emperor John VIII at the Council of Florence in 1439. Both men might be described as pragmatic pro-unionists, who believed that reunion could be achieved without the Eastern Church sacrificing its theological and liturgical patrimony. Patriarch Joseph of Constantinople, who died during the Council of Florence, and the scholar Bessarion, who attended the same council, supported the union on more theological grounds. Bessarion subsequently converted to Catholicism and was created a cardinal, and there were other prominent converts to Catholicism, such as the Emperor John V and Demetrios Kydones, as just mentioned. On the other hand, there were hardline opponents of reunion, such as Bishop Mark of Ephesus at the Council of Florence, and Metrophanos who succeeded Joseph as patriarch of Constantinople soon after the end of the same council. Monastic communities, which were influential in society and public opinion, were largely and sometimes vociferously opposed to reunion. In the middle, among less well-known and high-profile figures, there evidently existed a wide range of beliefs and approaches and no doubt plenty of indifference to the possibility of reunion – it was not an issue to which most people gave frequent attention. Nevertheless the decisive rejection by the Orthodox Church of the reunion negotiated by its leaders at the Council of Florence in 1439, despite the quite generous terms of the settlement and despite the mortal peril from the advance of Islamic forces in which Constantinople stood at the time, shows that opposition to reunion – or, more positively, belief in the values and autonomy of Orthodoxy – was strong and widespread.

Despite the prevailing opposition to formal reunion with Rome – at least to the terms offered by the leadership of the Catholic Church – contacts and mutual concern between the two Churches remained quite strong during the later Middle Ages. The serious and continuing negotiations for reunion, right up to the Council of Florence, are one proof of this interest; the translations into Greek of Western works of theology are another; there were many contacts at less official or public levels.

Russia. The period 1350 to 1550 was a golden age for the Orthodox Church in Russia, notably in the realms of spirituality, missionary zeal and religious art. The decline of Tartar suzerainty over Russia, already mentioned, and the Church's leading role in the opposition to Tartar rule, formed the context for this remarkable renaissance.

Already in the thirteenth century, Russian missionaries were notable for their work of evangelization among the Tartars and the pagan tribes of the north and north-east of the vast continent. In the fourteenth century the most remarkable figure was St Stephen, Bishop of Perm (1340–96), who worked among the Zyrian tribes. Famous for his holiness, he also strove for inculturation. He learned the local languages and used the native runes in his writings. An icon painter of note, he portrayed a God of beauty as well as of truth. He worked away from regions that were affected by Russian military and political conquests, thereby both preserving the purity of evangelization and avoiding many cultural compromises.

Sergius of Radonezh (1315–92) is widely regarded as the greatest national saint of Russia. Of noble birth, he and his brother Stephen became monks and together founded the monastery of Holy Trinity in the forests to the north of Moscow. Sergius was elected superior of the community in 1334 and was restored to this position after a period of conflict with his brother and resulting exile. The monastery soon became the most famous reli-

gious centre in Russia. It was responsible for the foundation of some 40
other monasteries during Sergius's lifetime and another 30 soon after his
death; thus it formed the spearhead and model in the monastic revival in
late medieval Russia, after the destruction of many monasteries during the
Tartar invasions of the country. Most of the monasteries were founded in
the forests of north Russia, as far as the White Sea and the Arctic Circle.
Since towns often grew up around them, the monasteries proved crucial
to the spread of Orthodox Christianity and Russian civilization into these
remote regions. In his life and teaching Sergius proclaimed the importance of prayer, work and community life, and he forbade his monks to beg.
Prayer was both liturgical, following the services of the Church's liturgy,
and private: Sergius was renowned as a mystic. His lifestyle was simple
and austere: he dressed as a peasant and even while abbot he looked after
the kitchen garden. Yet he played a major role in the political and social
life of his time, intervening in several disputes between Russian princes in
order to prevent civil wars. He encouraged Archduke Dmitri of Muscovy
in his resistance to the Tartars, and Dmitri's crucial victory over them at
the Battle of Kulikovo in 1380 was attributed to his advice and prayers. In a
remarkable way he combined the spiritual and social dimensions of monasticism – a mystic who yet encouraged close cooperation between Church
and state. He declined the offer to become archbishop of Moscow in 1378.
His life and visions were recorded by his contemporary, the monk Epipha-
nius. Sergius was buried in the church of Holy Trinity monastery, where his
tomb quickly became a centre of pilgrimage. Already venerated as a saint in
his lifetime, he was soon canonized by the Russian Church and proclaimed
patron of Moscow and later of all Russia.

Other notable monastic saints were Nilus of Sora (Nil Sorsky, 1433–1508)
and Joseph of Volokolamsk (1439–1515). Nilus was a monk of an eremitical community in the forests beyond the Volga river; Joseph was abbot of
the large and wealthy monastery of Volokalamsk. The two men clashed
openly at a synod of the Russian Church in 1503. Nilus spoke out against the
ownership of lands by monasteries, which at the time owned a huge proportion of the land in Russia, perhaps as much as one-third of it, while Joseph
replied in defence of monastic lands. The majority at the synod agreed with
Joseph, but Nilus had some support at the synod and more in the country. During the sixteenth century these differences developed into a major
controversy between those (called 'Possessors') who supported monastic
ownership of lands, and those ('Non-Possessors') who agreed rather with
Nilus. Evidently the dispute had been simmering in the later Middle Ages
and it represented two differing approaches to monasticism. Abbot Joseph
and the Possessors supported an ideal of organized and disciplined commu-

nities of monks, with emphasis on liturgical observance, social service and some political involvement. Nilus and the Non-Possessors, on the other hand, stressed contemplative and ascetic ideals, more in line with the traditions of Mount Athos and under the influence of Byzantine hesychasm. Nilus himself had lived for a while as a monk on Mount Athos and knew the hesychast tradition at first hand. In the fourteenth century Sergius of Radonezh appeared to have synthesized the two approaches, but the cracks were developing in the fifteenth century and they became open fissures afterwards. Nevertheless the Russian Church showed itself broad-minded in canonizing as saints both Nilus and Joseph and thereby recognizing the validity of both ideologies of monasticism.

The two centuries beginning around 1350 were a Golden Age in Russia for religious art. During this time the iconographic traditions of Byzantium were developed further by Russian painters. Monks of Holy Trinity and its many daughter monasteries were specially active and qualified in this regard. Appropriately, perhaps the finest and best known of all Orthodox icons, the Holy Trinity by Andrei Rublev (1370–1430), was painted in honour of St Sergius and placed in his monastery at Radonezh.

Bulgaria, Serbia and Romania. Monasticism flourished in these countries in the later Middle Ages, even though they were increasingly subject to Islamic government. The influence of Byzantine monasticism, especially of Mount Athos, remained strong and the tradition of hesychastic prayer was influential in some communities. In Bulgaria the best-known monasteries were Paroria, which had been founded by Gregory of Sinai in the 1330s and became an international centre in the Orthodox world, attracting disciples to the life of prayer, and Kilifarevo in the mountains near Trnovo, which was founded in the mid-fourteenth century by Theodosius of Trnovo with the support of the Bulgarian tsar. Serbia was notable for its royal foundations and in the late fourteenth century Nicodemus, who was half Serb and half Greek, and who had been a monk in the Serbian community of Chilandari on Mount Athos, was responsible directly, or through his inspiration, for the foundation of various monasteries in the Wallachia region of the country, most notably the monastery at Tirmana. The patriarchate of Serbia was created within the Orthodox communion in 1346, and this new status of the Serbian national Church was recognized by Constantinople in 1375.

Conclusion. The above treatment of the Orthodox Church has been sketchy. Something has been said about Christianity in the remnants of the Byzantine Empire and in Russia, though even in these regions the focus has been upon the institutional Church and monasticism; little has been said about the religion of the laity. For other countries the story has been limited to the main events affecting the outward development of the Church. Part of the problem is the perennial one: lack of relevant evidence – especially relating to popular religion – about communities that do not enjoy freedom of religion. In such circumstances, evidence of religious practice is less likely to be recorded, and more liable to destruction, than in communities that are in control of their social and political environment. This problem most obviously affects our knowledge of the Orthodox Church in countries that lay under Muslim rule. The second difficulty relates to the current state of research. Only recently, and only gradually, are the relevant archives and publications of Eastern Europe and Western Asia becoming extensively known to Western scholars, especially in material relating to popular religion. Within 20 years, maybe sooner, the present short section should be rewritten in a much better and fuller form.

Other Eastern Churches

Several major and enduring schisms within the Christian community predated the rupture between the Orthodox and Catholic Churches in 1054. During the later Middle Ages, therefore, the resulting Churches were in schism – or out of communion – with both the Orthodox and the Catholic Church. They constituted important communities within Christianity. The principal groups numbered five: the so-called Nestorian Church, which emerged from Nestorius's rejection of the Council of Ephesus in 431 on the grounds that it paid insufficient attention to the humanity of Christ; and four Churches that had rejected the Council of Chalcedon in 451 on the opposite grounds that it paid too much attention to the humanity of Christ, too little to his divinity, namely the Armenian, Syrian (or Jacobite), Coptic and Ethiopian Churches.

Asia and the Nestorian Church

The Nestorian Church – which was also called the East Syrian or Chaldean Church on account of its early centre at Edessa in eastern Syria – spread rapidly and widely, its missionaries reaching India and China at an early date. The rise of Islam subsequently drove a wedge between the Church's original territories bordering the Mediterranean and its new lands in the east. The branches became severed from the roots. As a result, by the later Middle Ages, Nestorianism (as it may be called for convenience, though its disciples regarded themselves rather as belonging to the true and orthodox church) appears to have constituted a number of somewhat fragmented communities, with some traditional loyalty to Nestorius, rather than a coherent Church; though it is difficult to construct a true picture because so little of the surviving evidence comes from the Nestorian side.

The Western Church made a number of vigorous and imaginative attempts to establish contact with Nestorian communities in various parts of Asia. The attempts made before 1300 have been outlined in the previous volume of this History. Most of our information about these communities, as well as the fragile establishment of the Catholic Church in the same regions, after 1300 just as before, comes largely from the accounts written about them by Western missionaries.

In the Crimea and its neighbourhood, Franciscan missionaries had established a number of houses in the late thirteenth century, and in the early fourteenth century they baptized the Khan Toqtai (1300–12) and several members of his household. Franciscan missionaries were also working among the Bashkirs, but the conversion of the Khan Uzbek (1312–40) to Islam halted their endeavours. Nestorian Christians had generally enjoyed toleration and even favour within the domains of the Mongol Tartars, but the conversion of the latter to Islam in the fourteenth century made their situation much more precarious.

A fleeting reunion between Rome and the Nestorian Church in Iraq may have occurred in the early fourteenth century. The Nestorian patriarch Jahballaha III of Baghdad sent an embassy to Rome and in 1304, in a letter addressed to Pope Benedict XI, professed readiness to accept papal primacy and to enter into union with Rome. There appears, however, to have been no follow-up. During the fourteenth century Islamic rule brought persecution and martyrdom to both Catholic and Nestorian Christians, though the Dominicans and Franciscans were able to maintain a number of friaries in the region.

Marco Polo (1254–1324) of Venice, the most famous traveller of the Middle Ages, gave some account of Christianity in China, revealing the survival of the Nestorian Church in the vast country and the desire for Western missionaries. According to his *Travels* (or *Book of Marvels*), his father and uncle visited the Great Khan Kublai (1260–94), who asked them to request the pope to send him a hundred Christian missionaries. The papacy responded with several missions. The first to arrive was led by the Franciscan friar John of Montecorvino, who delivered a letter from the pope to Kublai's successor Timur (1294–1307) and then began his apostolate among the Nestorian Christians in northern Tenduc. Opposition from the Nestorians persuaded him to move to Khanbaliq (later Beijing). There he was able to establish a sizeable Christian community of Mongols and Chinese, assisted by his Franciscan colleagues Arnold of Cologne and, later, Odoric of Pordenone, who wrote a graphic account of his three years in Khanbaliq. In a letter of 1305 John recounted the successes of the mission. He emphasized the importance of catechetical and liturgical formation – he had translated the Psalms and the New Testament into a native language (probably Uighur, or Mongol written in Uighur characters) and trained a boys' choir that delighted the khan – and then he asked for assistance. In reply, Pope Clement V named him archbishop of Khanbaliq in 1307 and sent six bishops who were to consecrate him as archbishop and then to take up dioceses that John was to assign to them. He directed the mission until his death in 1328, by which time there were said to be some 30,000 Christians in China.

The conversion of the Mongols to Islam, completed under Tamerlane (c.1357–1405), proved burdensome for both Nestorians and Catholics. In China, the situation of Christians became very difficult after the nationalistic Ming dynasty came to power in 1368. There, a Venetian visitor in 1473 found neither churches nor Christians – maybe an exaggeration but nevertheless indicative of the dire situation. Nestorians remained in Persia, as witnessed by John of Montecorvino who visited the region on his way to India and on to China. In India he visited the Christians in the south-west of the country in 1292, as did the Dominican friar Jourdan Catalani some 30 years later. Both men encountered there a vigorous Christian community, which had Nestorian links inasmuch as the head of the Church and sometimes other bishops were sent to the community by the Nestorians of Edessa. Indeed it was in this region that the Nestorian Church was to make its most lasting impression.

Armenian Church and reunion

Partly owing to internal wars in which the country was involved at the time, Armenia did not send representatives to the Council of Chalcedon in 451. As a result of this fateful absence, the Armenian Church never recognized the teaching of the council – which was to prove crucial to the dogmatic development of both the Orthodox and Catholic Churches – and formally rejected it in the year 555, on the grounds of its non-representation at the council. Subsequently, during the Middle Ages, the Armenian Church sought to protect its independence from the ecclesiastical and political ambitions of Constantinople and the advances of Muslim Turks and Tartars. One of the results in the later Middle Ages was a certain rapprochement with Rome on the part of western Armenia, which constituted a semi-autonomous kingdom and was commonly called Cilicia or Lesser Armenia.

A synod at Sis in Cilicia in 1307 accepted in principle reunion with Rome, despite strong opposition from some of the clergy. Cordial relations between Lesser Armenia and the papacy continued during the reign of Pope John XXII, who gave encouragement to a synod to discuss reunion which was convened by King Oshin at Adana in 1316. Another synod at Sis in 1346 pronounced in favour of reunion with Rome, even though Greater Armenia remained opposed to the proposal. Two events then intervened. First, the Black Death struck Armenia with particular ferocity in 1349. Secondly, Cilicia effectively lost its independence in 1375 and was ravaged by the Tartar army of Tamerlane. Thereafter it was a country under foreign occupation.

The prospect of reunion with the Catholic Church resurfaced in the fifteenth century and climaxed at the Council of Florence in 1439. Negotiations for the reunion had begun at the Council of Basel in 1434 but they were interrupted by the tensions between the council and Eugenius IV. Eugenius resumed the negotiations when he transferred the council to Florence. A delegation from the Armenian Church, including representatives from the Church's widespread diaspora beyond Armenia, reached the city in 1439. In the resulting decree of reunion, *Decretum pro Armenis*, the substantial concessions came from the Armenian side: notably, recognition of the Council of Chalcedon and later ecumenical councils, and of medieval Catholic teaching on the seven sacraments. Even so, there was generous recognition of the relative autonomy of the Armenian Church for those who accepted the reunion. Initially there was some acceptance of the decree in Lesser Armenia but much less in Greater Armenia. Any likelihood of full corporate reunion quickly disappeared, and further possibilities were overshadowed by the Muslim occupation of most of the country, though a small minority of the Armenian Church has remained in communion with Rome ever since.

Syrian or Jacobite Church

This Church was sometimes called the Syrian Church inasmuch as it derived from the rejection of the Council of Chalcedon by a substantial group of Christians in Syria, sometimes the 'Jacobite Church' after Jacob Baradeus, the community's brilliant organizer and missionary in the sixth century. The Church continued to expand after Baradeus, mainly eastwards, into Mesopotamia and Persia, Afghanistan, Turkestan and Sinkiang, but also westwards as far as Cyprus. It excelled in organization with a network of dioceses and there developed a liturgy based on Syriac, which was the common language of most of its members. The Church played a large part in the renaissance of Syriac scholarship in theology, philosophy, history and science – Bar Hebraeus was a notable polymath scholar in the late thirteenth century. However, Tartar invasions led by Tamerlane in the late fourteenth century proved very damaging. Many churches and monasteries were destroyed, organizational structures were dislocated and the number of faithful was greatly reduced. About the same time, internal divisions, including a schism lasting from 1364 to 1394, further weakened the Church's membership and integrity.

The fifteenth century brought the reunion of a section of the Syrian Church with the Catholic Church towards the end of the Council of Florence (by which time the council had moved to Rome). It followed the reunions with the Orthodox and Armenian Churches at the same council. Archbishop Abdala of Edessa was sent to Rome by the head of the Syrian Church, Patriarch Ignatius, to discuss the prospect of reunion and after long discussion the decree of reunion, *Multa et admirabilia*, was proclaimed in September 1444. Abdala agreed to accept, on behalf of the patriarch, the teaching of the Catholic Church, including that of Christ's two natures, human and divine, which had been proclaimed by the Council of Chalcedon. The fruits of the decree, however, were disappointing. Only a small section of the Syrian Church accepted the reunion and the mainstream of the Church continued along its separate path.

Coptic and Ethiopian Churches

The Coptic and Ethiopian Churches should be taken together since they were so closely linked. The Coptic Church – meaning principally the Church of Egypt – had been a powerhouse of the early Church, providing many of the most eminent theologians, a tradition of martyrs, and leadership for the whole Church in the ascetical and monastic movements. Refusal to accept the decision of the Council of Chalcedon meant the Church there gradually moved into schism with the rest of Christendom. Two centuries later the Arab conquest of Egypt gradually led to the conversion of the large majority of the population to Islam. By the later Middle Ages, Christians were few in number and the Church remained out of communion with both Rome and Constantinople. The Church of Ethiopia, which had started as the junior partner to the Egyptian Church, came to assume an almost equal, even senior role in the partnership.

Ethiopia had been evangelized by missionaries from Egypt, and the tradition whereby the principal bishop of Ethiopia was appointed by the patriarch of Alexandria in Egypt, and remained subordinate to him, continued throughout the Middle Ages. The Ethiopian Church followed the Coptic Church in its rejection of the Council of Chalcedon. However, whereas Egypt and neighbouring lands were conquered by the Muslim Arabs and largely converted to Islam, Ethiopia to the south retained its political independence and Christian heritage through the medieval period. Indeed the period 1270 to 1530 is regarded as a Golden Age for Christianity in Ethiopia.

The era began with the arrival on the Ethiopian throne of Yikunno Amlak in 1270. He had been educated by monks and he proved to be both an able ruler and a promoter of Christianity in his realm. His grandson Amda Siyon (1314–44) continued in a similar vein and expanded the kingdom both to the south-west and towards the coast. Under him was written the national epic *Epos Kebra Nagast* ('The Glory of Kings'), which traced his dynasty back to Solomon. The zenith of Ethiopian Christian culture was reached under Zara Yakob (1434–68), who sought to make his kingdom both thoroughly Ethiopian and truly Christian. He imposed Christianity on the peoples of the recently acquired territories, promoted monasticism and Christian literature and promulgated a law code that included monogamy.

The period witnessed two major monastic personalities who led reforms of monasticism in the nation, which in turn contributed much to the religious revival of the time. Takla Haymanot (1215–1313) was responsible for the building of Debra Libanos, which became the leading monastery in the country, and for composing its monastic Rule. The second leader was Ewostatewos (1273–1352), whose principal monastery was Debra Maryam in Tigre province. He was a controversial figure inasmuch as he urged observance of the Sabbath in addition to Sunday. When he failed to get the approval of the patriarch of Alexandria, he went into exile in Armenia and died there 14 years later. For a long time his disciples were persecuted and excluded from the priesthood, but eventually Zara Yakob rehabilitated them and recognized their Sabbath observance as a specific Ethiopian characteristic. The monks of both these two traditions contributed much to the work of evangelization in the country, in both its original heartlands and the newly acquired territories, and to the development of the Ethiopic liturgy. The liturgy continued to be celebrated in Ge'ez, the ancient language of the country.

Zara Yakob sent a delegation to the Council of Florence and a formula of reunion was reached at the council in 1442. Subsequently, however, the terms of the reunion did not meet with widespread approval in Ethiopia and, as a result, only a small fraction of the Ethiopian Church entered into communion with Rome.

CHAPTER 7

Christendom and the Non-Christian World

This chapter explores the attitudes of Christians, principally those living in Western Christendom, towards followers of the other two major world religions that impinged upon them, Judaism and Islam, as well as towards the pagan subcultures that lay within the boundaries of Christendom.

Tolerance of other religions had a place, yet it would be wrong to regard it as an absolute ideal in a modern sense, either among Christians or among followers of other faiths. For the Christian leadership, certainly, a paramount obligation was to preach the Gospel and thereby bring good news to the non-Christian world. Such zeal, and the accompanying hard work and attention to detail, were well expressed by Decree 24 of the Council of Vienne (1311–12), even though its recommendations proved too demanding for their full implementation. The decree, which was addressed in the name of the pope, using the papal 'we', declared as follows:

> Among the cares lying heavily on us there is one on which we reflect constantly: how we may lead the erring into the way of truth and win them for God with the help of his grace. ... We are in no doubt that to attain our desire, the word of God should be fittingly explained and preached to great advantage. ... We desire earnestly that holy Church should be well supplied with Catholic scholars acquainted with the languages most in use by unbelievers. These scholars should know how to train unbelievers in the Christian way of life, and to make them members of the Christian body through instruction in the faith and reception of sacred baptism.

> In order, then, that skill in these languages be attained by suitable instruction, we have stipulated, with the approval of the sacred council, that schools be established for the following languages wherever the Roman Curia happens to reside and also at Paris, Oxford, Bologna and Salamanca. That is, we decree that in each of these places there should be Catholic scholars with adequate knowledge of Hebrew, Arabic and Chaldaic. There are to be two experts for each language in each place. They shall direct the schools, make faithful

translations of books from these languages into Latin, and teach others those languages with all earnestness, passing on a skilled use of the language, so that after such instruction others may, God inspiring, produce the harvest hoped for, propagating the saving faith among the heathen peoples.

The salaries and expenses of these lecturers in the Roman Curia will be provided by the Apostolic See, those at Paris by the king of France, and those at Oxford, Bologna and Salamanca by the prelates, monasteries, chapters, convents, exempt and non-exempt colleges, and rectors of churches, of England, Scotland, Ireland and Wales, of Italy, and of Spain, respectively. (*Decrees*: 380–1)

Judaism

Judaism long predated Christianity; indeed Christianity grew out of Judaism. Communities of Jews were to be found in many towns in Europe during the early Middle Ages. Relations between Christians and Jews in Western Christendom, which had never been easy but had experienced quite a warm *convivencia* during the eleventh and early twelfth centuries, deteriorated sharply during the century or so before the beginning of our period. The Fourth Lateran Council of 1215 and other thirteenth-century legislation, both ecclesiastical and civil, had restricted the freedom of Jews in a variety of ways and they were subjected to burdensome taxes. In various towns there were pogroms of Jews, often sparked off by accusations that Jews had tortured and murdered a boy while re-enacting the sufferings and crucifixion of Christ. Jews were expelled from various countries in the late thirteenth century, most notably from England and France, on the orders of their respective kings, in the 1290s.

The later Middle Ages witnessed further deterioration in the situation. The fifteenth century saw more massacres of Jews accused of killing a Christian boy, notably those focusing on the deaths of Andrew of Rinn in 1462 and Simon of Trent in 1475. Other assaults followed discoveries of Jews allegedly desecrating the Eucharistic host, as portrayed in ghoulish detail in a series of six paintings by Paolo Uccello. Pogroms also occurred in the aftermath of the Black Death in 1347–50, which was widely attributed to the poisoning of wells by Jews – at Basel in Switzerland, and Speyer, Worms, Cologne, Mainz and other places in Germany. Later, various towns and principalities in Germany followed the example of the kingdoms of France and England in expelling Jews: Strasbourg in 1368, the Palatinate in 1390, Freiburg in 1401 and 1424, Speyer in 1405 and 1435, Trier in 1418, Mainz in 1420 and several times later, and Cologne in 1423. Altogether, many Jews were expelled from the Rhineland and southern Germany. In England the only Jews who were officially allowed to remain were those who converted to

Christianity; a house for such converts was established in London. In Spain the *Reconquista* of the country brought many hardships to the substantial Jewish population. Many were pressurized into converting to Christianity and then lived under suspicion, while many others left Spain altogether. In Italy Jews remained relatively secure. A substantial number of the Jews expelled from various countries found refuge in Eastern Europe, notably Poland. On balance, however, the number of Jews in Western Christendom declined further in the later Middle Ages, falling from the peak of perhaps half a million, or 1 per cent of the total population, in the mid-thirteenth century.

The Council of Basel's 'Decree on Jews and neophytes' (7 September 1434) provides a remarkably informative statement of the attitude of Church authorities, at the highest level of a general council, towards Jews. The decree addresses 'other infidels' as well as Jews, but evidently it had the latter principally in mind:

> This holy council, following in the footsteps of our saviour Jesus Christ, desires in deepest charity that all may acknowledge the truth of the Gospel and thereafter abide in it faithfully. By these salutary instructions it desires to provide measures whereby Jews and other infidels may be converted to the orthodox faith and converts may remain steadfast in it. The council therefore decrees that all diocesan bishops should depute persons well trained in Scripture, several times a year, in the places where Jews and other infidels live, to preach and expound the truth of the Catholic faith in such a way that the infidels who hear it can recognize their errors. They should compel infidels of both sexes who have reached the age of discretion to attend these sermons under pain both of being excluded from business dealings with the faithful and of other apposite penalties. But the bishops and the preachers should behave towards them with such charity as to gain them for Christ not only by the manifestation of the truth but also by other kindnesses. The council decrees that Christians, of whatever rank or status, who in any way impede the attendance of Jews at these sermons, or who forbid it, automatically incur the stigma of being supporters of unbelief.

> Since this preaching will be more fruitful in proportion to the linguistic skill of the preachers, we decree that there must be faithful observance of the constitutions of the council of Vienne, which ordered the provision in certain universities of teachers of Hebrew, Arabic, Greek and Chaldean languages [see pp 173–4]. So that this may be more adhered to, we wish that the rectors of these universities should add to what they swear to on taking office, that they will endeavour to observe the said constitution. It should be clearly laid down, at the councils of the provinces in which these universities are situated, that the teachers of the said languages are to be adequately compensated.

Furthermore, renewing the sacred canons, we command both diocesan bishops and secular powers to prohibit in every way Jews and other infidels from having Christians, male or female, in their households and services, or as nurses of their children; and Christians from joining them in festivities, marriages, banquets or baths, or in much conversation, and from taking them as doctors or agents of marriages or officially appointed mediators of other contracts. They should not be given other public offices, or admitted to any academic degrees, or allowed to have on lease lands or other ecclesiastical rents. They are forbidden to buy ecclesiastical books, chalices, crosses and other ornaments of churches under pain of the loss of the object, or to accept them in pledge under pain of the loss of the money that they lent. They are to be compelled, under severe penalties, to wear some garment whereby they can be clearly distinguished from Christians. In order to prevent too much intercourse, they should be made to dwell in areas, in the cities and towns, which are apart from the dwellings of Christians and as far distant as possible from churches. On Sundays and other solemn festivals they should not dare to have their shops open or to work in public. (*Decrees*: 483–4)

Attention then turned to those who converted to Christianity:

If any of them [Jews and other infidels] wishes to be converted to the Catholic faith, all his goods, both movable and immovable, shall remain intact and unharmed in his possession. ... Bishops should exhort Christians to aid these converts and should support them from the income of churches, as far as they can, and from what passes through their hands for the benefit of the poor, and they should defend them with fatherly solicitude from detraction and invective.

Since by the grace of baptism converts have been made 'fellow citizens with the saints and members of the household of God' [Ephesians 2.19], and since regeneration in the spirit is of far greater worth than birth in the flesh, we determine by this edict that converts should enjoy the privileges, liberties and immunities of the cities and localities in which they are regenerated by holy baptism, which others obtain merely by reason of birth and origin. Let the priests who baptize them and those who receive them from the sacred font carefully instruct them, both before and after their baptism, in the articles of the faith and the precepts of the new Law and the ceremonies of the Catholic Church. Both they and the bishops should strive that, at least for a long time, they do not mingle much with Jews or infidels lest, as occurs with convalescents from illness, a small occasion may make them fall back into their former perdition.

Since experience shows that social communication between converts renders them weaker in our faith, and has been found to damage much their salvation, this holy council exhorts local ordinaries to exercise care and zeal that they are married to born-Christians, in so far as this seems to promote an increase of the faith. Converts should be forbidden, under severe penalties, to bury the dead according to the Jewish custom or to observe in any way the Sabbath and other solemnities and rites of their old sect. Rather, they should frequent our churches and sermons, like other Catholics, and conform themselves in everything to Christian customs. Those who show contempt for the above should be delated to the diocesan bishops or inquisitors of heresy by their parish priests, or by others who are entrusted by law or ancient custom with inquiring into such matters, or by anyone else at all. Let them be so punished, with the aid of the secular arm in need be, as to give an example to others. (*Decrees*: 484–5)

The decree reveals a blend of kindness and severity, persuasion and intolerance – a strange mixture of motives. There was the desire for the conversion of Jews to Christianity, but pain and bewilderment too that so few Jews were seeing the light – revealing a sense that Christianity was self-evidently true and therefore Jews must be culpable in blinding themselves to the obvious. There was a certain fear of Jews and recognition of their intelligence and sophistication, hence the prohibitions against converse and mixing with Jews on the part of both native Christians and Jewish converts to Christianity; also a sense of the inferiority of Christians, in various practical ways, with respect to Jews.

The period saw plenty of polemical literature against Jews. For example, *Pharetra fidei Catholicae contra Iudaeos* ('Quiver of the Catholic Faith against Jews') written by the Dominican friar Theobald of Paris; *Tractatus contra perfidos Iudaeos* ('Treatise against the Perfidious Jews') by the German Dominican Peter Schwarz (d.1481); and *Fortalitium fidei* ('Fortress of the Faith') by the Spanish Franciscan convert from Judaism, Alfonso de Spina (d.1491). Raymond Lull's (d.1315) *Liber de gentili et tribus sapientibus* ('The Gentile and Three Wise Men') was exceptional in that it carefully avoided invective against Jews. There were in addition popular preachers who denounced the iniquities of Jews and stirred up anti-Semitic sentiment, notably John of Capestrano and Bernardine of Siena (d.1444). The texts of mystery and passion plays contained crudely anti-Semitic passages.

But there was the other side of the coin, hinted at in the decree of Constance. In its very prohibitions, the decree implied that much *convivencia* was in fact taking place, in business and within the household and 'in festivities, marriages, banquets and baths'. Evidently there was also a measure of esteem for Jews. Even the polemical writers and preachers implicitly recognized this dimension. Secular and ecclesiastical authorities gave more support to Jewish communities than the decree of Constance might suggest, admittedly often from material motives – because Jews were useful to them as sources of taxation, as money-lenders and as reliable officials. Both the Emperor Charles IV and Pope Clement VI sought to protect Jews against the charges of causing the Black Death. Some humanist scholars, most notably Giovanni Pico della Mirandola (1463–94) and Johannes Reuchlin (1454–1522), learned Hebrew and engaged with contemporary Jewish scholarship. The Council of Vienne had encouraged much wider teaching of Hebrew, even if the motive was the conversion of Jews. The city of Florence was a centre of interest in Kabbala and other forms of Jewish theosophy. Although there was no return to the ecumenism of the eleventh and early twelfth centuries, nevertheless a judicious reading of the sources points to a more positive assessment than exclusive emphasis on the restrictions, expulsions and massacres would suggest.

Islam

Christianity felt gravely – even mortally – threatened by Islam throughout the later Middle Ages. It was felt most obviously in the eastern regions of Christianity: by the Orthodox Church, culminating with the capture of Constantinople in 1453, and by other Eastern Churches in Asia and North Africa. The threat came principally from Arabs and Turks and other peoples who had converted to Islam at an early date. The conversion of the Tartars to Islam in the fourteenth century identified the threat from this people, too, with the faith of Mohammed. While the challenges impinged principally upon the Orthodox and other Churches of the East, they also menaced the eastern borders of Western Christendom. Even in 1500 there seemed no halt, and no effective answer, to the advances of Islam from the East. In Western Europe, it is true, the later Middle Ages witnessed the decline and fall of Islamic power in the Iberian peninsula, but this was exceptional. Almost everywhere else Islam seemed on the advance, Christianity in retreat.

The frustration and impotence of Christendom was felt intimately through the failure of the crusades. The last Christian stronghold in the Holy Land, the city and fortress of Acre, had been captured by Muslim forces in 1291. Crusades to recapture Jerusalem and the Holy Land continued to be called at the highest levels, of popes and kings, throughout the later Middle Ages, but either the calls fell on deaf ears or the small expeditions that were organized met with failure. Symptomatic of the sense of frustration, right at the beginning of the period, was the suppression of the order of the Knights Templar, which had played a central role in the crusades, at the Council of Vienne in 1311–12 (see p 5). Homosexual practices among the knights were among the reasons given for the suppression, but in reality the order was being made a scapegoat for the failure of the crusades.

The same Council of Vienne spoke more directly about recommended

Christian attitudes towards Muslims. Its Decree 25 somewhat parallels the Council of Basel's decree on Jews, though it is still more hostile. There is no attempt at dialogue, and the sense of Christian fear and suspicion of Muslims comes through strongly. Basic lack of knowledge of Islam appears in the grave error of suggesting that Muslims (who are called Saracens) adore (Latin, *adorent*) Mohammed:

> It is an insult to the holy name and a disgrace to the Christian faith that in certain parts of the world subject to Christian princes where Saracens live, sometimes apart, sometimes intermingled with Christians, the Saracen priests, commonly called Zabazala, in their temples or mosques, in which the Saracens meet to adore the infidel Mohammed, loudly invoke and extol his name each day at certain hours from a high place, in the hearing of both Christians and Saracens, and there make public declarations in his honour.
> ...
>
> These practices cannot be tolerated any further without displeasing the divine majesty. We [the pope], therefore, with the sacred council's approval, strictly forbid such practices henceforth in Christian lands. We enjoin on Catholic princes, one and all, who hold sovereignty over the said Saracens and in whose territory these practices occur, and we lay on them a pressing obligation under the divine judgement that, as true Catholics and zealous for the Christian faith, they give consideration to the disgrace heaped on both them and other Christians. They are to remove this offence altogether from their territories and take care that their subjects remove it, so that they may thereby attain the reward of eternal happiness. They are to forbid expressly the public invocation of the sacrilegious name of Mohammed. (*Decrees*: 380)

There was no relenting in the official line. Just after the end of the period, another general council of the Western Church, Lateran V (1512–17), proposed a new crusade with these words:

> Our intense desire for this campaign against the evil and implacable enemies of the cross of Christ is indeed implanted in our hearts. ...
>
> Our aim is to crush the Turks and other infidels standing firm in the eastern and southern regions. They treat the way of true light and salvation with complete contempt and totally unyielding blindness. They attack the life-giving cross on which our Saviour willed to accept death ... and they make themselves hateful enemies of God and most bitter persecutors of the Christian religion. Strengthened by defences not only spiritual but also temporal, we may be able, under God's guidance and favour, to oppose the bitter and frequent sallies by which, in wild rage, they move savagely amidst Christian blood. (*Decrees*: 610, 651)

At the academic level, interest in Islamic thought and Muslim scholars reached a low point. There was very little open debate between Christian and Muslim intellectuals such as had characterized the twelfth century – as evidenced by Abelard and Peter the Venerable. The condemnations of Thomas Aquinas, Siger of Brabant and other scholars at Paris university in the late thirteenth century, for their alleged enthusiasm for the Arab scholars Avicenna and Averroes, had further distanced Christianity from the Islamic world (though Averroes was regarded as a heretic by many Muslims). The widely used *Impugnatio Alcorani* ('Refutation of the Koran'), written by the Dominican friar Ricoldus de Monte Croce in the early fourteenth century, was a refutation of the errors of Islam rather than an attempt at dialogue. There was some interest in Averroism at Paris university in the fourteenth century, led by John of Jandun, and at Padua university in Italy during the Renaissance, but these were revivals on a minor scale. Duns Scotus and William of Ockham, perhaps the sharpest minds and most influential philosopher-theologians of the early fourteenth century, did not continue the interest in Arab scholarship that their illustrious predecessor Thomas Aquinas had shown. Scotus, indeed, looked forward to the disappearance of Islam. Hearing of a defeat of the army of the sultan of Egypt (which Scotus attributed to the year 1300, though it occurred in December 1299), he wrote thus (*Ordinatio*, Prologue, 2.1.112) by way of explaining Islam's longevity:

> Concerning the permanence of the sect of Mohammed, that sect began more than six hundred years after the law of Christ and, God willing, it will shortly be brought to an end, since it has been greatly weakened in the year of Christ 1300 and many of its believers are dead and still more have fled, and a prophecy among them states that their sect is to be brought to an end.

The language barrier between Arabic and Turkish, the principal languages of the Muslim world confronting Christianity, and Greek and Latin, the two main common languages of Christendom, East and West, obviously obstructed communication between followers of the two faiths. But whereas earlier the West had produced translations of major Islamic works into Latin – the Koran had been translated into Latin under the direction of Peter the Venerable, and there were Latin translations of works of Avicenna and Averroes – there appears to have been much less enthusiasm for communication of this kind in the later Middle Ages.

In Western Christendom, the Islamic world was encountered largely at a distance and impersonally. Only in the Iberian peninsula and parts of the Mediterranean world were Christians living in substantial numbers alongside Muslims. As a result, Muslims for most Christians were more an abstract concept than real individuals – rather as people living in communist countries were experienced by Westerners before the fall of the Iron Curtain. Official statements, including Church documents, may give a more hostile view than many people actually held. It is significant that Margery Kempe was well impressed by the Muslims she encountered in the Holy Land (see p 99).

In the East, Christians lived in much closer contact with Muslims and were, for the most part, subject to their government. There was, doubtless, much good yet unrecorded cohabitation. Muslim rulers granted a fair measure of toleration to Christians, especially where they were numerous. There were more positive acts of cooperation, such as Sultan Mohammed's help with the installation of the patriarch of Constantinople (see p 159). Nevertheless there was economic and social as well as religious pressure on Christians to convert to Islam, and many Christians must have felt the humiliation of living as second-class citizens in lands that their ancestors had once ruled. The Muslim Tartars, moreover, brought persecution and destruction to many Christian communities.

In short, the experience of Muslims was radically different for Eastern and Western Christians, yet for both the relationship with Islam was quite fraught.

Paganism, magic and witchcraft

Paganism

De Heidense Middeleeuwen, edited by Ludo Milis, was first published in 1991 and the English translation, *The Pagan Middle Ages*, appeared in 1998. The collection of essays argued that paganism remained a potent force during the Middle Ages, hidden beneath a veneer of Christianity. The book summed up, in a rather provocative manner, various trends among historians who considered that the Christian nature of medieval Europe had been exaggerated. Some subsequent studies argued in a similar direction. As mentioned in the Introduction (see pp xxiii–xxiv), writers in the Reformation and Counter-Reformation traditions, and indeed during the Enlightenment, had reached somewhat similar conclusions much earlier, though there was a significant difference inasmuch as these earlier writers were arguing that late medieval people had failed to maintain the high ideals of Christianity – whether in doctrine or in practices or in both – and as a result had lapsed into forms of paganism, rather than that paganism had survived from earlier times, into the later Middle Ages, as an organized and coherent alternative religion.

To some extent the issue is one of definition. The word 'pagan' conveys a rather wide and derogatory meaning, literally someone from the 'countryside' (Latin, *pagus*), as distinct from the more sophisticated early Christians who lived mainly in towns. To own the description 'pagan', with the connotation of non-Christian, was to risk persecution and death. So, unsurprisingly, people who openly claimed to be pagans were hardly to be found during the later Middle Ages. There is no clear evidence, during this period, of a well-organized and institutionalized movement that might be called paganism. But did it exist in more hidden forms?

An important consideration is the Incarnation: Christ, in taking human nature, proclaimed the basic goodness of creation. Accordingly there is no sharp distinction between Christianity and the rest of life. Reformation and Counter-Reformation, in seeking to purify the Church of superstition and abuses, ran the risk of drawing the distinction too sharply and of projecting it and the accompanying accusation of paganism back onto the later Middle Ages. A classic, extreme case was the later unease with the nude in Renaissance art: the figures in Michelangelo's 'Last Judgement' in the Sistine Chapel in Rome were covered with drapes in the late sixteenth century on the grounds that without them the painting was too pagan. A great strength of late medieval religion was precisely that it entered into so much of life so fully.

The section on 'Minimal obligations' (see pp 71–89) argued that many people lived at the lower end of Christian commitment, at least in the eyes of the Church authorities. Where their hearts and minds lay remains largely closed to investigation, but there is little to suggest that, in their relative lack of enthusiasm for Christianity, they were positively embracing paganism. Even so, that many were perceived to be almost lapsing into paganism shows that this alternative to Christianity was taken seriously by the orthodox.

Magic and witchcraft

Can the same considerations as for paganism be applied to magic and witchcraft? Yes and no. In terms of magic, everyone accepted the possibility of intervention by persons and forces beyond this world and there was often only a thin line – in terms of verification – between the invocation of good and bad spirits: the difference might be just a matter of opinion. Whereas paganism was a rather vague label and was used only rarely as a judicial accusation, witchcraft and magic were thought to be identifiable and appeared, as a result, much more frequently and specifically in court cases and other records.

One of the most famous trials involving witchcraft and magic was that of Eleanor Cobham, Duchess of Gloucester, and various people associated with her, in 1441. The records of the trial reveal the complexity of the issues, the pressure from the prosecutors that the evil practices be identified and their sense of the seriousness of the matters involved, and also the requirement that the miscreants be punished severely and in public. At the same time there are touches of humanity and understanding, most notably on the part of 'most of the people' who had 'great compassion' on Dame Eleanor. The account, from an anonymous English chronicle, reads as follows:

In the month of July [1441], Master Roger Bolingbroke, who was a great and skilful man in astronomy, and Master Thomas Southwell, a canon of St Stephen's chapel, Westminster, were taken as conspirators of the king's [Henry VI's] death. For it was said that Master Roger should labour to consume the king's person by way of necromancy, and that Master Thomas should say Masses in forbidden and unsuitable places, that is, in the lodge of Hornsey Park near London, upon certain instruments with which Master Roger should ... use his craft of necromancy against faith and good belief, and he assented to the said Roger in all his works. And on Sunday the 25th of the same month, the said Roger, with all his instruments of necromancy, stood on a high stage above all men's heads in St Paul's churchyard while the sermon lasted. ... And the Tuesday next Dame Eleanor Cobham, Duchess of Gloucester, fled by night to the sanctuary at Westminster. Wherefore she was held suspect of certain articles of treason.

In the meantime Master Roger was examined before the king's council, where he confessed and said that he wrought the said necromancy at the instigation of Dame Eleanor, to know what should befall her and to what estate she should come. Wherefore she was cited to appear before certain bishops of the king ... in St Stephen's chapel, Westminster, to answer certain articles of necromancy, witchcraft, heresy and treason. ...

And this same time was taken a woman called the witch of Eye, whose sorcery and witchcraft Dame Eleanor had long time used. By such medicines and drinks as the witch made, the said Eleanor compelled the duke of Gloucester to love her and to wed her. Wherefore, and also because of relapse, the said witch was burnt at Smithfield.

Dame Eleanor appeared before the archbishop of Canterbury and others and received her penance in this form: that she should go the same day from Temple Bar with a meek and demure countenance to St Paul's cathedral, bearing in her hand a taper of one pound, and offer it there at the high altar. And the following Wednesday she should go from the Swan in Thames Street, bearing a taper, to Christ Church in London, and there offer it up. And the Friday following she should go likewise from Queenhithe, bearing a taper of the same weight, to St Michael in Cornhill, and there offer it up. Which penance she fulfilled and did right meekly, so that most of the people had great compassion on her.

After this she was committed again to the wardship of Sir Thomas Stanley wherein she remained all her life afterwards, having yearly 100 marks assigned to her for her findings and costs: whose [Stanley's] pride, covetousness and lechery were the cause of her confusion. (*EHD*, iv: 869–70)

Trials of women accused of witchcraft increased notably in the fifteenth century. Whereas previously they had mostly involved individual cases, increasingly in the fifteenth century they became collective trials of many suspects. Even so, the number of accused was well below the high point reached in the late sixteenth and early seventeenth centuries. Often, too, the ecclesiastical authorities protected women from unjust accusations. The papacy was generally reluctant to give the Inquisition authority in matters of witchcraft, though papal bulls in 1398 and 1484 granted a measure of such authority to inquisitors. Inasmuch as it was thought to involve an overt or tacit pact with the devil, witchcraft was a very serious matter.

The large-scale trials of the fifteenth century were concentrated inside quite a small region within and around the Alps. The century also saw the production of a number of treatises outlining the diabolical danger posed by witchcraft and recommended procedures for dealing with it. These works presented witchcraft as a widespread and coherent phenomenon and so helped to fuel the extensive witch-hunts that followed later. The best known was *Malleus maleficarum* ('Hammer of Witches'), which was written by the German Dominican friars Heinrich Kramer and Jacob Sprenger and published in 1487. It was to remain the most influential work of its kind into the seventeenth century.

The reality of magic and witchcraft was acknowledged by everyone. The perceived danger was magnified by prosecutions and by those who systematized the threat into a grand design; on the other hand, it was diminished by an innate caution in the matter on the part of most Church authorities and by the good sense of most of the laity. All those involved believed they were dealing with a serious issue. A great strength of late medieval religion was the space it gave to imagination and the sensual. It is not surprising that the purifications of these areas on the part of both Reformation and Counter-Reformation led to a marked increase in the number of women who were identified, by both Catholics and Protestants, as witches.

Conclusion

William Langland, writing in late fourteenth-century England, introduced the vision of Piers Plowman thus:

> A fair field full of folk, found I there between,
> Of all manner of men [people], the mean and the rich,
> Working and wandering as the world asketh.
> (*The Vision of Piers Plowman*, Prologue, lines 17–19)

This book, too, has centred on people. The later medieval Church was essentially a community of individuals, richly diverse yet united – both firmly and fragilely – in appreciation of the Christian mystery and struggling with it.

The Western Church was a very extensive and sophisticated institution, involving an elaborate hierarchy and affording manifold opportunities for Christians to grow in, and practise, the faith. By the later Middle Ages it was an old establishment, with a history stretching back well over a thousand years. In a sense the institution had acquired a life of its own, and there was the danger that means would become ends. We have seen both the conservatism and the remarkable creativity of the Church of the time, its ability to hold on to and adapt well-tried formulae as well as to develop new movements. Notwithstanding the important institutional dimensions, the Church meant essentially people, the whole Christian community, the *communitas fidelium* (community of the faithful) in the language of the time.

This emphasis on people may seem obvious, unnecessary to labour. However, as outlined in the Introduction, the later medieval Church – principally the Western Church – has been instrumentalized in past historiography. It has been treated too much as a prelude to the Reformation and Counter-Reformation and thereby has run the danger of becoming a concept, an explanation of later developments. In recent years this Church has been studied more in its own right, less in terms of historiographical preoccupations. As a result, the richness and diversity of Christians of the time have been explored with much profit, notably by Anglophone historians. The present book follows in this tradition and, it may be hoped, makes some further contribution to it.

The later Middle Ages brought a notable increase in the amount of surviving evidence, in comparison with the immediately preceding centuries. The increase is particularly marked with regard to popular religion. As a result, it is possible to enter into the beliefs and religious practices of significant numbers of lay people in the Western Church during the last two centuries of the Middle Ages. The present work has tried to explore some of this fascinating material in depth and from a variety of viewpoints.

This volume is the third of seven in the I.B.Tauris History of the Christian Church. By the end of the period covered in it, the Church was already three-quarters of the way through its history to date. However, the later Middle Ages marks a fundamental turning-point in the history of Christianity, in some sense the half-way mark. For the first 1,500 years Christianity had been largely confined to the Mediterranean world and to northern and Central Europe. Thereafter Christianity spread to all corners of the globe and became a world religion. The sixteenth century brought, too, a radically new situation within the Western Church through the fragmentation into Catholic and Protestant communities. The late Middle Ages, therefore, marks for the Church both the culmination of the long medieval period and the background to the great transitions that followed. In this way the period forms a crucial hinge in both Church history and world history.

The first two chapters of the book looked at the more obviously institutional dimensions of the Western Church of the time: Church councils, the secular clergy at various levels from pope to junior curate, and religious orders. A remarkably extensive and sophisticated establishment emerges, all for a population roughly equivalent to that of the United Kingdom today. There was diversity, energy and creativity among the people who made up this institution and managed its manifold branches. Yet they would surely have seen themselves as following ways of life even more than as servants of an organization. Many sympathetic and fascinating personalities appear, alongside plenty of human frailty and sinfulness. In terms of institutional developments, the conciliar movement is particularly notable. While the movement faltered within the Church, it had a profound and lasting influence on the development of secular representative institutions in the West, and thereby on world history.

Chapter 3 focused on the laity, the large majority of the members of the Church. We saw the wide range and varying intensity of participation on the part of the laity, from minimal observance to exceptional religious experiences. Mystics of the time represented one of the foremost developments in the spirituality and prayer-life of the Church. Women featured prominently in this development. For the most part, religion blended remarkably harmoniously with other dimensions of life, through guilds and confraternities, processions and pilgrimages, various forms of community life, more individual devotions and lifestyles, and through relaxation and enjoyment. The period may justifiably be called the 'Age of the Laity' in the Church.

Chapter 4 focused on learning and various forms of culture. The later Middle Ages was a time of wide learning and great curiosity. Universities were designed principally for the clergy and they produced a number of notable intellectuals, both those who were primarily associated with a university, such as Duns Scotus and William of Ockham, and many others who spent some time in university studies. The number of universities and schools grew significantly during the period. In addition, there were many other channels for growing in knowledge, from reading books – which was often done in a communal context – to the liturgical services of the Church. Finally, there were the brilliant academic and artistic achievements of the early Renaissance, which formed an integral part of the late medieval Church.

Chapter 5 studied dissenting movements and the official Church's response to them. Cathars and Waldensians were less prominent than they had been in the thirteenth century. The most serious challenges of the time came from John Wyclif and the Lollards in England, and Jan Hus and the Hussites in Bohemia. Wyclif anticipated in his writings most of the teachings that were to come to the fore in the sixteenth-century Reformation. While these dissenting movements were important, and are essential to an understanding of the late medieval Church, they remained relatively small and confined to particular countries. The parameters of orthodoxy were sufficiently wide and attractive to contain the large majority of the population. The Church could be brutal in its repression of heresy, but its actions in this regard must be considered within the framework of accepted norms of the time as well as its concern to preserve orthodoxy. Even so, there is reason to believe that the laity were generally more tolerant, less dogmatic, than Church authorities in this regard.

Chapter 6 treated all too briefly the Orthodox Church and various other Churches that were partly separate from the Catholic Church. Together they may have counted a quarter of the total Christian population of the time. The Orthodox Church was distinguished by its heritage and direct links with the early Church. In its original heartlands it came to be increasingly a Christian community living under Muslim government. In these occupied areas, nevertheless, the Orthodox Church retained remarkable vitality, while in other countries, most notably Russia, it grew and flourished. All the other, smaller Churches likewise felt the pressure of the expansion of Islam. It was the Church of Ethiopia that perhaps best preserved its independence as well as its religious and cultural heritage.

The last chapter looked at the attitudes of Christians towards outside religions and beliefs, and towards the people who adhered to them. Judaism and Islam were the two most prominent faiths of this kind; paganism, magic and witchcraft formed subcultures that are difficult to evaluate but which were taken seriously by the Church authorities. Regarding Islam especially, there was a noticeable difference in the experience of Eastern and Western Christians. In the West, Muslims were to be found for the most part on the borders of Christendom, whereas in the East they formed the majority of the population in many countries where Christians lived. There was some *convivencia*, sometimes willing and sometimes perforce, probably more than the scanty surviving evidence of good relations suggests. Nevertheless the later Middle Ages was a time when Christians of both East and West showed relatively little understanding or sympathy regarding other faiths and religious practices. This lack contrasts with their remarkable curiosity and creativeness regarding beliefs and practices that fell within the Christian framework. The contrast may partly be explained by the great pressure that Christians of both East and West experienced. Their worlds seemed to be threatened by both internal and external perils, and in these circumstances it is understandable that a society should think first of its own survival and much less, positively, of outsiders.

We may end by returning, full circle, to one of the central questions posed in the Introduction. Why was the later medieval Church followed by the Reformation? The question remains intriguing yet difficult to answer. On the one hand, within the late medieval Church many of the seeds of both Reformation and Counter-Reformation may be discerned: these epoch-making movements in Church history represent both developments from within the late medieval Church and reactions against its perceived failures. Yet had they known, late medieval Christians would have been surprised, I think, at the precise forms these developments were to take. However, the Holy Spirit was considered to be Lord of both history and surprises.

Bibliography

This selective bibliography lists the most important modern publications in English, and a few in other languages, as well as other works that are referred to in the book.

General works

Encyclopedias and dictionaries

Dictionary of the Middle Ages, ed Joseph Strayer (New York, 1982–89), 13 vols.
Encyclopedia of the Middle Ages, eds A. Vauchez, B. Dobson and M. Lapidge (Cambridge, 2000), 2 vols.
New Catholic Encyclopedia (Detroit, 2nd ed, 2002), 15 vols.
The Oxford Companion to Christian Thought, ed Adrian Hastings (Oxford, 2000)
Oxford Dictionary of National Biography, ed H.C.G. Matthew and Brian Harrison (Oxford, 2004), 60 vols.
The Oxford Dictionary of the Christian Church, ed F.L. Cross and E.A. Livingstone (Oxford, 3rd revised ed, 2005)

Other general works

Barry, Colman J. (ed), *Readings in Church History* (Westminster MA, revised ed, 1985), 3 vols. in 1
Classics of Western Spirituality (Mahwah, Paulist Press). This fine series provides the main texts in English translation, together with an introduction and notes, of many spiritual writers and mystics of the later Middle Ages.
Duffy, Eamon, *The Stripping of the Altars: Traditional Religion in England, c. 1400–c.1580* (New Haven and London, 1992; 2nd ed, 2005)
English Historical Documents, vol. 4 (1327–1485), ed A.R. Myers (London, 1969)
Fliche, Augustin, and Martin, Victor (eds), *Histoire de l'Eglise* (Paris, 1946–), vols. 12–15. These outstanding volumes remain fundamental to an understanding and appreciation of the later medieval Church.
Hamilton, Bernard, *Religion in the Medieval West* (London, 1986)
___, *The Christian World of the Middle Ages* (Stroud, 2003)
Huizinga, Johan, *Herfsttij der Middeleuwen* (Leyden, 1919). English translation, *The Waning of the Middle Ages* (London, 1924)
Jedin, Hubert (ed), *History of the Church*, vol. 4, *From the High Middle Ages to the Eve of the Reformation* (London, 1981)
Knowles, David, and Obolensky, Dmitri, *The Christian Centuries*, vol. 2, *The Middle Ages* (London and New York, 1969)

Oakley, Francis, *The Western Church in the Later Middle Ages* (Ithaca and London, 1979)

Pantin, W., *The English Church in the Fourteenth Century* (Cambridge, 1955)

Southern, R.W., *Western Society and the Church in the Middle Ages* (Harmondsworth, 1970)

Swanson, R.N., *Religion and Devotion in Europe, c.1215–c.1515* (Cambridge, 1995)

Tanner 1984; see under Chapter 2

___, 'Piety in the Later Middle Ages', in Sheridan Gilley and W.J. Shiels (eds), *A History of Religion in Britain* (Oxford, 1994), pp 61–76

Chapter 1. Papacy and Councils

Crowder, C.M.D., *Unity, Heresy and Reform 1378–1460: The Conciliar Response to the Great Schism* (London and New York, 1977)

Decrees of the Ecumenical Councils, ed Norman Tanner (Washington DC and London, 1990), 2 vols.

Duffy, Eamon, *Saints and Sinners: A History of the Popes* (New Haven and London, 1997; new ed, 2001)

Figgis, J.N., *Studies in Political Thought from Gerson to Grotius, 1414–1625* (Cambridge, 1907)

Gill, Joseph, *The Council of Florence* (Cambridge, 1959)

Kelly, J.N.D. (ed), *The Oxford Dictionary of Popes* (Oxford, 1986)

Morrissey, T., 'The Decree *Haec Sancta* and Cardinal Zabarella', *Annuarium Historiae Conciliorum* x (1978), pp 145–78

Oakley, Francis, *Council over Pope? Towards a Provisional Ecclesiology* (New York, 1969)

Tanner, Norman, *The Councils of the Church: A Short History* (New York, 2001)

Tierney, Brian, *Foundations of the Conciliar Theory* (Cambridge, 1955)

Chapter 2. Clergy and Religious Orders

Eco, Umberto, *Il nome della rosa* (Milan, 1980). English translation, *The Name of the Rose* (London, 1983)

Greatrex, Joan (ed), *The Vocation of Service to God and Neighbour: Interests, Involvements and Problems of Religious Communities and their Members in Medieval Society* (Turnhout, 1998), especially the articles by James Clark (St Albans abbey), Nicholas Heale (John Lydgate of Bury St Edmunds abbey) and Anthony Marett-Crosby (Robert Joseph of Evesham abbey).

Harriss, Gerald, *Cardinal Beaufort* (Oxford, 1989)

Heath, Peter, *The English Parish Clergy on the Eve of the Reformation* (London, 1969)

Knowles, David, *The Religious Order in England* (Cambridge, 1957–60), 3 vols.

Lawrence, Hugh, *Medieval Monasticism: Forms of Religious Life in Western Europe in the Middle Ages* (London and New York, 2nd ed, 1989)

___, *The Friars: The Impact of the Early Mendicant Movement on Western Society* (New York, 1994)

Newett, M.M., *Canon Pietro Casola's Pilgrimage to Jerusalem in the Year 1494* (Manchester, 1907)

Tanner, Norman, *The Church in Late Medieval Norwich 1370–1532* (Toronto, 1984). This work provides the basis, and full documentation, for the section 'A case study: Norwich'.

Chapter 3. Laity

Abbott, Christopher, *Julian of Norwich: Autobiography and Theology* (Cambridge, 1999)

Brundage, James A., *Law, Sex and Christian Society in Medieval Europe* (Chicago, 1987)

Clay, Rotha M., *The Hermits and Anchorites of England* (London, 1914; Detroit, 1968).

Edwards, J., 'Religious Faith and Doubt in Late Medieval Spain: Soria *circa* 1450–1500', *Past and Present* cxx (1988), pp 3–15

Helmholz, Richard, *Marriage Litigation in Medieval England* (Cambridge, 1974)

Kempe, Margery, *The Book of Margery Kempe*, ed S.B. Meech and H.E. Allen (Early English Text Society, ccxii, 1940)

Le Roy Ladurie 1978; see under Chapter 5

McLean, Teresa, *The English at Play in the Middle Ages* (Kensall Press, no date)

Murray, Alexander, 'Piety and Impiety in Thirteenth-Century Italy', in G.J. Cuming and Derek Baker (eds), *Popular Belief and Practice* (Studies in Church History, Cambridge, 1984), pp 83–106

Newett 1907; see under Chapter 2

Pantin 1955; see under General works

Reynolds, Susan, 'Social Mentalities and the Case of Medieval Scepticism' *Transactions of the Royal Historical Society*, 6th series, i (1991), pp 21–41

Simons, W., *Cities of Ladies: Beguine Communities in the Medieval Low Countries, 1200–1565* (Philadelphia, 2001)

Sumption, Jonathan, *Pilgrimage* (London, 1975)

Tanner, Norman, 'Making Merry in the Middle Ages', *The Month*, September–October 1996, pp 373–6. This article is the basis of the section 'Relaxation and enjoyment'.

___ and Watson, Sethina, 'Least of the Laity: The Minimum Requirements for a Medieval Christian', *Journal of Medieval History* xxxii (2006), pp 395–423. This article provides the basis, and full documentation, for the section 'Minimal obligations'.

Toussaert, Jacques, *Le sentiment religieux en Flandre à la fin du Moyen Age* (Paris, 1960)

Chapter 4. Knowledge and Culture

Catto, J.I. and Evans, R. (eds), *Late Medieval Oxford*, The History of the University of Oxford, vol. 2 (Oxford, 1992)

Copleston, Frederick, *A History of Philosophy* (London, 1946–75), vols. 2

(Augustine to Scotus) and 3 (Ockham to Suarez)
Evans, G.R. (ed), *The Medieval Theologians* (Oxford, 2001)
Janson, H.W., *History of Art* (New York, 4th ed, 1991)
The New Oxford Companion to Music, ed Denis Arnold (Oxford, 1983), 2 vols.

Chapter 5. Heresy and Dissent

Hudson, Anne, *The Premature Reformation: Wycliffite Texts and Lollard History* (Oxford, 1988)
Kaminsky, H., *A History of the Hussite Revolution* (Berkeley and Los Angeles, 1967)
Lambert, Malcolm, *Medieval Heresy* (Oxford, 3rd ed, 2002)
Le Roy Ladurie, Emmanuel, *Montaillou: Cathars and Catholics in a French Village, 1294–1324* (London, 1978)
Spinka, Matthew, *John Hus at the Council of Constance* (New York, 1965)
Tanner, Norman (ed), *Heresy Trials in the Diocese of Norwich 1428–1431* (Camden 4th series, xx, 1977)
Wakefield, Walter L., and Evans, Austin P., *Heresies of the High Middle Ages* (New York, 1969)

Chapter 6. Eastern Churches

Baur, John, *2000 Years of Christianity in Africa* (Nairobi, 1994; revised ed, 1998)
Hussey, J.M., *The Orthodox Church in the Byzantine Empire* (Oxford, 1986)
Ware, Timothy, *The Orthodox Church* (London, revised ed, 1993)

Chapter 7. Christendom and the Non-Christian World

Chazan, R., *The Jews of Medieval Western Christendom 1000–1500* (Cambridge, 2006)
Kieckhefer, R., *European Witch Trials: Their Foundations in Popular and Learned Culture 1300–1500* (London and Berkeley, 1976)
___, *Magic in the Middle Ages* (Cambridge, 1994)
Milis, Ludo (ed), *De Heidense Middeleeuwen* (Brussels, 1991). English translation, *The Pagan Middle Ages* (Woodbridge, 1998)
Tanner, Norman, 'Christianity vs "Paganism"? Reflections on Medieval Europe', *The Month*, February 2000, pp 60–5
von Sicard, H., *Medieval Christian Perceptions of Islam* (New York, 1996)

Useful journals

Catholic Historical Review
Journal of Ecclesiastical History
Journal of Medieval History
Le Moyen Âge
Mediaeval Studies
Medium Aevum
Revue d'histoire ecclésiastique

Index

This selective index covers the principal persons, places and subjects mentioned in the book.